D1165644

THE CIVILIZATION OF THE AMERICAN INDIAN SERIES

Ritual of the Bacabs

RITUAL

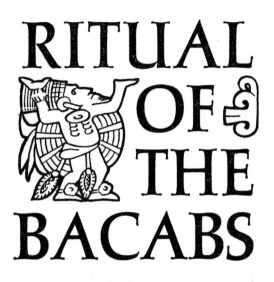

OF THE
BACABS

Translated and Edited
BY RALPH L. ROYS

UNIVERSITY OF OKLAHOMA PRESS : NORMAN

By Ralph L. Roys

The Ethno-Botany of the Maya. New Orleans, 1931.

The Book of Chilam Balam of Chumayel (translator and editor). Washington, D. C., 1933.

The Titles of Ebtun. Washington, D. C., 1939.

The Indian Background of Colonial Yucatán. Washington, D. C., 1943.

The Maya Chontal Indians of Acalan-Tixchel: A Contribution to the History and Ethnography of the Yucatán Peninsula (with France V. Scholes). Washington, D. C., 1948.

The Political Geography of the Yucatán Maya. Washington, D. C., 1957.

Ritual of the Bacabs: A Book of Maya Incantations (translator and editor). Norman, 1965.

LIBRARY OF CONGRESS CATALOG CARD NUMBER: 65–11227

PREFACE

T HE MANUSCRIPT ENTITLED the "Ritual of the Bacabs" was so named by William Gates, because of its frequent mention of these deities. It consists largely of medical incantations, but there are also a few intended for other purposes. Nearly all the incantations are written in a single hand, which could well be of the last half of the eighteenth century, but this is not certain. The last twenty-three pages contain mostly ordinary medical prescriptions, and the last two are written on the back of a printed Indulgence dated 1779.

From the language of these incantations it would appear that they were copied from a much older manuscript, which might have been written during the first part of the seventeenth century or possibly even earlier.

The first published description of the "Ritual of the Bacabs" was by Alfred M. Tozzer in 1921; but I am indebted to Alfred L. Bush, associate curator of manuscripts of Princeton University Library, for an account of the later history of the manuscript. Most of it is from unpublished papers of William Gates.

The Princeton codex of the "Ritual of the Bacabs" was discovered in Yucatán during the winter of 1914-15 by Frederic J. Smith. Gates, who acquired it at this time, has stated, "How he ever got even to hear of it or see it, much less acquire it, is simply a mystery." In 1930 it was purchased from Gates by Robert Garrett, a distinguished collector of manuscripts; and it remained in his possession in Baltimore until 1942, when he deposited it temporarily at the Institute for Advanced Study at Princeton. In 1949, at Garrett's direction, the manuscript was transferred as a gift to the Princeton University Library to join Garrett's other manuscript collections there.

In 1941 through the kindness of Ruth Lapham Butler, custodian of the Edward E. Ayer Collection in the Newberry Library in Chicago, a photocopy of the manuscript of "The Ritual of the Bacabs" was made available to me; and from this the present study has been made.

It is with gratitude that I acknowledge my obligation to John D. Barrett, president, and the Bollingen Foundation for a fellowship grant which enabled me to prepare the manuscript for publication.

I am indebted to the late A. V. Kidder, to H.E.D. Pollock, and to the Carnegie Institution of Washington for assistance in obtaining needed material and other aid during my preliminary studies of the Bacabs manuscript. I have turned to E. W. Andrews for help in the identification of fauna names. Gordon R. Willey has kindly supplied me with photographic material from the Peabody Museum, Harvard University. W. B. Cook, Jr., has read the translation of these incantations and commented on them from the standpoint of a psychiatrist. Verne Ray has advised me regarding a fundamental difference between the attitude of the Yucatecan writer of these incantations and that of a shaman in the Pacific Northwest.

Throughout the preparation of this study I have turned constantly to J. E. S. Thompson for information and criticism, and I am deeply indebted to him for his assistance.

RALPH L. ROYS

Seattle, Washington
April 5, 1965

INTRODUCTION

Thanks to our one-sided emphasis upon the so-called natural causation, we have learned to distinguish what is subjective and psychic from what is objective and "natural." For primitive man, on the contrary, the psychic and the objective coalesce in the external world. In the face of something extraordinary it is not he who is astonished, but rather the thing which is astonishing.

—C. G. Jung[1]

MEDICINE WAS CLOSELY ASSOCIATED with benevolent magic in pre-Spanish Yucatán. In spite of the disapproval of the latter by the Christian missionaries, this association continued throughout the colonial period and indeed down to the present time. Many medical treatises written in Maya have come down to us, but the largest, which is written in Spanish, is entitled *"Yerbas y hechicerías Yucatán"* ("Herbs and Enchantments of Yucatán"). I was unable to find in it any incantations or other references to magic that I could recognize, but the wording of the tile is sufficient evidence of a close association of medicine with magic in people's minds.

Landa writes of "the priests, the physicians and sorcerers, who are all the same thing."[2] This appears to have been true of the doctors and shamans, but the priesthood was a different and higher profession. Nevertheless, the priests and shamans co-operated, for we read in an account of a ceremony: "On the following day the physicians and the sorcerers assembled in one of their houses with their wives, and the priests drove away the evil spirit. Which being done they opened the bundles of their medicine, in which they kept many little trifles, each having his own little idols of the goddess of medicine, whom they

---

[1] Quoted from *Modern Man in Search of a Soul* (1933), 124–51. The chapter from which this is taken is entitled "Archaic Man."

[2] *Landa's "Relación de las cosas de Yucatán"* (edited by A. M. Tozzer), 153–54.

ix

called Ix Chel. And so they called this festival Ihcil Ix Chel, as well as some small stones called *am* [spider], of the kind they used for casting lots."

In another passage we read: "There were also surgeons, or, to be more accurate, sorcerers, who cured with herbs and many superstitious rites."[3]

In a report by the corporation of the city of Mérida in 1579 we find an account of some of the poisonous snakes of Yucatán, following which we read: "Formerly in the time when they were pagans, they took measures to cure themselves of this poisoning by means of spells and enchantments. There were great sorcerers [*encantadores*], and they had their books for charming and enchanting them. With a few words that they recited they charmed and tamed poisonous serpents; they caught and held them in their hands without their doing them any injury."[4]

Unfortunately the Bacabs manuscript contains no formula for subduing a serpent, although snakes in the abdomen, even including a rattlesnake, are fully treated. We do, however, find incantations for charming a poisonous spider and a scorpion (MS, pp. 157, 160).

In the gathering described by Landa, where both priests and shamans were present, we are told that it was the former who first exorcised the evil spirit (*demonio*), after which the shamans proceeded with their own business. We do not know which evil spirit this was. From the respectful terms in which Hun Ahau, the lord of Metnal, the underworld, is addressed in these incantations, it would seem unlikely that he was meant in Landa's account. Indeed, among the Mexicans his counterpart. Mictlantecuhtli, was treated with great respect.[5]

In spite of the efforts of the Spanish clergy, in colonial times the doctors and shamans do not seem to have been driven underground as the native priests were. This is deplored in a book by Sánchez de Aguilar, *Informe contra idolorum cultores del Obispado de Yucatán*, which was first published in 1639.

[3] *Ibid.*, 94   [4] *Relaciónes de Yucatán*, I, 67; hereafter designated as *RY*.
[5] Fr. Bernardo de Sahagún, *Historia general de las cosas de Nueva España*, I, 283–85.

It seems likely that the shamans took over some of the functions of the old priesthood, but there is little evidence of it in the "Ritual of the Bacabs." Obviously one of the important functions of the priesthood was to pray to the gods. In these incantations, however, although the names of various deities are often respectfully cited, we find few, if any, supplications. Although the shaman repeatedly addresses the four Bacabs as gods, he gives them peremptory orders, often in harsh language. At times he seems to threaten them or even curse them for their responsibility in connection with the creation of the personified diseases which he is exorcising. In these incantations he even states that he bats and tosses them about like a ball in a game (MS, pp. 26, 117, 185).

In one incantation, it is true, the shaman briefly commands Bolon-ti-ku, the nine gods of the underworld, and Oxlahun-ti-ku, the thirteen gods of the heavens, to behead and to flay an offending spirit; but this seems exceptional (MS, pp. 135-36).

Aside from his commands to the Bacabs and the exception just noted, the shaman accomplishes his purposes through his own power and not that of the gods. He does not oppose the deities; indeed, he is usually reverent; but his field of action is a different one.

A disease is considered to be a semipersonified being. Although, so far as I can tell, it does not assume human form, it understands commands and can be impressed by the words of the shaman. In many cases the name of a disease is an indication of the form it is believed to take. Almost at the beginning of the *Book of Chilam Balam of Kaua* is a picture of a macaw with a large snake between its claws. It carries the caption: "This is a picture of spider-snake-macaw-wind-seizure; purple-macaw-wind-seizure; . . green-macaw-wind-seizure is its name." The Kaua is a late manuscript and by this time, early in the nineteenth century, diseases with fauna names had become confused with the personified winds (*malos aires*) so prominent in modern Maya medicine. Except for the Kaua manuscript, I have as yet found little or no mention of these evil winds in the colonial literature of Yucatán.

Somewhat as a knowledge of the origin and past history of a

criminal often enables the authorities to check his activities, similarly the power of the shaman reciter appears to have been derived from his complete knowledge of the evil spirit which is the disease. So he tells what he knows, in order to exorcise it. He recounts its parentage, often only on the mother's side. He tells of the lustful impulses which inspired its disgraceful conception and shameful birth; and he goes on to relate the circumstances of its origin. He also recites the names of its bird, its tree, and the tree that was its arbor. Sometimes he even adds the name of the vine that was the "binder" in the construction of the arbor. Maya wooden structures are often said to be "bound" rather than built.

To every person was ascribed a fauna called a *mut* ("omen") and also a certain tree, both referring to the name of the day on which he was born. In the colonial Maya literature we find several short calendars which show such a correlation.[6] The fauna cited in these calendars include the rattlesnake, shark, jaguar, and possibly the dog, but by far the greater number consisted of birds.

The word *mut* usually means "news" or "general report," but it is also the name of a bird of the Cracidae family.[7] In Chontal and other lowland Maya languages, however, *mut* is a general term for "bird." In the Bacabs manuscript the word *mut* is almost always accompanied by *ch'ich'*, the usual Maya word for "bird." In these incantations, however, many insects are also called "birds," apparently for ritual purposes. In a general way the contexts in the Bacabs manuscript indicate the same significance as in the Kaua manuscript, except that in the Bacabs manuscript the *mut* is never anything but a bird or an insect.

It seems possible that the evil insects from Metnal, the underworld, by means of which the modern practitioner of black magic is believed

[6] Alfredo Barrera Vásquez, "Horóscopos mayas ó el pronóstico de los 20 signos del tzolkin según los libros de Chilam Balam de Kaua y de Mani," *Registro de Cultura Yucateca*, Vol. I, No. 6, pp. 4–33; A. Barrera Vásquez and S. Rendón, *El Libro de los Libros de Chilam Balam*; J. E. S. Thompson, *Maya Hieroglyphic Writing: An Introduction*, 70; Book of Chilam Balam of Kaua, 11, 12, 14, 21, 22; Codex Pérez, 94–95.

[7] T. Maler, "Explorations of the Upper Usumacintla and Adjacent Regions," *Memoirs* of the Peabody Museum, Vol. IV, No. 1, p. 132.

to inflict illness upon his victim, are referable to some of the insects called "birds" in our incantations. This, however, is uncertain.[8]

Birds and insects are often cited in our incantations, and snakes or lizards are occasionally mentioned; but it seems remarkable that only rarely do we find the name of a mammal. The large number of alleged idols observed by the first Spaniards might be at least partly accounted for if they included the birds and insects ascribed to individual persons.

Landa tells us: "They had such a quantity of idols that even those of their gods were not enough; for there was not an animal or insect of which they did not make a statue, and they made all these in the image of their gods and goddesses."[9] Some of them, however, may have represented Maya patronymics. Out of some 250 of the last that have come down to us, about 31 can be recognized as plant names; 12 as names of mammals; 12 as birds; 6 as insects; 4 as fish; and two are the general terms for snakes and iguanas. There are no doubt others, which I am unable to identify.[10]

In the calendars that I have cited a certain tree is ascribed to every person, its species apparently depending on the name of the day on which he was born. Such trees are also assigned to the personified diseases treated in these incantations. The trees are probably considered to be feminine; the names of many of them are sometimes preceded by the feminine prefix, *ix* or *x*. Few Maya plant names are preceded by the masculine prefix, *ah* or *h*. When it is assigned to the personified disease, the tree itself is also personified, for we read: "Who is your tree? Who is your bush?" On one occasion the shaman declares, apparently to the spirit that he is exorcising, "Shortly ago I disparaged you to your tree, to your bush" (MS, p. 138).

Closely associated with the personified tree in this manuscript is the arbor (*dzulbal*, also called *dzulub*), which is named for some species of tree or shrub. In the Chumayel manuscript, where the

---

[8] Cf. Appendix B.

[9] *Landa's "Relación de las cosas de Yucatán,"* 110.

[10] Ralph L. Roys, "Personal Names of the Maya of Yucatán," Carnegie Institution of Washington *Publication 523*, pp. 42–44.

dzulbal is also called a *pasel* ("small hut") in the same context, the arbor is ascribed to the "first men" of certain lineages in the ritual of a lineage—cult.[11]

Frequently, though by no means always, the arbor is associated with an *acantun* ("stone shaft") and, less often, an *acante* ("wooden shaft"). On these there is sometimes a splotch of blood. At times we also read of a *maxcal* plant, which Standley describes as resembling the maguey, which is also said to have blood on it, possibly a reference to its spine, which might be used in connection with a blood sacrifice. These features are apparently considered to be within an enclosure of some sort, for we read of four entrances or openings to the *acantun*. These details are also usually accompanied by a mention of birth or procreation (MS, pp. 5, 33, 46–47, 64).

The references to the *acantun* with its related features, including its association with birth, remind us of Landa's account of the idol-makers and the ceremonies with which they carved and brought their gods to life.

He tells us: "When the wood had arrived, they built a hut of straw, fenced in, where they put the wood and a great urn in which to place the idols and keep them there under cover, while they were making them. They put incense to burn to four gods called *acantuns*, which they located and placed at the four cardinal points. They put what they needed for scarifying themselves or drawing blood from their ears, and the instruments for sculpturing the black gods, and, with these preparations, the priest and the Chacs and the workmen shut themselves in the hut and began their work on the gods, often cutting their ears and anointing those idols with the blood and burning their incense, and thus they continued until the work ended."[12]

In the Madrid Codex,[13] we see illustrations of the process of carving wooden idols. It would appear that here we have a birth ceremony for the new gods.

In pagan times the four Acantuns were prominent symbols, or

---

[11] Ralph L. Roys (trans. and ed.), *The Book of Chilam Balam of Chumayel*, 63–74.
[12] *Landa's "Relación de las cosas de Yucatán,"* 160.
[13] Pages 95d, 96d, 97b, 98b.

idols as Landa calls them, during the New Year ceremonies for the birth of the year. To each year was ascribed a certain Acantun associated with a color and one of the cardinal points, or world quarters. For the east was the Chac ("red") Acantun; for the north was the Sac ("white") Acantun; for the west, the Ek ("black") Acantun; and for the south, the Kanal ("yellow") Acantun.

For the year ascribed to the east: "There were many people who drew their blood, cutting their ears, and anointing with their blood the stone of the god called Chac Acantun, which they had there. Here they took boys and drew blood from their ears by force, making gashes in their ears. They kept this statue until the unlucky days had passed and meanwhile they burned incense to it."[14] A somewhat similar procedure was followed for the north, west, and south years.[15] Landa does not tell us explicitly that these were birth ceremonies for the years, but it would seem clear that such was the case.

Here the question arises what was the fundamental significance of the *acantun*. In a considerable number of these incantations the origin of the evil spirit is ascribed to "the lust of creation [*ch'ab*]" and "the lust of darkness [*akab*]." From the various contexts it seems plain that *ch'ab* is the male principle and *akab*, the female. Although the phrase is often a stereotyped one, slight variations sometimes occur, when these two forces are cited. For example, in an incantation for "erotic seizure" (MS, p. 30), referring to the female principle, we read of "the lust of birth [*al*]" instead of darkness (*akab*). Also in incantations for "snake-pulsation" (MS, pp. 130–31) and for "a worm in the tooth" (MS, pp. 169–70) we find practically the same thing. These appear to be synonymous for *akab*.

For *ch'ab*, the male principle, one equivalent seems to be *cit* ("father") and another, *mehen* ("begetting") (MS, pp. 176, 199); and in an incantation for gout the word *acantun* is paired with *akab*, taking the place of *ch'ab* (MS, p. 91). This would seem to account for the presence of the word *acantun* in the various passages dealing with begetting.

[14] Landa's "Relación de las cosas de Yucatán," 144.
[15] Ibid., 141, 146.

It is more difficult to account for the term *acante* ("wooden shaft"), which I have not found elsewhere.

As we have seen, Landa tells of the medicine bundles of the shamans and their contents. We find much the same thing in an incantation to charm a certain poisonous spider named *am*. Here the "small stones" mentioned by Landa are called "green spider of wood" (*yax am-te*) and "green spider of stone" (*yax am-tun*); and the goddess Ix Chel is repeatedly cited (MS, pp. 157–60). Her image is not mentioned, but in other incantations for various complaints we read of a "red modeled female figure" (*chacal pat ix uinic*) and a "female figure" (*ix uinic* and *ix uinicil*) (MS, pp. 31, 97, 132). Since Ix Chel was the only goddess of medicine recorded for Yucatán, I would ascribe these expressions to her. Among the Chontal of Tabasco, whose language is very similar to Maya, Ix Chel was often called only "the woman."[16]

Throughout these incantations we find frequent mention of a "wooden man" (*uinicil-te*) and a "stone man" (*uinicil-tun*). These, I believe, were the same figure, sometimes of wood and sometimes of stone. There are some indications that they were properties of the shaman. The various contexts suggest that this figure represented the patient, or in one case where no cure is involved, it might be the patron for whom the incantation was recited.

Sometimes these figures are said to be green (*yax*), and in one case the stone man is reported to be white and black, according to the color ascribed to a symptom in the complaint. In an incantation for drying a running sore, when it is supposed to be dried up, the shaman, apparently addressing these two figures, calls them, "Dry one of wood, dry one of stone!" (Cf. MS, pp. 43, 61, 75, 81, 88, 90, 92, 97, 144, 149–51, 157).

Two other objects cited in these incantations might also be properties of the shaman. These are the fan and staff, which were

<hr/>

[16] France V. Scholes and Ralph L. Roys, "The Maya Chontal Indians of Acalan-Tixchel: A Contribution to the History and Ethnography of the Yucatán Peninsula," Carnegie Institution of Washington *Publication 560*, 57; cf. Thompson, *Maya Hieroglyphic Writing: An Introduction*, 47–48.

sometimes symbols of rulership among the Mayas. On the Xiu family tree the founder is portrayed with a fan in his hand. Its handle ends in the head of a serpent (*can*), which makes it a rebus for a heavenly (*canal*) fan.[17] In the Chumayel manuscript an illustration intended to be that of a Maya head-chief portrays him as a Spanish dignitary holding a staff of office.[18] In the incantations we find repeated threats that the shaman will slap the evil spirit with a heavenly (or snaky, a pun) fan and staff, or that he will cast him into the wind of the fan and staff (MS., pp. 24, 108–11, 114, 119).

In both the Spanish and the Maya accounts of the native religion we read of a supreme deity. The Motul Dictionary contains the following item: "*hunab ku*: the only living and true God, the greatest of the gods of the people of Yucatán, of whom there was no image, because, they said, there was no conception of his form, since he was incorporeal." The Vienna Dictionary (f. 129r.) gives a similar account of a god said to be the most important of the Maya deities; but he is named Colop-u-uich-kin ("snatcher-of-the-eye-of-the-sun"). Elsewhere we find this name only in the Bacabs manuscript, where it is repeated a number of times; and here a creator god seems to be implied in the contexts, but it may be the evil spirit that he has created.

In these incantations we also read of Colop-u-uich-akab ("snatcher-of-the-eye-of-the-night"). Although the sun was usually regarded as the head of the Maya pantheon, it would seem plain that an eclipse was caused by a still higher power.[19]

Most of these incantations are to cure a patient; and to do so, it is usually considered necessary to banish the evil spirit. He may be consigned to Metnal, the foul-smelling abode of the dead in the underworld (MS, pp. 9–10).

In some cases he is cast or falls "behind the sky," "to the place of," "to the house of," or "to the door of the house of" one of the four Pauahtuns. These may have been the wind gods, who reside at the

---

[17] Sylvanus G. Morley, *The Ancient Maya*, pl. 22.

[18] Roys, *The Book of Chilam Balam of Chumayel*, 3.

[19] Cf. Glossary of Proper Names.

four cardinal points, or world quarters (MS, pp. 49–55). According to other passages, he is cast into the wind of the fan and staff, presumably of the shaman, and falls behind the sky to the places of Ix Kuknab, Ah Bolon-yocte, Uaxac-yol-kauil, or Ix Co-ti-pan. The first three of these names also occur elsewhere in colonial Maya literature (MS, pp. 22–24).[20]

In incantations for asthma the sensation of drowning is emphasized by references to bodies of water. The banished spirit is to fall to an "east shore," an "east lagoon," or a "south estuary." He is also said to fall at the place of Ix Macanxoc. I am unable to translate the last, but it is of interest, since Macanxoc, now a part of the ruins of Cobá, was named for Lake Macanxoc, which lies beside the ruined site (MS, pp. 65, 79).

One interesting device of the shaman, apparently designed to magnify the importance of the occasion in the minds of the patient and any others present, is to liken a symptom to a cosmic phenomenon. In an incantation for a certain pulsation of the abdomen it is said of the evil spirit, "Then he caused the sun to pulsate; he caused the moon to pulsate; he caused the stars to pulsate [or twinkle]."

Nearly one-third of the Bacabs manuscript is devoted to incantations for various so-called seizures. The term is *tancas*, a contraction of *tamacas*, which is the name of a number of complaints. Among these are madness, frenzy, numbness, spasm, and falling sickness. It is defined as "a frenetic malady which strikes dumb, crazes, and deafens the person who has it."[21] Strangely enough, *tamacas* was also the name of the Milky Way.

Some seizures are named for fauna, such as the deer, *hunpedzkin*-reptile, jaguar, macaw, monkey, *oo*-bird, tarantula, and wasp. Others are ascribed in these incantations to certain kinds of people, such as drunkard-seizure, madness-seizure, and traveler-seizure. Erotic behavior is mentioned in a number of cases, where it is not indicated by the name of the complaint. Apparently it was regarded as a particularly obnoxious symptom.

[20] *Ibid.*
[21] *Diccionario de Motul.*

The sun god was perhaps best known as Kin-ich Ahau ("sun-eye lord").[22] In these incantations he is sometimes called Kin Chac Ahau ("sun great lord"); and, as we have seen, the eclipse-god is named Colop-u-uich-kin ("snatcher-of-the-eye-of-the-sun") or Kolop-u-uich-kin ("wounder-of-the-eye-of-the-sun"). Both of these sometimes appear as malevolent deities. The macaw, which was associated with the sun in the worship of the latter at Izamal, is blamed for seizure in these incantations; and the eclipse deity is said to be the creator of "wasp-seizure" (MS, pp. 25, 51). Both the sun god and the eclipse deity are named as the "father" of "jaguar-macaw-seizure," *anal-ḳaḳ*, which is an ulcerous eruption, and another complaint resembling a wasp-sting (MS, pp. 106, 108, 134). *Anal-ḳaḳ* is associated with the sun god probably because the syllable *ḳaḳ* ("eruption") is a homonym for "fire" in Maya.

In a number of cases, where erotic conduct is one of the symptoms of the disorder, it is understandable to find the origin of the evil spirit associated with the lust (*cool*) or lewd madness (*coil*) of creation (*ch'ab*) and darkness (*aḳab*), or birth (*al*) (MS, pp. 5, 30, 45ff.); but it is more difficult to follow the train of thought when a similar origin is ascribed to asthma, a snake in the abdomen, or a tapeworm (MS, pp. 68, 129–30). In the *Book of Chilam Balam of Chumayel*, however, other diseases which would seem equally irrelevant are also said to be the consequence of libidinous conduct introduced by the Itzá.[23]

These incantations are much given to a literary device, possibly with somewhat the same intent as that of alliteration in English. This a frequent play on words of the same, or somewhat similar, sound, but with different meanings. They abound in puns, near-puns, and sometimes very bad puns, although with no intention of humor. The Maya language lends itself to such a device, for it contains many homonyms and other similar-sounding words.

This seems natural in the case of incantations, where a certain amount of mystification might be expected; but with the Maya it

[22] Thompson, *Maya Hieroglyphic Writing: An Introduction*, 124–48.
[23] Roys, *The Book of Chilam Balam of Chumayel*, 83.

extends even to alleged historical material. In the *Book of Chilam Balam of Chumayel* is an account of an Itzá invasion of Yucatán, which contains many examples of this device. Here are a few of them, which involve well-known place names:

> Ppole, "where the remainder of the Itza were increased in number [*ppolhob*]."
> Tixchel, "where their words and discourses were prolonged [*chelhi*]."
> Tzuc-oop (grove of *oop*-trees), "where they remained apart [*u tzucah ubaobi*] under the *oop*-trees."
> Kikil (place of the rubber trees), "where they contracted dysentery [*kik-naki*]."
> Ti-cooh (place of the puma), "where they haggled for what was dear [*coohi*]."
> Dze-mul (small mound), "where the grandfather . . . arrived to reconcile them [*dzemlah yol*]."
> Popola (water by the rushes), "where the mat [*pop*] of the *katun* was spread."[24]

In a number of cases homonyms appear as factors in Maya symbolism. On the upper border of one side of a platform in the Mercado at Chichén Itzá, and above a double procession of dignitaries, there is a relief carving of two rattlesnakes with symbols of the planet Venus in the undulations of their bodies. It would seem that we have here a pun on the terms *ahau-can* ("rattlesnake") and *ahau-caan* ("sky-lord"). Inasmuch as speech scrolls are issuing from the mouths of the two leaders of the processions, it seems possible that a third meaning for *can*, which is "speech," is indicated.

In a case of a complaint called "bones" there is general debility, and the patient feels that he is suffering from a loosening of the articulation of his joints. The shaman calls upon the chimney swift to knit the bones together firmly, just as it cements its nest to the wall of a well (MS, pp. 209–10).

To a patient suffering from gout it is explained that he is lying beneath a bed-cover of nettles and other prickly plants, which is also

---

[24] *Ibid.,* 16–17, 70–73.

infested with stinging ants. The shaman explains that he is now changing this cover for one composed of the tails of the quetzal, the macaw, and the oriole; and he intones: "Come, yawning! Come, winking! Come, snoring! Come, sinking [into sleep]! Come, blinking!" (MS, pp. 90–91, 94–95).

With the aid and advice of William B. Cook Jr., M.D., who is a practicing psychiatrist and has looked over the incantations, I have made the following deductions, although Dr. Cook is not responsible for all of them.

As in the case of European magic, a knowledge of an evil spirit gives the possessor certain powers over it. Here the shaman knows its bird, its tree, and its arbor, things which appear to be symbolic of its origin, although we do not know how this came to be.

The trust of the patient in the shaman is doubtless the source of his curative powers. Hypnosis, as the most dramatic example of the patient's faith in the doctor, may well have been an important part of his armamentarium. In many cases the puns, near-puns, and the frequent repetition of identical or similar-sounding syllables in a number of sequent polysyllabic words would tend to produce a somnolent state. All of the above factors would be apt to produce a hypnotic effect (cf. MS, pp. 94–95, 100).

It seems significant that the shaman often states that he is committing violence on the personified disease. Also, mental afflictions arouse more fear than physical ills, because the cause is more mysterious. These incantations provide an explanation of their source, and thereby the disease becomes less terrifying, possibly losing some of its potency. To the patient, the incantation would seem to describe a conflict between the shaman and the personified disease. Consequently, the shaman must assert emphatically that he is winning the contest.

To any modern Yucatecan who is familiar with the present Maya concepts of disease, it may be surprising to find in these incantations apparently only a single mention of the personified evil winds. At the present time these are held responsible for many, though probably not a majority of, illnesses. The modern beliefs concerning

xxi

RITUAL OF THE BACABS

these winds have been treated fully by the Redfields and by Alfonso Villa.[25]

Since the sixteenth century *ik* has been defined as "wind," "breath," and "spirit," but the immortal soul is *"pixan,"* and the Holy Ghost is *Cilich Pixan.* Although the term *ik* has always been associated with a pathology of the breathing passages, as well as with the winds that blow, the idea of personified evil winds as a cause of disease seems to have appeared only quite late in the literature of the colonial period.[26]

Today certain currents of air are dangerous to health, especially one that raises a spiral of dust. They have a personality of some sort, and the shaman can often influence or control them.

Besides these actual winds, there are the so-called winds. Some of these are thought to be little people, who perform petty mischief at night. Some of them act of their own volition, while others may be induced by spirits or sorcerers.

A number of the evil winds are named for fauna, such as *tzitz-mo-ik* ("purple-macaw-wind"), *citam-ik* ("peccary-wind"), and *am-can-mo-ik* ("snake-spider-macaw-wind"). Others take their names from the disease which they cause. Among these are *tancas-ik* ("seizure-" or "shock-wind"), *coc-ik* ("asthma-wind"), *mamuk-ik* ("debility-wind"), *kasap-tun-ik* ("anury-wind") and *ol-xe-ik* ("desire-to-vomit-wind"). It seems uncertain in many cases just how a wind occupies a patient's body, but recovery is dependent on its being forced to leave.

It is a matter for the shaman to decide whether or not the patient's illness has been caused by an evil wind and, if so, which particular wind has brought on the ailment.

An apparently exceptional mention of an evil wind occurs in an incantation for "erotic seizure" (MS, p. 32). Here we read: "I curse you, Yum-ac-uinic-ik" ("father-*ac*-man-wind"). Unfortunately the element, *ac* is a homonym with five different meanings. It could mean a certain grass, a turtle, a boar peccary, a dwarf, or a certain con-

[25] Robert Redfield and Alfonso Villa R., *Chan Kom, a Maya Village.*
[26] Roys, *The Book of Chilam Balam of Chumayel,* 206–208, 210.

stellation. The *ac-ek* ("turtle star") is explained as a constellation lying partly in Gemini.[27] It is shown in the Paris Codex, on the east façade of the Monjas at Chichén Itzá, and at Uxmal. The peccary is also present as a star-glyph on the Monjas façade.[28]

I find two other passages in the Bacabs manuscript which suggest the possibility of an old association of some sort between certain evil spirits and the winds. As I have already noted, in an incantation for what is called a certain "wasp-seizure" the offending spirit is consigned to the "door of the house" of the Chac ("red") Pauahtun behind the east sky, to that of the Ek ("black") Pauahtun behind the west sky, and to that of the Sac ("white") Pauahtun behind the north sky (MS, pp. 29, 49, 52–53, 55–56). I have suggested elsewhere that the four Pauahtuns might be wind gods, but this has not as yet been confirmed.[29]

The question naturally arises, how much will the "Ritual of the Bacabs" aid us in deciphering the hieroglyphic records? J. E. S. Thompson has discussed a few of the possibilities in this respect somewhat along the following lines.[30]

It seems unlikely that this manuscript will be of much aid in the decipherment of the carved inscriptions, which appear to be presentations of dates and calculations, in part historical. On the other hand, the three hieroglyphic codices which have come down to us are largely of a divinatory or prophetic nature, although the Dresden Codex also contains important astronomical data.

Here we find sacred almanacs giving lucky and unlucky days for various activities and covering such subjects as hunting, bee-keeping, crops, weather, and, which is most important to our present study,

[27] *Diccionario de Motul.*

[28] E. Seler, "Die Ruinen von Uxmal," *Abhandlungen der Königl. Preuss. Akad. der Wissenschaften, Jahrgang,* 1917, *Phil.-Hist. Klasse,* No. 3, pl. 29; E. Seler, *Gesammelte Abhandlungen zur americanischen Sprach-und Altertumskunde,* V, 230; Thompson, *Maya Hieroglyphic Writing: An Introduction,* 161.

[29] Roys, *The Book of Chilam Balam of Chumayel,* 67, 110; Thompson, *Maya Hieroglyphic Writing: An Introduction,* 161.

[30] "Symbols, Glyphs, and Divinatory Almanacs for Diseases in the Maya Dresden and Madrid Codices," *American Antiquity,* Vol. XXIV, pp. 349–64; "A Blood-drawing Ceremony Painted on a Maya Vase," *Estudios de Cultura Maya,* Vol. I, 13–20; "Merchant Gods of Middle America," in *Homenaje al Ing.* (edited by Roberto Weitlander), II.

disease. We have strong evidence that the users of these books spoke a form of Yucatecan Maya very similar to the language of the "Ritual of the Bacabs."

There is a considerable body of colonial Maya literature, much of which is of value for the study of pre-Spanish history and contains a skeletal outline of the old lore, but not the esoteric material which we need to decipher many of the texts in the codices. The "Ritual of the Bacabs," on the other hand, contains a wealth of the materials missing in the other colonial Maya sources.

The pairing of the words *acantun* and *acante* is of much interest. In the Dresden Codex (pp. 26–28) this pillar is depicted rebus fashion. The shaft is surmounted by heart-shaped foliage and has a snake (*can*) twisted around it. It stands on a *tun*-sign, which can mean "stone" or "rock." The outline of the pillar includes the symbol for "wood" (*te* or *che*); and *acan* is the name of a plant with heart-shaped leaves. The whole can be read *acan* (*can*)*te*. The *tun*-sign could indicate either *acantun* or the pile of rock on which we are told the pillar was set up. In the latter case it could be read "the *acante* [on] a rock pile."

Mr. Thompson also suggests that the "Ritual of the Bacabs" may throw more light on certain passages in the codices which treat of diseases, particularly skin complaints (Maya, *ḳaḳ*).[31] The last appear to have been in the charge of the goddess of medicine and childbirth.

One incantation is for "traveler-seizure" (*ah oc-tancas*). Here are references to subjects associated with traveling merchants, such as the cross-roads and the fan and staff which were symbols of the merchant gods of Middle America.

Some of the numerous names of gods and other mythical beings may well be appelatives of well-known deities.

So far as I can learn, only a single curing incantation has been recorded prior to the discovery of the Bacabs manuscript. Here I give my own translation, but it differs only slightly from that of Rejón García.

[31] Thompson, "Symbols, Glyphs, and Divinatory Almanacs for Diseases in the Maya Dresden and Madrid Codices," *American Antiquity*, Vol. XXIV, 349–64.

"The seizure [*tancasil*] of the sick person shall go to Metnal [the underworld]! Who removes his seizure? I remove his seizure, because I possess the miraculous power [*mactzil*] to remove it. Let them go to Metnal: sudden death, cold, pain in the side [*auat-mo*, "macaw-screech"], leprosy, asthma, retention of the urine. They shall go to Metnal! Who removes his seizure? I remove his seizure, because I have the miraculous power to remove it. They shall go to Metnal: vomiting, blood-vomit, hiccough, epilepsy, ulcer, fainting."

Text: *Xiic û tancasil ҟohan metnal. Maix luҟsic û tancasil? Ten luҟsic û tancasil tumen yan ten mactzil in luҟsic. Xicoob metnal che tun cimil, zizhalil, auatmó, chac hauay, tuziҟ, ҟal uix, xic metnal. Maix luҟsic û tancasil? Ten luҟsic û tancasil tu men yan ten û mactzil in luҟsic. Xicoob metnal xé, xeҟiҟ, tuҟub, bocan, sac cimil,* etc.[32]

Discussions with Professor Verne F. Ray, who has made a special study of shamanism in the Pacific Northwest, have led me to realize the unusual significance of the absence in the Maya incantations of prayers to the deities, although the deities are frequently cited. The Bacabs are given orders, admonished, and sometimes even cursed; but I can find no instance of a deity being supplicated.[33]

I have already mentioned a tendency in these incantations to bring together homonyms or other words of a similar sound but different meanings. Here, too, the scribe has often written only a single vowel, where the context might call for similar words with a double vowel. Consequently the translator must choose between two meanings, both of which may have much in their favor. An effort has been made both in the translation and in the notes to indicate some of these ambiguities. Sometimes, though not as often as we might wish, the doubtful word appears in a stock phrase, which is also found in other contexts elsewhere in the colonial Maya literature. This can be a great help.

Of the last twenty-four pages of the Bacabs manuscript, eighteen

---

[32] M. Rejón García, *Supersticiónes y leyendas Mayas*, 54.

[33] Cf. V. F. Ray, *Primitive Pragmatists: The Modoc Indians of Northern California*, 42–71.

are devoted to medicine and plant lore, three contain what appears to be a fragment of an incantation, and three are blank pages. None of this material has been transcribed or translated in the present volume.

I have attempted to make the translation as literal as possible, but the paragraphing and the punctuation are my own. Slash marks indicate the end of a page in the manuscript, and the numbers in the margin show the beginning of the manuscript pages.

In the original manuscript each incantation has its own title, which has been italicized in the translation. In a number of instances the title is immediately followed by a short comment on the nature of the disorder or, more rarely, a brief instruction regarding the actual treatment to be employed. For example, an incantation for asthma is preceded by the direction that a hot stone be wrapped in certain leaves and placed on the abdomen of the patient. Such digressions, however, are rare.

CONTENTS AND ILLUSTRATIONS

ILLUSTRATIONS

Ritual of the Bacabs

A BOOK OF MAYA INCANTATIONS

I

4   *The words for jaguar-macaw-seizure* (balam-mo-tancas[1]);
the madness (coil) *of the seizure*

Hun Ahau![2] Unique Can Ahau![3] Can Ahau would be the creation. Can Ahau [Hun Ahau] would be the darkness, when you were born.

Who was your creator? Who was your darkness?[4] He created you, did Kin Chac Ahau, Colop-u-uich-kin ("sun great lord, snatcher-of-the-eye-of-the-sun"),[5] when you were born.

Who was your mother? Who was your begetter, father, when you were born? Chacal ("red") Ix Chel, Sacal ("white") Ix Chel, unique point of the lancet, unique point of the genitals.[6] That was your mother; that was your begetter, your father.[7]/

[1] *Tancas* (written *tamacaz* or *tamcaz* in the Maya dictionaries) is here translated as "seizure," but it was also the name of the Milky Way. In this manuscript it indicates such disorders as frenzy, epilepsy, convulsions, falling sickness, and numbness.

[2] Hun Ahau ("one lord") could mean either the day of that name, as a time period, or the name of the lord of the underworld, Metnal, the abode of the dead. (See Glossary of Proper Names.) Where it is considered to be the day name, it is transcribed "1 Ahau"; otherwise it is written out.

[3] Can Ahau could be either the day 4 Ahau or, more rarely, the equivalent of Caan Ahau ("sky lord"). Here the association of Can Ahau with darkness is considered to be an error of the scribe.

[4] These two terms, creation (*ch'ab*) and darkness (*akab*), recur throughout the manuscript. From their contexts I infer that the former is the male principle and the latter, the female.

[5] Colop-u-uich-kin ("snatcher-of-the-eye-of-the-sun") is explained in the Vienna Dictionary as the name of the greatest of the Maya gods, who was incorporeal. Here and elsewhere in this manuscript this name is coupled with Kin Chac Ahau ("sun-great-lord") in such a way as to indicate that they are considered to be the same deity, but this would seem impossible. (See Glossary of Proper Names.) It seems possible that Colop-u-uich-kin is named here partly because of the resemblance of his name to "lust of creation" (*u cool ch'ab*), an epithet applied to the disease.

[6] This association of the flint lancet (*ta*) with the male genitals (*ton*) also occurs in the Maya katun prophecies. Since *ta* could also have other meanings, it is of interest that its near synonym, *tok* ("flint or "flint knife"), appears in the same association (Roys, *The Book of Chilam Balam of Chumayel*, 56, 156; "The Maya Katun Prophecies of the Books of Chilam Balam," 40, 51).

[7] Many parts of this manuscript deal with semi-personified seizures, and most of

5   Raised behind it, raised behind the tree, the *maxcal* (fl.), where you were born, lust of creation, lust of darkness. *Kanch'ah*-snake, there in the trees, *ḳanch'ah*-snake there in the rocks, when you were born, lust of darkness.

Drunkard-seizure (*ah-ci-tancas*) are you. Lust of creation (*u cool ch'ab*), madness are you. Cock-macaw-seizure (*ah-mo-tancas*) are you. Deer-seizure (*ceh-tancas*) are you.

Who is your tree? Who is your bush? What was your arbor, when
6   you were born?[8]/ The red *tancas-che* ("seizure tree"), the white *tancas-che*, the black *tancas-che*, the yellow *tancas-che*, the red *ḳantemo*-tree, the white *ḳantemo*, the black *ḳantemo*, the yellow *ḳantemo*.[9] These were your trees, you, macaw-seizure. The red *has-max*-tree, the white *has-max*, the black *has-max*, the yellow *has-max*, the red *ḳoḳob-max* ("*ḳoḳob*-snake-monkey"), etc.; the red *nicte-max* ("erotic-monkey"), etc. These are your trees; erotic-seizure, monkey-seizure, are you, madness-seizure./

7   It would be at the place of Ix Hun-pudzub-kik ("lady needle-remover-of-blood"), Ix Hun-pudzub-olom ("lady needle-remover-of-clotted-blood").[10] Removed is creation (*ch'ab*), removed is darkness (*aḳab*), from the bond of its force at the place of Ix Hun-pudzub-kik, Ix Hun-pudzub-olom. There he took his force, at the place where he vomited water, [if] not water, then clotted blood. Traveler-seizure! Drunkard-macaw-seizure! Anteater-snake-seizure (*chab-can-tancas*)! How?

Cast them away, ye four gods, ye four Bacabs, to fall at the place of/

---

such incantations contain references to the evil and disgraceful nature of their origin. The unidentified *maxcal*-plant is reported to resemble the maguey; thus it would appear to have had spines that would be useful in blood sacrifices.

[8] Everybody was associated with a tree or bush and also with an arbor named for a tree or bush. The former was personified. These were in some way relevant to the name of the day on which a person was born. As we shall see later, everyone was also associated with a so-called bird, which might sometimes be an insect. (Kaua MS, pp. 11–12, 14, 21–24; Codex Pérez, pp. 94–95; Barrera Vásquez and Rendón, *El Libro de los Libros de Chilam Balam*, 189–94.)

[9] Note that these plant names contain the elements *tancas* ("seizure") or *mo* ("macaw").

[10] The word *olom* ("clotted blood") can also mean merely "blood," but the usual word for the latter is *ḳik*.

8 Kan-kinich ("yellow sun-eye"), *kan-ch'ah*-snake clotted blood;[11] at the place of Ix Hun-tah-acay clotted blood. Cast ye them still, ye four gods, ye four Bacabs, to fall at the place of Ix Co-tancas-ek ("lady mad-seizure-star"). Four days prostrate at the place of Ix Co-tancas-ek. There he bit the arm of the madness of creation, the madness of darkness; then he licked the blood on the *maxcal*-plant; then he licked the blood on the *acantun*.[12]

9 Then cast ye still/ the lust of creation, the lust of darkness, ye four gods, ye four Bacabs. He would fall into the heart of Metnal (the underworld), at the place of the father of Can-yah-ual-kak ("vigorous-enemy-of-fire"), Ix Ma-uay ("lady detrimental-one"), Ix Mac-u-hol-cab, who keeps closed the opening in the earth.[13]

These then are his mother, his lewd father, when he arrives in the heart of Metnal. Loudly resounds the clamor of his birds. How were ye all created, ye four gods, ye four Bacabs? This is to be recited by Can-yah-ual-kak, the four gods, the four Bacabs./

10 The cry of his bird, his bird of tidings,[14] because of Ix Ma-uay, who

[11] The *kan-ch'ah* is described as a large nonpoisonous snake, and its name, "orange-red-drop," suggests strongly that it was red spotted. Here, apparently, it is cited as a symbol of the blood sacrifice mentioned in the following lines.

[12] The *acantun* ("stone set up on a foundation") was a monument, also considered to be a god, erected to honor the birth of each New Year at one of the four ritual entrances to a town and anointed with the blood of worshipers. *Acantuns* were also set up at the four cardinal points around the fenced hut where the idol makers smeared them with their own blood. In these pages we shall read of splotches of blood on an *acantun*. (Cf. *Landa's "Relación de las cosas de Yucatan,"* 146–47, 308–309; Roys, *The Book of Chilam Balam of Chumayel,* 111–14.) I surmise that the "arbors" elsewhere mentioned in this manuscript were considered to be ceremonial huts, like those used by the idol makers.

[13] These appelations, Can-yah-ual-kak, Ix Ma-uay, and Ix Mac-u-hol-cab, recur in the manuscript, but they are hard to explain. It has been suggested that they are associated with an opening in the earth leading down to Metnal, the underworld (communication, J. E. S. Thompson). From two copies of a colonial Maya calendar we can piece out what may be a reference to such an opening. "[On the day of] Hun Ahau comes forth a fearful [stench of] putrefaction from Metnal" (Tizimin MS, p. 41; Codex Pérez, p. 140). Possibly Ix Ma-uay ("detrimental lady") is to be associated with Ix Hun Ahau, the consort of Hun Ahau, lord of Metnal.

[14] The word *mut*, translated as "bird of tidings," has a double meaning. It is defined as "news" or "what is being said," but it is also the word for "bird" in Chontal and other languages of the Maya stock. Today *mut* is the name of a bird of the Cracidae family (Maler, "Explorations of the Upper Usumacintla and Adjacent Regions," *Memoirs* of the Peabody Museum, Vol. IV, No. 1, p. 132).

keeps the opening in the earth. The red *chiichii*-bird, the white *sipip*-bird, the red *sipip*, the *ko*-bird of the sky, the *ko* of the clouds.

I bring notice that you fall into the heart of Metnal, lewd-seizure. How? Macaw-seizure, how? Jaguar-seizure, how? How about the lust of creation, ye four gods, ye four Bacabs? . . . This is blood then,
11   clotted blood then,/ on the tree of cock-macaw-seizure.

This is to be recited, when you address the four gods, the four Bacabs, because of Ix Ma-uay, who keeps closed the opening in the earth.

Cast ye the needful with the paraphernalia,[15] ye four gods, ye four Bacabs. Cast it into the slightly soured *atole*. Remove it all into the opening of his harsh breathing. When it enters into the opening, cast in the virgin cacao. Thus, when it enters the opening, cast in the virgin kernels. Thus, when it enters into its front, cast in the virgin
12   *chankala*-herb./ The exterior part: Can-yah-ual-kak. This would enter into its face [or front]. Cast in the *cumux-can* (fl.?). That would be seated in its cartilege (or bone). Cast in the snake-venom. Thus it would enter his throttle to needle-point out the blood. Cast in the *batcan* (fl.?). Cast in the *halal-kan* [*halal-can*, fl.?]: . . . Cast in the *dzii-kan* (*dzin-can*-herb?). That enters to fill out his back. Cast in the *kokob-tok* ("*kokob*-snake-flint," fl.?). That would enter into his tooth. . . ./

[There is no page 13, but page 14 is probably a continuation of page 12. It is badly faded and has not been translated.]

II

15   *The words for traveler-seizure* (ah oc tancas)

He vomits; lax are his bowels; there is fever also. This is traveler-seizure; there is babbling also. In the name of Dios, the father.

[The day] 4 Ahau would be the creation. [The day] 4 Ahau [1 Ahau] would be the darkness. Then were born the heart of creation, the heart of darkness.

---

[15] It seems possible that the last half of MS page 11 (beginning with this sentence) and all of page 12 belong to another incantation and were inserted here by error of the Maya scribe.

He comes from the fifth layer of the sky, the offspring of the *ƙo* in the Tzab (the "snake-rattles constellation," the Pleiades), the *ƙo* in the clouds. I strike him dumb, traveler-seizure. This would be that he understand it, that he ... traveler-seizure .../

[There is no page numbered 16.]

17 This is to be recited, the command for him in the heart of the sky here.

Thus the white *oo*-bird is his bird, the red *oo*-bird. So then his tree comes from the heart of the sky.

Who, then, is his mother? He would be the offspring of the fire-colored rainbow (*chel*), the offspring of the fire in the sky, the off-spring of the fire in the clouds. How?

The force of the friction at the tip of the fire[-drill?] just before Kin Chac Ahau ("sun great lord") vomits because of him; shortly before Ix Bolon Can ("lady nine-sky") vomits because of him. I curse you, seizure! This would be recited; this would be his insolent

18 speech;/ this would be recited: his command in the heart of the sky here.

So then the white *oo* is his bird, the red *oo* then. His tree comes [from] the heart of the sky.

Who, then, is his mother? He would be the offspring of the fire-colored rainbow, the offspring of the fire there in the sky, the offspring of the fire there in the clouds, the force of the friction at the tip of the fire[-drill], just before Kin Chac Ahau vomits, just before Bolon Can vomits because of him. I curse you, seizure. This would be recited, his insolent speech.

19 Well defended would he be by a powerful/ defense. It would be by the mighty sun, the mighty cloud.

He would fall at the four crossroads, at the four resting places, at the place of Ix Ho[1]-can-be ("lady four crossroads"), at the place of Yum Ho[1]-can-lub ("father four-resting-places"). This would be recited by Ix Ho[1]-can-be, Ix Ho[1]-can-lub.

This would be the order to traveler-seizure. How? This would be the order, shortly before, for us here.

The red *oo* is his bird of tidings. Thrown to the wind of creation, the wind of the staff, the wind of the fan.[16] He would fall behind the sky . . . at the place of Bolon Choch ("nine" or "many releases"). I curse you seizure./

[On pages 20–21 is a fragment of an incantation written in a different and more sophisticated hand; see Appendix A. The sequence of the text from page 19 falls on MS p. 22.]

22   These would be his kind words here, just before the vomiting of Sac-uayab-xoc ("white-demon-shark"), Sac-mumul-ain ("white-muddy-crocodile"), just before the vomiting of the four gods, the four Bacabs, because of the casting of the flint into the wind of the fan, into the wind of the red fan.

He would fall behind the east sky,[17] at the place of Ix Kuknab ("lady water-lily-sprout"), just before they would vomit, just before they would cry out. The offspring, how? of Ix Ti-ho-tzab ("lady at-the-five-rattles") from the fifth layer of the sky. Traveler-seizure, how?

The red *oo*, the white *oo*, are his bird, his bird of tidings (*mut*).

23   Ye gods, ye Bacabs!/ Cast ye him into the wind of the fan, into the wind of the staff. He would fall behind the south [sky] to the place of Uuc-chan-chuc, Ah Ik, at the place of Ah Bolon Yocte ("he of many strides"), falling headlong, the hair of his head [like] mad, just before he vomits. The hair-tail of his head just below, when he fell, when he was bound. The force of creation, directly, just before they would vomit.

[It was] *ix-malin*-cacao, when he fell, when he was bound, that gushed from the jar, foreign cacao from the neck of the jar. It gushed directly from its neck. This would be his command, directly, there

24   to your house./ It was knocking in the wind of the fan, in the wind of the staff.

This would be recited. It would fall at the place of the west arbor

16 The fan and more rarely the staff are cited in the katun prophecies as symbols of sovereignty (Roys, *The Book of Chilam Balam of Chumayel*; "The Maya Katun Prophecies of the Book of Chilam Balam," 37; Morley, *The Ancient Maya*, pl. 22). Among the Mexicans they were insignia of the merchants (Thompson, *Mexico Before Cortez*, 127, 132).

17 Falling figures are portrayed in the Dresden Codex (pp. 15b, 40b, and possibly 58c).

of Ix Co-ti-pan, at the place of Ix Tah-kab, at the place of U-lam-tzin [Olon-tzin].

This would be said by Ah Olon-tzin, the *oo*-bird. This would be said, when macaw-seizure received the order. How? In the fifth (*ho*) layer of the sky. The offspring of Ix Ti-tzab ("lady in-the-rattles-constellation"), the *ho* [*ko*] in the clouds, the *oo*-bird. How? These would be the four gods, the four Bacabs, because of traveler-seizure. How? His bird, his bird of tidings. How? He is to be cast into the wind of the fan, into the wind of the staff. He would fall,/ powerful Kauil, at the place of Uaxac-yol-kauil ("eight heart-of-food"), the guardian of the opening in the earth, almost, it would be, of Ix Hun Ahau.[18] Amen.

III

The incantation for macaw-seizure (mo-tancas) *and convulsions* (nunil-tancas); *also traveler-seizure* (ah oc-tancas) *and fever*

Whether it is his mouth, not his tooth, whether froth flows from his mouth, this is to be said. This is a certain command, which begins when you recite it. A very good command, a good incantation.

First 1 Ahau. Unique 4 Ahau would be the day. 1 Ahau would be the night. Then occurred the creation;/ then occurred the birth in the four divisions of the sky; then it occurred in the four divisions of the clouds.

Meanwhile, this would be said: I curse you, ye gods, ye Bacabs, when ye command the creation. The gods are to be declared; these would be the Bacabs. How great is his insolent talk, when you command him. This is the command of the gods; this is the command of the Bacabs: Seven heaps grasped! This would be said: I curse you, creation! *Koko*-bird! This would be his shameless talk; this would be his insolent speech.

What is your pain (or grief)? How? The *ko*-bird in the sky, the

---

18 Here the opening in the earth is associated with Uaxac-yol-kauil, apparently a maize god and possibly referring to the planted grain. It is also associated with Ix Hun Ahau, the consort of the lord of Metnal. (Cf. MS p. 81 below, where this opening is associated with "the guardian of the rear" of Yaxal Chac, the rain god.) Cf. Glossary of Proper Names.

27 *ko* in the clouds./ The son (*mehen*[19]) of Kinich Kak-mo ("sun-eye fire-macaw"), the offspring (*yal*) of the fire-colored rainbow (*chel*). Red was the ringed sun, red was the ringed moon, when he was born.

Now, when it progresses to his tooth (or beak?), split in the middle was his [effigy-]bowl, overturned at the opening to his *acantun*, when his birth occurred, when his creation occurred. I was his arbor, I was his bush, when his birth occurred, when his creation occurred.

This is to be recited: The *ek-acal* (fl.?), the *kantemo*-tree. You were his tree, the *punab*-tree, when his birth occurred, when his creation occurred. The red *pule*[20] is his bird of tidings (*mutil*). What is

28 the symbol of his tongue?/ This would be the claw of the red *lukub-tok* ("flint-remover," fl.?), the seed of the *sihom-takin* ("gold soap-berry tree"), the [bull's] eye of the white circle, the ear-stopper of tangled hair, the bowl of the ring of my buttock.

Then he saw the birth; then he saw the creation. This would be said: *Kanch'ah*-snake-blood, *kanch'ah*-snake-clotted-blood, on the wooden haft (*kabalte*), the stone haft (*kabaltun*),[21] where he licked it for breakfast. The red *kuxub* (arnotto), when he breakfasted. Then he saw the birth, then he saw the creation. Then he ate (or bit) the

29 *potz*,[22] when the birth occurred, when he husked the staff,/ when he ate the *kanche* [*kamchi*,[23] "breakfast"], when the birth occurred.

He is to be cast to the place of Chac Pauahtun Chac; there where he took mixed blood, its force; there where he took the collected fire, its force; there where its burning occurred. Here I damaged it; here I cut it. This is to be recited.

[19] Here the use of the term *mehen* ("begotten son") deserves notice because it is so rare in this manuscript. Almost always any offspring mentioned is called *al* ("born one"), which is a reference to a female parent.

[20] I can find no record of any bird named *pule* or *pul*.

[21] *Kabal* has been defined, so far as I know, only as the primitive Yucatán potter's wheel. In this manuscript, however, it is sometimes referable to *kab* ("arm," "hand," or "handle"), and sometimes to another *kab*, which means "juice," "broth," or the liquor of something.

[22] I can find no meaning for *potz*. If *podz* were intended, it could mean something squeezed out, like pus from a sore or milk from a teat. *Podz* can also mean something slippery or muddy.

[23] *Kanche* means a stool or seat, and it is also the name of the button mangrove. Here the word seems to be merely a pun on the word *kamchi* ("breakfast").

This would be his wing, with which he damages it, with which he cuts it. Thus it would enter into the fan-wind of the door of the house. This would be the spine, which he cuts; so he enters the forest of saplings. Thus ends my chopping it with its bone. This is to be
30 recited./ He is to be cast into the place of Ix Hun Ahau. Amen.

IV
The words for erotic- (nicte-)[24] *seizure*

Mad will be the speech of the man because of fever. The man has an impulse to run because of his madness also.

Unique 4 Ahau is the day for the creation of the great fierce one. High (*can*) is the door of his green arbor,[25] where the origin (*sihil*) of the lust of birth (*u cool al*), the lust of creation (*u cool ch'ab*) took place. Firmly set was his red haft (*ḳabal*), when there occurred the
31 birth of the *on* ("*aguacate*"), the plumeria (*nicte*);/ when there occurred the birth of the hummingbird-plumeria (*dzunun-nicte*).

Then it was, when he took the head (or exterior) of the *acan*-plant to be squeezed over it. What then is its symbol? I seize the red modeled human figure (*chacal pat ix uinic*), the white modeled human figure.[26]

Thirteen turns are his circuit in the heart of the sky, while he vigorously seeks and finds the red *chichibe*-herb, the red *ḳutz* ("tobacco plant"), the white *ḳutz*, while I seize it. This is the symbol of the red *bacal-che*-shrub, the white *bacal-che*, the symbol of my

24 The plumeria (*nicte*) figures prominently in Maya literature as a symbol of eroticism (cf. Roys, *The Book of Chilam Balam of Chumayel*, 104). Only in this manuscript have I found an erotic significance for the aguacate (*on*) in Yucatán. In Mexico, where the name *auacatl* can also mean "testicle," it is considered to have aphrodisiac properties (P. C. Standley, *Flora of Yucatán*; Alsonso de Molina, *Vocabulario de la lengua Mexicana*, II, 9). The association of the arbor (*dzulbal*) with birth is plain.

25 In the Chumayel manuscript we read of ceremonial huts named for trees, but there associated with the lineage cults. The term *dzulbal* is employed (Roys, *The Book of Chilam Balam of Chumayel*, 63–64). We are reminded of the stone replicas of such huts over the doors of the south wing of the Monjas quadrangle at Uxmal (Holmes, 1895 not in bibliography, pl. 9; E. Seler, "*Die Ruinen von Uxmal*," *Abhandlungen der Königl. Preuss. Aḳad. der Wissenschaften, Jahrgang* 1917, *Phil.-Hist. Klasse*, No. 3, pl. 41). It would seem that the rooms behind them may well have been devoted to lineage cults.

26 The "modeled female figure" (*pat ix uinic*) suggests that it could have been one of the properties of the medicine man.

steeping the sweetness (or wine?) from the *sac-nicte*-tree ("white plumeria"), the bed-cover of the *sabac-nicte*-tree ("purple plumeria"), 32 the bed-cover of the *kan-mucuy-che*, the covering of its bed./ So that, how? with the juice of the *chichibe*-herb and the juice of the *sac-nicte*-tree I steeped it for him to drink.

Oh, I curse you, Yum-ac-uinic-ik ("father dwarf-man wind")[27] with erotic-seizure together. This would be recited over the man who talks very madly. He runs, afflicted with a convulsion (*hadz-ik*). This shall be recited over him, twice recited.

Then begins the bleeding of his tongue with a point of the *ci* ("maguey"), also the middle of his back. Then he is to be aspersed with medical herbs in hot water. Amen.

V

The words for tarantula-eruption (chiuoh-kak), tarantula-seizure (chiuoh-tancas)

Hun Ahau! Unique Can Ahau! Can Ahau would be the creation; 33 Hun Ahau/ would be the darkness.

Four (*can*) are the doors to his arbor; four are those to his *acantun*, where his birth occurred.[28] Four splotches of blood, four splotches of clotted blood [are] behind the *acantun*, the *acante* ("wooden monument"). Four were their flint lancets; four were their male genitals; four were their arbors, when his birth occurred.

What is his arbor? The *chiuoh-xiu* ("tarantula plant"), the white

[27] The expressions Yum-ac-uinic-ik and *hadz-ik* ("blown by the wind") would seem to anticipate the later theory of *malos aires* ("bad winds"), which is so important in modern Maya medicine. Elsewhere I first find *hadz-ik* in Beltrán's grammar, originally published in 1746 (cf. Pío Pérez, *Coordinación alfabética de las voces del idioma Maya que se hallan en el arte y obras del Padre Fr. Beltrán de Santa Rosa*, 29).

[28] Here we are reminded of Landa's account of the idol makers, who worked in a "fenced straw hut," which I take to be the same as the arbor (*dzulbal*) often mentioned in these incantations. There were *acantuns* at the four cardinal points, and they made blood sacrifices from their ears to anoint the idols (*Landa's "Relacion de las cosas de Yucatán*, 144, 147, 160). He does not mention the *acante* ("erected wooden shaft"). It is true that he tells of certain upright timbers which were associated with blood sacrifices and were set in the temple courts. He gives no Maya name, and it seems doubtful that they were the originals of the *Acante*, which is so often associated with the *acantun* in these incantations (*ibid.*, 114 and n.).

koch-plant, are his arbor. The red *xacatbe*-insect, the white *xacatbe*, are his birds.[29]

Who was his mother? He would be the offspring of Ix Bolon-che, Ix Bolon-ch'och'ol [a beetle?], Ix Paclah-actun, the offspring of Ix Yal-hopoch, the offspring of Ix Yal-sik-che, when he was born in the heart of the sky.

34   Say ye:/ Thrice hail seizure. This is to be said: Uoh! This would be the reply of Ix Uooh in the sky, Ix Uooh in the clouds.[30] He would be cast behind the east sky to the place of Chac Pauahtun. Who was his creator? His creator was Colop-u-uich-kin ("snatcher-of-the-eye-of-the-sun"), when it was damaged, snatched away.

These would be the words of Oxlahun-ti-ku ("thirteen-gods"). Say ye still: Thrice hail seizure! This would be said: Uoh! This would be his reply: *Tii ul*.[31]

The red *chiuoh*-tarantula, the white *chiuoh*, tarantula-blood,
35   tarantula-eruption-seizure. The red/ *koch*-plant, the white *koch*, are his arbor; the *chiuoh-xiu* is his arbor.

Cast yet him behind the south sky to the door of the house of Kan ("yellow") Pauahtun. Who was his creator? He created him, did Colop-u-uich-kin in the heart of the sky.

Say ye still: Thrice hail seizure! This would be said: Uooh! This would be his reply: *Tii ul*.

The red *chiuoh*-tarantula, the white *chiuoh*, tarantula-blood, tarantula-eruption, tarantula-seizure. Then clamored his bird, the red *xacatbe*-insect.

36   The yellow *koch*-plant, the black *koch*,/ the *chiuoh-xiu*, are his arbor. Very yellow would be the fruit of the *put* ("papaya"). The

[29] Here the *xacatbe*, an insect resembling a locust, is called a "bird." Frequently in these pages an insect is considered to be a "bird" for ritual purposes. The *koch*-plant may be associated with the tarantula because its name resembles that of another insect, *ix kochol*, described as a large wingless cricket.

[30] Ix Uoh is discussed in the Glossary of Proper Names. It might be a supernatural tarantula, since the latter is variously named *chi-uoh* and *co-uoh*, although only the former name appears in this manuscript.

[31] *Tii ul* is difficult to translate. I suspect that it is an affectation of a Chontal form meaning "bitten" or "biter." The Chontal appear to have been famous sorcerers. If so, the Maya equivalent would be *chi-ul*.

balam-ḵuch-ci ("jaguar-vulture-agave"): This enters into the anus of tarantula-eruption, tarantula-seizure. Then he took the rough exterior of the *chi* ("*nancen*").[32] This is his arbor, where he took his force.

He is to be cast behind the west sky, to the door of the house of Ek ("black") Pauahtun. Who is his creator, when he is damaged, when he is snatched away?

Say ye still: Thrice hail seizure! This is to be said: Uooh! This would be his reply: *Tii ul*.

The black *chiuoh*-tarantula, tarantula-blood, tarantula-eruption,/
37   tarantula-seizure. The black *ḵoch*-plant is his arbor; the *chiuoh-xiu* is his arbor. The black *xacatbe*-insect is his bird.

Tarantula-blood, tarantula-eruption, tarantula-seizure! Slap ye him still, when he bars off the seashore. Four days he burns it; four days he spoils the seashore. His birds clamored; the red *xacatbe*-insect, the white *xacatbe*, are his birds.

The red *ḵoch*-plant, the white *ḵoch*, they are his arbor; the *chiuoh-xiu* is his arbor.

38   Say ye still: Thrice hail seizure! This is to be said:/ Uoh! This would be his reply: *Ti ul*. How is it?

The red *chiuoh*-tarantula, the white *chiuoh*, tarantula-blood, tarantula-eruption, tarantula-seizure.

Four days he burns it: four days it burns on the seashore. The *tabcan* ("mangrove") would burn; the *yaxum*-tree[33] would burn. For four days stinks the fish in his arbor, when his birth occurred.

Slap ye him still! He would fall behind the north sky, at the door of the house of the Sac ("white") Pauahtun. Who was his creator? He created him, did Kolop-u-uich-kin ("wounder-of-the-face-of-the-
39   sun") in the heart of the sky,/ when he is to be removed (or burned?

---

[32] The reference to the *chi*-fruit would appear to be simply a partial pun on the word, *chi-uoh*, ("tarantula").

[33] Not only is the mangrove a common tree on the coast but my only report of the unidentified *yaxum*-tree placed it near the sea north of Ixil (communication, J. Martínez Hernández). The reference to burning may be due to the name of the complaint. *Chiuoh-ḵaḵ* ("tarantula-eruption") and could mean "tarantula-fire." This mention of the seashore might also be a rather far-fetched pun. The Maya word for sea is *ḵaḵ-nab*, and the word for shore is *chi*.

toc-hom). These would be the words of Oxlahun-ti-kuob ("thirteen-gods"): Thrice hail seizure! This would be said: Uoh! This is his reply: *Ti ul.*

The white *chiuoh*-tarantula, the yellow *chiuoh*, tarantula-eruption, tarantula-seizure! The red *koch*-plant is his arbor; the *tii-uoh-xoc* [*chiuoh-xiu*, fl.] is his arbor at the door of the house of Sac Pauahtun.

Slap ye him still! He would fall in the heart of the sky. Say ye: Evil (*kasil*) of creation, evil of darkness, when he shall deteriorate (*kas-hom*), when he shall be snatched away. Then he snatched away

40 the eye of the sun. Say ye still, this is to be said by him:/ Thrice hail seizure! [This would be said:] Uooh! This would be his reply: [*Ti ul*].

The black tarantula. Then clamored the red *xacatbe*-insect, the white *xacatbe*, his birds.

The red *koch*-plant, the white *koch*, the *chiuoh-xiu*, are his arbor in the heart of the sky. Give ye [it], with yourselves. Cast [him into] the rays of the sun.[34] There he took the force (or poison, *kinam*) of tarantula-blood, tarantula-eruption [literally, "tarantula-fire"], tarantula-seizure. Cast ye him into quicksand. Cast ye him still.

41 What is his symbol (*uayasba*[35]), when he departs into/ the heart of the sky? It would be the leaf of the *koch*-plant, his symbol, when he departed into the heart of the sky. There was the *uohil*[36] of the *xan*-palm, when it was bound, forcibly clasped by Ix Bolon-che, Bolon-ch'och'ol, Ix Cucul-patz-kin ("lady sunstroke"?), Ix Yal-hopoch. Four days it ripened yellow at the base of the red *koch*-plant.

[34] The phrase, *u matzab kin*, is translated as "rays of the sun," but its literal meaning is "eyelash of the sun." Another term for the same is *u mex kin*, literally "beard of the sun."

[35] It is difficult to determine the full significance of the term *uayasba*, here translated "symbol." It is explained in the Motul Dictionary as being the form, character, or symbol of a person. For example, we read: "The Holy Spirit descended upon them in the form [*uayasba*] of fire." *Uayaz* is defined as "that which passes suddenly, like a dream or vision." *Uaay* means a familiar spirit, which takes the form of an animal.

[36] It is evident that the syllable *uoh*, as part of the word *chi-uoh* ("tarantula") is here a word to conjure with. From the context, it would appear to be the interior of the trunk of the *guano* palm, as it is associated with the pith of a reed. Elsewhere we find some part of its trunk employed as a charm to hasten parturition (Roys, *The Book of Chilam Balam of Chumayel*, 15, 293).

There was the pith (*macapil*) of the *halal*-reed; there was the *uohil* of the *xan*-palm, when it was bound, when it fell. There he took the stopper (*mac*) of breath, the stopper (*mac*) of saliva.

42   Four days clamored the red/ *xacatbe*-insect, the white *xacatbe*. He damages the seashore.

Who is his creator? His creator is Kolop-u-uich-kin[37] in the heart of the sky

Say ye still: Thrice hail seizure! This would be recited: Uooh! This would be the reply: Uoh in the sky, Uoh in the clouds, *Ti ul.* How?

The red tarantula, tarantula-blood, tarantula-eruption [or -fire, a pun], tarantula-seizure. Then it enters into tarantula-water (*chiuoh-haail*) [on] the seashore.[38] The *oppol*-tree would burn; the *yaxum*-tree would burn. Four days rotted the fish, when he licks the froth of

43   the water that enters into/ the white saliva of tarantula-seizure. It falls on the baked savannah. The red coloring matter was crammed into his neck.

He would fall to the place of Som-pul ("violent casting"), Som-ch'in ("violent hurling"). There he took the obstruction in his throat to spoil (*ḳasic*) the red beaten water. That enters into the white saliva of tarantula-seizure, to be cast into the red liquid (*ḳabal*). There he spoils the wooden man, the stone man.[39] I grasp the bowl (*lac*) of my red genitals (*ton*), my white genitals, when it occurs that I vigorously squeeze it over the wooden man, the stone man.

Thirteen (*oxlahun,* supreme?) are my hail-waters, with which I

[37] Kolop-u-uich-kin ("wounder-of-the-eye-of-the-sun") seems obviously an arbitrary variation from the name, Colop-u-uich-kin, but it is quite in keeping with the spirit of these incantations. It is possible that these rhetorical devices could have had a hypnotic effect on the patient.

[38] It is hard to tell what is meant by *chiuoh-haail* ("tarantula-water"). A stream of that name flows into Laguna de Términos from the east side, and on it is a village of the same name (Scholes and Roys, *The Maya Chontal Indians of Acalan-Tixchel,* 224, map 3). We are reminded of the name of one of the natural wells at Bolonchenticul, which is Chimez-ha ("centipede-water") (C. H. Berendt, "*Nombres proprios en lengua Maya,*" f. 43v.).

[39] The "wooden man" and "stone man" (*uinicil-tun, uinicil-te*) appear a number of times in these incantations. In some instances the context seems to imply that they are properties of the medicine man and represent the patient (cf. MS p. 91 below).

44 assuage/ your force (or pain). I am your mother; I am your father. Great Can Ahau! Amen.

VI
The lewd madness of seizure (u coil tancas)

Unique 4 (*can*) Ahau is its day; unique 4 Ahau [1 Ahau] is its night; the lewdness (*coil*) of night, the lewdness of day, there in the sky (*caan*), there in the clouds.

Firmly established is his *acantun*. Four (*can*) days prostrate is the serpent (or shoot, *canil*) of creation.[40] Four days it turns about, [where it is] placed, planted. You are the lewdness of seizure. Curses upon you!

45 Ye gods!/ Ye Bacabs! Who are those who move noisily? The lewdness (*coil*) of creation, the lewdness of darkness. Who else are they also? There would be babbling seizure. Oh, who was your creator? He created you, did Kin Chac Ahau, Colop-u-uich-kin ("sun great lord, snatcher-of-the-eye-of-the-sun"), Colop-u-uich-akab ("snatcher-of-the-eye-of-night"). Then you blossomed forth at the hand of Colop-u-uich ("eye-snatcher"). Who created you? He created you, did Ix Hun-ye-ta ("unique point of the lancet,") Ix Hun-ye-ton ("unique point of the male genitals"). He gave you your force, Chac-dzidzib-kik ("red-cardinal-blood").

Who is the great bird of prey? The great one who pecks, the great *ah chuy* ("kite"), the great bird of prey. Who is your bird? The *ko*
46 in the sky, the *ko* in the clouds.[41]/ Who also are you? You are, how? macaw-seizure (*mo-tancas*). You are *cuyum*-snake-blood, madness-seizure, the moth-larva (*cuyil*) of the day, the snake (or shoot?) of the night, suppurating blood.

I suddenly grasp you for the fourth time in my incantation (*pedz*), when I stand erect.

[40] The expression *u canil ch'ab* could mean either the serpent or the offshoots of creation. Here the reference to planting (*pakal*) appears to support the latter interpretation.

[41] Here would seem to be definite evidence that the unidentified *ko* is considered to be a bird, although, as has been pointed out, some insects are called "birds" in this manuscript. It is possible also that there was either a star or a constellation named for such a bird.

Thirteen (or supreme?) are my fathers. How? Thus indeed I put him to sleep. Great Can Ahau! Amen.

VII
The words for kanpetkin-*wasp seizure;*[42] *its incantations*

Can Ahau alone! Unique Can Ahau! Can Ahau would be the
47 creation. Four (*cante*) are the doors to his arbor;/ four are the openings to his *acantun*. Four splotches of blood (*can tah k̟ik̟*), four splotches of clotted blood were behind the *acantun*, behind the *maxcal-*plant,[43] when his birth occurred. Four were the doors to his arbor, when the birth of the evil (*k̟asil*) of creation occurred.

Who was his creator? He created him, did Kolop-u-uich-kin ("wounder-of-the-eye-of-the-sun") in the midst of the sky, when his birds clamored. The red *pap*-jay, the yellow *tacay*-bird, are his birds. The *k̟an-dzul-mo*-macaw was his mother. [He was] the offspring of the *ix k̟antanen-k̟in*-insect ("yellow-fronted-sun"), the *k̟antanen-u* ("yellow-fronted-moon"). The offspring, he would be, of *oo*-bird-seizure (*oo-tancas*), born in the heart of the sky./

48 Say ye still. The evil (*k̟asil*) of creation! This is to be said: Thrice hail seizure! This is to be said: Uoh!

This would be the reply, how? of the offspring of the *uoh*[44] in the sky, the *uoh* in the clouds. The offspring of the *ix k̟antanen-k̟in*-insect, the ix *k̟antanen-u*. The offspring of the sky-*k̟ok̟o*, the cloud-*k̟ok̟o. Kanpetk̟in*-wasp-seizure: The red *k̟anal*-wasp, the red *tupchac*-wasp, the red *xanab-chac*-wasp, The *dzidzil*-wasp, wasp-blood, wasp-seizure.

49 What is his arbor? The *k̟ante-ceh*-tree,/ the *k̟ante-mo*-tree, the *k̟andzutob* (fl.?), the *k̟an-pocob* [*k̟an-pok̟ol*-tree?] are the binders of his arbor, when his birth occurs.

---

[42] Since *k̟an-pet-k̟in* means literally "yellow circular sun," many things cited here are yellow (*k̟an*), although the Maya word also covers things which we would consider to be red or orange.

[43] For similar references to the *maxcal*, the *acantun*, or blood sacrifices, see MS pp. 5, 8, 33 above.

[44] Heretofore the *uoh* has been found associated with the tarantula (*chi-uoh*); but here it appears in connection with a seizure ascribed to a wasp.

18

Cast ye him still behind the east sky, to the door of the house of Chac ("red") Pauahtun Chac.[45] He blooms red, he blooms white, at the door of the house of Chac Pauahtun Chac.

Who was his creator, when he arrived to be spoiled, to be snatched away? These would be the words of Oxlahun-ti-kuob ("thirteen gods"): Thrice hail seizure! This is to be said: Uoh!

50   This would be the reply of the offspring, how?/ of the *uoh* in the sky, and [the *uoh*] in the clouds. The ix *ḳantanen-ḳin*-insect, the ix *ḳantanen-u*, the offspring, how? of the *ḳan-dzul-mo*-macaw.

Then clamored the birds of seizure. The red *pap*-jay, the white *pap*, the yellow *tacay*-kingbird, are his birds. The *ḳan-dzul-mo*-macaw is the offspring of the *ḳo* in the sky, the *ḳo* in the clouds. He would be the offspring of drunkard-seizure, the offspring of *ah oo*-seizure, when he was born.

Slap ye him. He would fall behind the south sky. Who was his creator, . . . to be spoiled, to be snatched away? These would be the words by Oxlahun-ti-ku ("thirteen gods"). Speak ye still! Yellow-

51   colored (*ḳan pulen*) at the door/ of his arbor. Thrice hail seizure! This would be said by Oxlahun-ti-ku. Uoh! This would be the word, how? of the offspring of the *uoh* in the sky, the *uoh* in the clouds; the offspring of the ix *ḳantanen-ḳin*, the ix *ḳantanen-u*; the offspring of drunkard-seizure; the offspring of *oo*-bird-seizure; the offspring of the *ḳan-dzul-mo*-macaw.

Then was he born; then ripened yellow his saliva; then turned yellow (*ḳanhi*) his arbor.

Who was his creator? His creator was Colop-u-uich-kin in the heart of the sky.

52   He is to be cast to the door of the house/ of Ek ("black") Pauahtun behind the west sky. Who was his creator, when he was spoiled (*tu ḳashon*), when he was snatched away (*tu toc hon*)?

These would be the words of Oxlahun-ti-kuob. Yellow-colored, black-colored, at the door of his arbor. Say ye then: Thrice hail

---

[45] There has long been some doubt about the nature of the four Pauahtuns. Here the name, Chac Pauahtun Chac confirms their close association with the Chacs, or rain gods.

19

seizure! This would be said. Uoh! This would be the reply, how? of the offspring of Uoh in the sky, Uoh in the clouds. The offspring of traveler-seizure, the offspring of drunkard-seizure, the offspring of *oo*-bird-seizure, the offspring of the *ḳan-dzul-mo*-macaw.

Who is his arbor? The *ḳante-cech* [*ḳante-ceeh?*], the *ḳante-mo*-tree. The *ḳan-dzutob*, the *ḳan-dzocob*-palm, are the binders of his arbor.

53   Who is his creator? To the east/ is Chac Ahau, Kolop-u-uich-kin, in the heart of the sky. Cast him down. He would fall on the seashore.

There clamored his birds; the red *pap*-jay, the white *pap*-jay, the yellow *tacay*-bird are his birds. The *ḳan-dzul-mo*-macaw is his mother. The offspring of the *ḳo* in the sky, the *ḳo* in the clouds. Thus is his arbor: the *ḳante-cech* [*ḳante-ceeh?*], the *ḳan-dzutob*, the *ḳan-dzocob*, are the binders of his arbor.

Speak ye still! This is to be said by Oxlahun-ti-kuob: Uoh! This would be his reply: *Ti ul.* How?

54   *Kanpetḳin*-wasp-seizure. The red/ *ḳanal*-wasp, the red *tup-chac*-wasp, the red *xanab-chac*-wasp, the *dzidzil*-wasp, wasp-blood, wasp-seizure.

Who was his mother, when he was born? He would be the offspring of the *ḳo* in the sky, the *ḳo* in the clouds; he would be the offspring of the *ḳan-dzul-mo*-macaw, his mother, when he was born; the offspring of drunkard-seizure, the offspring of *oo*-bird-seizure, the offspring of fierce-man-seizure (*ah co-tancas*), *ḳanpetḳin*-wasp-seizure, the offspring of the *ḳantanen-ḳin*-insect, the *ḳantanen-u.*

During his birth, during his creation, he would enter into wasp-seizure (*xux-tancas*) on the seashore, where he was bound, where he fell, the evil (*ḳasil*) of creation.

55   Cast him behind the north sky/ to the door of the house of Sac ("white") Pauahtun. He budded white in his arbor. Who was his creator? There he was to be spoiled, snatched away.

These would be the words of Oxlahun-ti-kuob ("thirteen-gods"): Speak ye still! The evil (*ḳasil*) of creation. Thrice hail seizure! This would be said by Oxlahun-ti-kuob. Uoh. This would be the reply of the offspring, how? of the *uoh* in the sky, the *uoh* in the clouds: *Ti ul.* How? *Kanpetkin*-seizure, the red *kanal*-wasp, the red *tup-chac*-wasp, the *dzidzil*-wasp, wasp-blood, wasp-seizure.

56 Then clamored his birds. The red *pap*-jay is his bird. The *kan-dzul-mo*-macaw./ The mother of the offspring of the *kantanen-kin*-insect, the *kantanen-u.* The offspring of drunkard-seizure, the off-spring of madness-seizure (*co-tancas*), the offspring of *oo*-bird-seizure, when he was born, the evil of creation, the evil of darkness. He is to be cast into the very yellow-colored, the very red-colored eye (or face) of the sun in the heart of the sky. Who was his creator, when he damaged (*kasah*) the eye (or face) of the sun?

Speak ye still! This would be said by Oxlahun-ti-kuob: Thrice hail seizure! This would be said: Uoh! This would be the reply of the offspring, how? of the *uoh* in the sky, the *uoh* in the cloud, the off-
57 spring of the *kantanen-kin*-insect,/ the *kantanen-can* [*-caan*] ("yel-low-colored-sky"), the *kantanen-u* ("yellow-moon"). *Kanpetkin*-wasp-seizure, offspring of the *ko* in the sky, [offspring of] the *ko* in the clouds. Offspring of drunkard-seizure, offspring of *oo*-bird-seizure, when he was born.

Then clamored the red *pap*-jay, the white *pap*, the yellow (*kan*) *tacay*-bird. The *kan-dzul-mo*-macaw was his mother, when he was born, the evil (*kasil*) of creation, the evil of darkness. The *kante*-tree, the *kante-mo*-tree, the *kan-dzutob* (fl.), the *kan-dzocob*-palm: these were the binders of his arbor, when his birth occurred.

There he took the pain, there he took the force (or poison) of *kanpetkin*-seizure.
58 He is to be cast into quicksand./ He is to be cast into the heart of the sky. He falls behind the east sky to the door of the house of Chac ("red") Pauahtun.

Who was his creator? Thus he was spoiled. These would be the words of Oxlahun-ti-kuob: Say [ye still]: Thrice hail seizure! This would be said. Uoh!

This would be the reply of the offspring, how? of the *uoh* in the sky, the *uoh* in the clouds. Give ye the trappings. Cast down would be the *xux-dzocob*-palm ("wasp-*dzocob*-palm"). There is his mother.

Cast [down] would be the *dzacal-mo-pasismo* ("*dzacal*-macaw-

59 spasm").[46]/ That enters into his *holbal* ("head" or "outer part"?). Cast [down] would be the husks of the food. That enters into the *yubal* ("cloak") on his back. Cast down would be the curled (or rolled) *dzoc* (fl.?). That would enter into his . . . . Cast down would be the virgin needle of Uuc-metlah Ahau. That enters into his sting. Cast down would be the virgin sieve of Uuc-metlah Ahau. That would occur when Oxlahun Calab ("13x160,000" [eternity?]) sleeps; that would occur when you sleep. The evil (or sperm, *kasal*) of creation, the evil (or sperm) of darkness.

60 There his birds clamored. The *kan-dzul-mo*-macaw is his mother,/ the offspring of the *kantanen-kin*-insect, the *kantanen-u*, the offspring of drunkard-seizure, the offspring of *oo*-bird-seizure, when he was born. For four days he made the round of the seashore. The *oppol*-tree would burn; the *tabche*-tree ("mangrove") would burn; [the crackling of] its bark would resound. For four days the fish would stink, when the birth of the evil (*kasil*) of creation shall occur. It would enter where the wasps are, on the fold of the seashore, when the damage (*kasul*) of creation fell.

The *kantemo*-tree, the kantecech [*kante-ceeh?*], the *kan-dzutob* (fl.), the *kan-dzocob*-palm are the binders of his arbor.

He spoils (*kasic*) it on the red savannah; there the hot sand would be crammed into his throat. He would arrive at the place of Som-ch'in, Som-pul ("sudden hurling, sudden casting"), where he takes the

61 *thutz*[47] of his (or its?) neck. He spoils/ the red beaten water, when he is being modeled [like clay]. He spoils the red potter's wheel (*kabal*), when his birth occurs, when he is being shaped (or modeled).

You saw my coming, but you did not see my going.

Shortly ago I extinguished your force over the wooden man, the stone man. Thirteen (or supreme) are my hail-waters, when I extinguish your force. Thirteen are my whirlwinds, when I extinguish your force.

Shortly ago I created 8,000 *pap*-jays, 8,000 *ch'el*-jays. Shortly ago I

---

[46] *Dzacal* usually means "cure," but it can also mean "poison," which would seem more applicable here.   [47] I can find no meaning for *thutz*.

created 8,000 *tacay*-birds.[48] This was the symbol of my hand (or arm), when I stood erect to extinguish your force over the wooden man, the stone man.

Hun Ahau! Unique Can Ahau! Amen./

62–63   [Manuscript pages 62–63 contain part of an incantation in a different hand. See Appendix A.]

VIII

64   *The words for asthma* (coc); *an incantation* (sian) *for asthma*

Unique Can ("four") Ahau! Can Ahau would be the creation, Hun Ahau would be the darkness, during his birth. Four days would he ruffle (*lothic*) his arbor; four days would he ruffle the *maxcal*-plant; four days would he ruffle his *acantun*,[49] during his birth, during his creation, by means of Oxlahun-ti-ku, by Bolon-ti-ku ("nine gods").

Who is his mother? The *uoh* in the sky, the *uoh* in the clouds. The biter (*ix nap*) in the sky, the biter in the clouds.

He would be cast down by Ix Hun-sipit-caan ("lady unique-discharged-from-the-sky"), Ix Hun-sipit-muyal ("from-the-clouds").

65   He would/ fall to the east shore, to the east lagoon.

Four days he ruffles (*lothic*) the red wooden trough (*tente*[50]); four days he ruffles the red lake (*koba*); four days he ruffles the face of the red Ix Chel,[51] the white Ix Chel, the yellow Ix Chel; four days he ruffles the face of the red Itzamna.

Who was his creator, who was his darkness, when he was born? The throbbing of birth would be the creation of the asthmatic one, when he was born, shortly before he was born.

Alas for chest-asthma! Alas for throat-mucus! Alas for biting-chest-

[48] It is hard to account for this mention of 8,000 birds. We are reminded of a clay idol at the town of Tadziu, which was named Hun-pic-ti-dziu ("8,000 cowbirds"). (Ralph L. Roys, *The Political Geography of the Yucatán Maya*, 76; *Relaciónes de Yucatán*, I, 186–87.)

[49] Another word for asthma is *loth-coc*, and the mention of ruffling (*lothic*) is a play on words. Apparently the sound of ruffling is associated with that of asthmatic breathing, but it is difficult to understand how the *acantun* could be ruffled.

[50] *Tente* is translated as though it were *chemte* ("wooden trough" or "wooden canoe"). A Chontal form is sometimes affected in this manuscript.

[51] Here Ix Chel is apparently associated with one of the four Itzamnas who brought the rain. *Chel* can mean rainbow.

asthma! Alas for the time shortly before his birth! Alas for hollow-
66 tree-fire-asthma (*hobon-che-kak-coc*)!/ Alas for head-asthma, nose-
pinching-asthma, severe asthma (*can coc*), yellow-dove-asthma (*kan-
mucuy-coc*)! Alas for brush-fence-asthma! Alas for consumptive
asthma! Alas for granary-asthma! Alas for wild-gourd-rattle-asthma!
Alas for rattle-asthma! Alas for gasping-asthma! Alas for purging (?)
asthma! Alas for *cuyum*-snake-asthma! Alas for nose-obstructing
asthma! Great causer of pain! Great fearsome one!

He would fall at the place of flat-stone-asthma (*sintun coc*), at the
place of nose-obstructing asthma, speechless asthma. This then would
be his mother. Alas, venom-fire-asthma (*saban-kak-coc*)! So he would
fall at the place of the *hunpedzkin*-reptile. Then fell *dzi*-blood, *dzi*-
vein.[52]/

67   Then he licked the poison on the back of the *hunpedzkin*-reptile.
Thereupon he took the pain of its force, four days stretched out, four
days curled up. He would fall to the place of *sinic*-ant-blood, *sinic*-
ant-humor; there he took their poison. This would be [from] the
back of their mother[53] [or "bedroom," a pun].

He would fall to the place of the red *xulab*-ant; he would fall to
the place of the red flint knife; he would fall to the place of the
red[-hot] coal; he would fall to the place of the red trough (or canoe).
There would be turning back and forth. So I grasp the bowl (*lac*),
then, of the fire (or eruption, *kak*) of my foot. So I would stand, then,
68 erect over the red wooden/ man, the white stone man.

Thirteen (or supreme) are the sprinklers, with which I sprinkle
the seashore. Whose is all the water? My property, it is said. Suck
up the asthma, is the reply, behind his *acan*-plant, behind his *maxcal*-
plant, at the opening to his *acantun*. Cast ye him, is the command of
his bird. This is the reply: he is cast to the place of Ix Macanxoc.

He would have taken for his mother the red *puhuy*-bird, his bird,
the *ix-huytok*,[54] when he suffers from diarrhea. This is the cry of
his bird.

[52] I can find no applicable meaning for *dzi*. Possibly *dzil* ("crammed") is intended.
[53] For a mention of poison on the back of a fauna, see also MS p. 157 below.
[54] I can make nothing out of *xhuy-tok*. *Tok* means "flint." One of the Xiu rulers
was named Ah Zuy-tok, but I cannot translate the name.

I stand erect. This is what stops his nostril. This is the lewdness (*coil*) of creation, the lewdness of darkness./

69   Thirteen are the stoppers, with which I stop the nostril of [the lewdness of] creation, the lewdness of darkness.

What is his bird? Who is his bird of tidings? The red *coco-can*-trogon, the white *coco-can*, the black *coco-can*, the yellow *coco-can*, the red *coc-ye*-bird, the white *coc-ye*, the black *coc-ye*, the yellow *coc-ye*.

Who created him? His creator is my *coc bal tun*,[55] the offspring of Ix Uoh in the sky, the offspring of Ix Culum-can, the offspring of Ix Co-pauah-ek, the offspring of Ix Hun-meklah ("lady unique-all-embracer"), the offspring of Ix Hun-sipit-muyal ("lady cloud-releaser"), the offspring of Ix Oc-tun-xix ("lady cement-pillar"?), Ix Ocom-tun ("lady stone-pillar")/ [Page 70, which follows, contains a short medical prescription in a different hand for diarrhea, and page 71 is blank. Page 72 apparently continues the incantation for asthma,

72   but there may be a break in the sequence of the text.] in the Tzab ("snake-rattles-constellation"), in the *ƙo* in the clouds. Who created him, when he was born? Ye four gods! Ye four Bacabs! Behead him, husk his shell! He would be beheaded by the four gods, the four Bacabs.

Then he would enter into *ƙaƙ-bacil* ("fire-" or "eruption-phthisis"). Then he would enter into the vault (*actun*), its slippery part. Then he would enter into the vault, its door. Then he would enter into the vault, its front; Then he would enter into the vault, its rear. Then he would enter into the buried part of the vault. Then he would enter into the base of the vault, its base.

The gold spindle[56] would be the tail of the gold turtle (*ac*). It

73   enters into the front of the gold shell (or scab?);/ it enters into the back of his eye. Cast down is the bad (or imitation) crystal (or

---

[55] *Coc bal tun* is difficult to translate. *Coc* could mean "deaf," "scanty," or "indigent"; but here it appears to be a play on *coc* when it means asthma.

[56] For spindle, the word in the text is *pech'eb*, which could mean "crusher," but I have corrected it to *pechech* ("spindle"). Cf. MS p. 20 in Appendix A, intrusive material, where we read of the gold spindle of Ix Hun Ahau, which is said to be the symbol of a tail.

mirror). It enters into his face. Cast down would be the white *bob*.[57] This would enter into the circle (or retina) of his eye. It would be cast down the white gullet (*lukub*, "swallower"), the red gullet. It would enter to the upper tooth, to the lower tooth.

The viscous poison (*cabil*) of the yellow [phlegm] is to be cast out. There he would take its force (or poison). There it would be cast into the [white] opening, the red opening. There he took the slippery substance (*holol*) of the throat. There he took the froth of the mouth. There he took the pack-net (or burden) of the pain, when he was seized.

74 Who is his tree? Who is his bush?/ The red *loth-coc* (fl., "spasm-asthma"), the red *bilim-coc* (fl., "extreme asthma"), the red *bacal-ac*-tree, *xihil-ac* [*xich'il-ac*-plant]. These would be his tree; these would be his bush. Four days he ruffles the red *ox-loth* (fl.? "much ruffled"), the red *bilim-coc*, the red *bacal-ac*, the red *coc-che* ("asthma-tree"), the red *xich'il-ac*, the red *sihom-che*-tree, gold is its fruit.

There is a change in the opening of his throat. The tongue of the butterfly-bead (*pepen-kan*)[58] would clack; it would enter his heart. The imitation jewel (*kas tun*) would enter his gall. A cord of strong thread would enter into his bowels. A finger-ring (or thimble) would
75 enter into his rectum. A garment,/ a mantle, would enter to his back. A white mat would enter to his front (or breast). . . . Tix-pic-dzacab ("lady-8,000-generations"), Tix-ho-dzacab ("lady-five-generations").

[Like] a puma (*coh*) is his mouth,[59] when it pains. It enters into the virgin-needle when it pains, when he is sleepless, when he does not curl up, the wooden man, the stone man, because of it. I cast you out by the power of the fan, by the power of the staff. Oh, ye Bolon-ti-ku ("nine gods")!

He would arrive at the north shore, the north estuary. Four days
76 would he ruffle (*lothic*) the red beaten water; four/ days he ruffles the

---

[57] The *bob* is variously defined as a certain unidentified animal, an unidentified tree, or the flowering stalk of the henequen.

[58] In this context the *pepen-kan* ("butterfly-red-bead") might be a figurative name for the uvula.

[59] For another example of the word for puma (*coh*) in a similar context, see the Chumayel manuscript, p. 88 (Roys, *The Book of Chilam Balam of Chumayel*, 149).

white beaten water, the black beaten water, the yellow beaten water. Four days he ruffles the red broth (*kabal*); four days he ruffles the white broth, the black broth, the yellow broth. Four days would he ruffle the face of Sacal ("white") Ix Chel; four days would he ruffle the face of Sacal Itzamna.[60]

Who, then, are his birds? What, then, are his birds of tidings? The

77 red *coco-chan*-trogon, the white *coco-chan*, the black *coco-chan*,/ the yellow *coco-chan*; the red *coc-ye* [-bird?], the white *coc-ye*, the black *coc-ye*.

He would arrive at the west shore, the west estuary. Four days he would ruffle the face of Ekel ("black") Ix Chel. Four days he would ruffle the face of Ekel Itzamna. He would fall to the place of Tan-sacal-chakan ("middle of the white savannah"). Four days he would ruffle the face of Ix Bolon-puc ("lady nine" or "many-hills"). Four days he would ruffle [the face of] Ah Tabay; four days would he ruffle [the faces of] Hun-pic-ti-ku ("8,000 gods").

78 Then he would be beheaded/ by Hun-pic-ti-ku. He would enter the vault to arrive at the place of Ah Can-chakan "lord-high-savannah," at the place of Ah Can-tzuc-che ("lord-high-clump-of-trees"). Then he would be beheaded by Ah Can-chakan, by Ah Can-tzuc-che.

Then he would enter the stalks of *ac*-grass. Four days would he be at the place of Ix Kan-kinim-tun, Ix Kan-kinim-te.[61] He would arrive at the place of Ah Som-ch'in ("sudden caster"), Ah Som-pul ("sudden thrower"). There he took the shoots of the *chi*-plum; there he took the shoots of the *pul*-guava.[62] There he took his force (or pain)./

79 Four days he took the red *tukbil-acan* ("hiccough-groaning") the

60 For the association of the goddess Ix Chel with the Itzamnas, see MS p. 65 above; also J. E. S. Thompson, "The Moon Goddess in Central America," Carnegie Institution of Washington *Publication 509*, Contribution 29; and *Maya Hieroglyphic Writing: An Introduction*, 11 ff.

61 I suspect that Ix Kan-kinim-tun and Ix Kan-kinim-te are meant to be the same as Ix Kan-kinib-tun and Ix Kan-kinib-te on MS p. 120 below. The meaning of the latter two expressions, however, is very different from the former.

62 The names of these fruit trees, *chi* and *pul*, seem to be introduced only as puns on the names Ah Som-ch'in and Ah Som-pul.

white *tukbil-acan*, the black *tukbil-acan*, the yellow *tukbil-acan*. Then he took his white (faint) sighing. Then he took the flatulence of your asthma. Then he took his white saliva, his white (faint) yawning, his white (pathological?) sweat. Then he took his fainting (*sac cimili*, "white dying"), when he suffered, when he was seized [by the attack].

He would arrive at the south shore, at the south estuary. Four days he would ruffle the yellow beaten water. Four days he would ruffle the face of Kanal ("yellow") Ix Chel, Kanal Itzamna, when he would arrive at the place of Ah Bolonte Uitz ("lord-nine-mountains")./

80 Then he was beheaded;[63] then he entered to the open chest-trough, its opening. Then he entered to the bottom of the trough, then to the back of the trough, its back. Then he entered to the front of the trough, its front.

For four days he would drink the juice of the red tobacco (*kutz*), the white tobacco, the black tobacco. Then he would be asleep; then he would be curled up. He would arrive at the place of the unique planting-stake (*ch'icib xul*). He would arrive at the . . . . There he would crunch its leg; there he would eat its arm.

81 He would arrive at the place/ of Chac-uayab-cat [Chac-uayab-cab].[64] He would arrive at the place of Chacal ("red") Ix Chel, Sacal ("white") Ix Chel, Ekel ("black") Ix Chel, Kanal ("yellow") Ix Chel. Then he damaged the wooden man, the stone man.

He is thrust, falls, into the left eye, how? of seizure, submerging asthma. This is to be recited. The left of the mat. The submerging ended; virginal was the submerging. Raised was the left of the mat[65] by him

He would arrive at the place of Ix Ma-uay ("lady detrimental-

---

[63] This mention of decapitation reminds us of the separate preservation of the heads of the Cocom rulers (*Landa's "Relación de las cosas de Yucatán,"* 131). The open chest-trough (*maben hol chem*) sounds like a colonial coffin without a lid. Later we shall see a mention of a "bound burial" of the sort customary in pre-Spanish times (MS p. 120 below).

[64] I feel sure that Chac-uayab-cat ("great-demon-jar") is an error for the more familiar Chac-uayab-cab ("great-demon-bee"). See Glossary of Proper Names.

[65] The left of the mat. Maya *dzic* or *dziic*, defined as "left" and also as "sinister."

one"),[66] the stopper of the opening in the earth, the guardian of the rear of Yaxal Chac. The coolness of my foot, the coolness of my hand, when they were seized, the wooden man, the stone man./

82   Unique Can Ahau! Amen.

IX
The breaking of severe asthma (can-coc)

A flat stone is to be heated and wrapped in the *ix koch*-plant, very hot, [and placed] on the abdomen, on the skin of the sick person. These are the words for breaking it.

Black charcoal is my symbol. I break it on the back of Itzam-cab ("earth-lizard"), for severe asthma. My close companion is Suhuy-kak ("virgin-fire"), when I break severe asthma. Who is the binder of his

83   bush? The white *mudz-coc*-plant is the binder of his bush./ Hun Ahau! Can Ahau!

X
The words for hunpedzkin-*reptile seizure* (hunpedzkin tancas)

Unique 4 Ahau was when he was born. One time was his day (*kin*); one time was his night. One day was he born; one day he stirred in his mother's womb.

Who was his mother? The offspring of Ix Hun-ye-ta ("lady unique-point-of-the-lancet"), Ix Hun-ye-ton ("lady unique-point-of-the-genitals"), Ix Hun-lah-dzib ("lady unique-writing"), Ix Hun-lah-uoh ("lady unique-glyph").

Who was his mother? The offspring of Ix Hun-dzalab-caan ("lady unique-seal-in-the-sky"), Ix Hun-dzalab-muyal ("lady unique-seal-in-the-cloud"), Ix Hun-tzelep-kin ("lady unique-turn-of-the-day"). Ox Hun-tzelep-akab ("lady unique-turn-of-the-night").

---

[66] For Ix Ma-uay, see MS p. 25 above and n. Here the mention of Yaxal Chac, the rain god, suggests that rain water was prevented from penetrating the hole in the earth which led down to Metnal. (Cf. Thompson, *Maya Hieroglyphic Writing: An Introduction,* 272, 286.)

[67] *Kalo* seems to mean "haste," or "hasten." *Dza ex kalo* is defined as "*da os prisa vosotros*" (Motul Dictionary). In the *Crónica de Calkiní,* however, the term *kalo* is applied to the deputies of the *batab,* or chief.

Who are his *kalo* (deputies)?[67] This is to be said: First (or green) *huh*-iguana, first *itzam*-lizard, first *haamcab* [*ah-am-cab*, "spider-bee"?], first *bekech*-lizard.

84   Where did he take his equipment?/ There he took it, at the place of his father, Kin Chac Ahau Itzamna. Where did he take the viscous poison of his back?[68] Curled up in the *nicte*-flower, in the heart of the *xuchit*-flower. Where did he take my *am*-spider? At the place of Ix Yaxal Chuen. There he took the red *yax-cab* (fl.?). Where did he take his face-stripe? There he took it, at the place of the white hail in the heart of Chuen.[69] There he took the red soot, the white, the black soot, the yellow soot.[70] That enters into the surface of his stripe. The *sihom*-seed of gold. That enters into the face (or eye) of the virgin
85   spindle. That enters/ into the tail of the thimble (or ring). It enters to the bottom of the strong cord; it enters into his intestines.

Who are his *kalo*? This is to be said: The *hunpedzkin*-sky (*hunpedzkin-caan*[71]), the *hunpedzkin*-("deadly-")*calam*-snake, the *hunpedzkin-kokob*-snake, the *hunpedzkin-taxinchan*-snake, the . . . *calam*-snake, the *ix paclah-actun*-(snake?), the ix *mumuc-sohol*-(snake?).

Who are his kalo? There ends the painting (or spotting?) on the back of these *hunpedzkin*-[reptiles]. Painted (or spotted) is the house (*na*) of the *kin*-insect (or sun?) Bandaged (*hunpedz*, a pun) is the back of the house of of the *kin*-insect (or sun?), painted on the back, hard-pressed (*hunpedzac*), on the house of darkness (*akab*), painted (or spotted) on its back.

86   What is the place of the creation of the red *kanal*-wasp?/ The white, the black, the yellow *kanpetkin*-wasp? The red *iche-uinic*-wasp? The white, the black, the yellow *iche-uinic*-wasps? The red *tup-chac*-wasp: The yellow *tup-chac*-wasp?

---

[68] Poison on a creature's back is also mentioned in the spider incantation (MS p. 157 below).

[69] This association of hail with Chuen would seem to confirm the idea that the latter is related to the north.

[70] Soot (*sabac*) was made from burning a certain tree. Here, apparently, it refers to face-painting. We are to consider these four colors only in a ritual sense.

[71] *Hunpedzkin-caan* is obviously a pun on the name of a snake (*can*).

There they took their places. There, was created the great stinger. This is the place of the red *sinic*-ant, the white, the black, the yellow *sinic*-ant. The red *hoch'*-ant, the white, the black, the yellow *hoch'*-ant. There, enters the *hoch'*-can ("*hoch'*-snake"), [one of] the *hunpedzkinil* ("deadly ones"). This is the place of the red *calam*-snake, the white, the black, the yellow ones.

How ended the painting (or spotting) of their backs? You saw whether their stinging occurred. I did not see it; I did not view it, when their stinging occurred. Shall I be stung on my back?/

87   Who was his tree? Who was his bush, when his birth occurred? The red *hunpedzkin* (fl.) was the tree, the *hunpedzkin* was his bush, when he damaged his arbor. Who was his arbor? The red *hunpedzkinche* ("tree"), the *hunpedzkin-yaban* ("bush").[72] One day he is curled up at the door of his arbor, one day he turns about in the heart of the sky. There he spoiled the lintel (*pacabil*) of his father. One day, seated (*pacan*) on the lintel of his father,[73] he spoiled the eye of the sun (*kin*), . . . [also] the eye (or face) of the moon. One day the face

88   of the sky/ was bitten (or stung) by him. Then he was beaten on his tail, on his head-part. How is this to be said? How does he not go for the gentle opening of his heart?[74]

He goes to be beheaded, when he damaged the green wooden man, the green stone man, when he damages the *kabal*. One time it was *chuen* by him. At one time there was the *acantun*, the *acante*, a great splotch of blood behind the *acantun-acante*.[75] One time there was a great rainstorm, a great whirlwind with rain.

89   Who is my symbol, I say, when the red *ek-pip*-hawk, the/ white, the red *hunkuk*-eagle were set up? How is my symbol? My claw is the red tarantula-flint (*chiuoh tok*). This is my claw, I say, when I

[72] Pío Pérez (*Coordinación alfabética*) lists five flora that are named for the *hunpedzkin*-reptile.

[73] This spoiler of the eye of the sun and that of the moon (unless there were two of them) must be an eclipse god. The mention of a lintel suggests that the shaman had seen the sun and the moon portrayed in the doorways of their respective houses.

[74] It is of interest to speculate what is meant by the gentle opening of the heart ("*ti ppebel u pucsikal*") and whether it is a reference to human sacrifice.

[75] For the *acantun* and *acante*, see note 12 above; but it is difficult to see the relevance of a windstorm.

31

flay you, when I arrived to seize the green *huh*-iguana, the green *itzam*-lizard. I stand ready to seize the green *huh*-iguana.

I stand ready to break the . . .[76]; the red *tok-pap* ("flint-*pap*-jay") is my symbol. Then I broke it in the face of the sun; I broke it in the face of the moon, over Yaxal Chac. My symbol. What is my symbol? I say, when arrived the wooden divider (*hatzabte*), the stone divider 90 (*hatzabtun*),[77] when [I] remove it over/ the green wooden man, the green stone man.

Unique 4 Ahau was when his birth occurred, when his creation occurred, by his father, by his mother. Amen.

XI
The words for gout (chibal oc)

I stand ready to demolish the red ant, the white, the black, the yellow ones. I stand ready to demolish the red spiny *tzah*-shrub, the white, the black, the yellow ones. The cover of the bed of the green wooden man, the green stone man![78] From it I remove the red *hoch'*-ant, the white, the black, the yellow ones. That enters into the *hoch'*-can ("boring-snake"), my *hunpedzkin*-[reptile].

91 From it I remove the red *ppoppox*-nettle,/ the white, the black, the yellow ones, over the green wooden man, the green stone man. From it I remove the red *lal*-nettle, from the cover of the *acantun*, from the cover of darkness (*akab* [the womb?]) where he was born.

Shortly ago, how? I changed the cover of your bed. What, then, is the new cover of your bed? Its cover is the tail of the *yaxum*-quetzal; its cover is the tail of the *op*-macaw. Ten are its covers. Oh, nine are its covers, thirteen are [its] covers. [Its cover is] the tail of the *kubul*-oriole, the tail of the *yaxum*-quetzal, which I put there to cover the bed of the wooden man, the stone man.[79]

[76] I am unable to translate the words *u cuch bob lo puben*.

[77] It is hard to tell what is meant by the "divider" (*hatzab*).

[78] The reference to the cover of the bed of the wooden man and the stone man suggests that both of these represent the patient.

[79] Here the healer changes an irritating bed-cover for a soothing one. Not only does this cover lie over the wooden and stone man, it also lies over the *acantun* and darkness (*akab*). In this association with *akab*, the *acantun* is substituted for *ch'ab*, the male principle, which is usually the companion of, and a sort of counterpoise to, "darkness," the female principle.

From it I remove the great stinger. What is the great stinger?
92 Red/ is its small flower; white is its raceme. Oh, what is its equipment (or weapon) when it stings (*chibal*)? A red pointed instrument (*cheeb*), a white, a black, a yellow one. This entered into its sting, when it stung. I stand ready to destroy its force (or pain); the great destroyer am I. [There was] fire below, smoke above,[80] when I destroyed the great stinger over the green wooden man. I destroyed it in the face (or eye) of the sun, in the face (or eye) of the moon.

Red piercer (*hulub*[81]) in the sky, white piercer in the sky; red
93 piercer in eruptions; white, red piercer in the *calam*-snake,/ [in] the *sac-la*-nettle, where it stung. I stand ready to seize the great stinger. I stand ready to pull it by its cord (*ḳan*). I stand ready to destroy the binding of the snake (*can*) the *hunpedzḳin-caan*, when it is bound, when it is seized, Oh, red *hunpedzḳin*! Four (*cante*) are my red releases, my white releases.

Who is my symbol[82] when I stand erect? The red *eḳ-pip*-hawk, the red *hun-ḳuḳ*-eagle. White is my symbol, when it arrives, the wooden separator (or distributor), the stone separator.

But oh! My companion is the great sleeper over the green wooden
94 man./ But oh! My companion is the great *balam-caan*[83] over the green wooden man, the great stone man. What is the great sleeper? I removed the great stinger (or pain-causer) [from] over the green stone man, the green wooden man. Shortly ago I placed a new cover on his bed.

Come, now, yawning! Come, now, winking! Come, now, snoring! Come, now, sinking [into sleep]! Come, now, blinking!

First unique 4 Ahau! 1 Ahau! This was when his birth occurred, when his creation occurred, by his father, by his mother.

---

[80] The mention of fire below and smoke above to destroy the stinger suggests the destruction of a wasps' nest in a high place.

[81] *Hulub* ("piercer") is something with which one can pierce, as with an arrow; thread, like a needle; or string, like fish or beads.

[82] Here it would appear that the "symbol" (*uayasba*) can be a living creature as well as an inanimate object (cf. MS p. 41 above).

[83] *Balam-caan* ("jaguar-sky"). I have thought this was meant for *balam-chan*, the name of a reptile (Roys, *The Ethno-Botany of the Maya*, 338); but here and on MS p. 99 below such an interpretation would not fit the context.

33

His green cover is the tail of the *yaxum*-quetzal; his green cover is the tail of the *kubul*-oriole. I changed the cover of his bed to destroy

95 [the pain]. Great sleeper! I remove the great stinger (or biter)./ Come, yawning'! Come winking! Come, snoring! Come, sinking [into sleep]! Come, blinking! Come snoring![84]

Unique Can Ahau! Can Ahau! Amen.

XII

The words for hunpedzkin-*vein* (*or humor*), *its incantations*

I enter then, how? to cool your heart (or spirit). It is to enter into the white hail-cooled, the red hail-cooled water, into the white spring, into the red source. The red is its symbol, the white is its symbol, when I destroy your force (or pain)./

96 Thus in the white hail-cold, the red hail-cold, thus in the white spring I extinguish your force. Thus in the white spring, in the red spring, I come to do [you] harm. The great harm-doer am I.

Then arose the red cock-*mo*-macaw partly (*xotena*), the red macaw entirely (*cotena*), the white macaw partly (*xotena*). I am the bird's mother, your bird of tidings. I am your red *ek-pip-pam* ("hawk toucan"), [your] white *ek-pip-pam*. The beak! The beak!

I stand ready to set erect the red *sinic*-ant [*sinic-che*-tree?] the red/

97 [prickley] *tzaah*-tree, the white *tzaah*-tree, the red *ya*-sapote, the white *ya*-sapote, the red *ppoppox*-nettle, the white *ppoppox*-nettle.

What is the symbol for the change of bed-cover? This is the red *hoch'*-ant, the red, the white *hoch'*-ant, *hooch'*-ant-blood, an abscess, when I break it on the face of the sun, on the face of the moon.

The red piercer (*hulub*) in the sky, the red piercer in the cloud, the red piercer in the *calam-snake*. Thus he stung above the wooden man, the stone man. The great stinger! The red *ix-uinic* ("female

98 figure"?) is/ his charge.

Oh, what is the equipment, the red pointed thing (*cheb*), that enters his sting (*ach*), when he stings? I stand over the wooden man, the stone man. I cool his force (or pain). I stand ready to break the

---

[84] The end of this incantation strongly suggests an attempt to produce a hypnotic sleep. (Cf. MS p. 100 below.)

binding of the snake (or "shoot," *can*), the *hunpedzkin-can*. Four (*can*) times was he bound; four times was he seized.

I grasp the bowl (*lac*) of my red release (*choch*). I untied the binding of the *caan* ("sky," "snake," "shoot"?), the *hunpedzkin* 99 [*can*?]. I grasp/ the bowl of the of the cock-birds (*ah ch'ich'il*), the red *ek-pip*-hawk. Thus then was the seizure of the binding of the snake, the *hunpedzkin*-snake (or -shoot?).

First Can Ahau! Unique Can Ahau!

Here, now? I now grasp the bowl of my great *balam-caan*. I call upon the great sleeper, then. How? Shortly ago I removed the stinger, when I changed his bed-cover. What then is his new bed-cover? Its green cover is the tail of the *yaxum*-quetzal; its green cover is the tail of the *kubul*-oriole, when I change his bed-cover./

100 I summon the great sleeper. I remove the stinger. Come ye, dozing! Come, yawning! Come, winking! Come, blinking! Come, dozing! Come, sinking [into sleep]! Come, snoring!

Unique Can Ahau! Hun Ahau! Unique Can Ahau!

[Gloss:] Eruption (*kak*) on a sick person.

XIII
The words for erysipelas (hobonte kak)

[Mostly illegible. This incantation also mentions a small ulcer named *anal-kak*.]

101
XIV
The incantation for eruptions, fever, seizures

I curse you, minor seizures! What eruptions are to be distinguished? How? Alas! Eruptions on the head and body, "entering" eruptions, ulcerous eruptions, feverish eruptions. These are . . . by their mother, by their father. They took her for their mother, alas: 102 Ix Hun-ye-ta ("lady unique-point-of-the-lancet"),/ Ix Hun-ye-ton ("lady unique-point-of-the-genitals").

Four days he turns about. This is his arrival. Oh! Over the wooden man, the stone man. Oh! Shortly ago I broke the force of the great fierce one. Oh! . . .

35

He does not sleep; he does not curl up. No, alas! Erysipelas-eruption.

Here are three small heaps of sand (or filings?). Alas, it enters into his precious stones (*tunilob*). What of their rasping? This is the course for *holom*-wasp eruptions. Oh! What of their bones? Alas, what of their bleeding? This is the course for red perforating eruptions (*chac-hulubte-kak*)./

103 Alas, six folds in the heavens; alas, six folds in Metnal. He is to be cast behind the north sky, alas. This was the heating by the heat of the cave, by the heat of the water, when they returned to be propagated by their mother, by their father. What, alas, was the lust of birth, the lust of creation? Who created them? Alas, the father created them.

Who are the *bobote*-eruptions? Alas, who is your bird, the bird of tidings of the eruptions? This is his creation, alas, red *mo*-macaw, the

104 white *mo*, the black *mo*./ Oh! Created by the *chac*-("red")*dzidzib*-bird, the white *dzidzib*, the black *dzidzib*, the black *dzidzib*. This is its cleansing, alas, by the red *mo*-macaw, the white *mo*, the red *ppocinbe*,[85] the white *ppocinbe*. These are the birds, these are the birds of tidings (*mut*), of eruptions. How? They are to be cut off. How? Alas!

Who is your tree? Who is the bush of the eruptions? Alas, it is to be created by the red *colonte*-woodpecker. This is to be created by him.

105 The red *nix-che*-tree. This is the arrival of the red *chacah*-tree./ This is the arrival, alas, of the eruptions. They return because of their mother, because of their father, alas.

Who is the coolness of my hand, alas, when I arrive, oh, to break the great fierce (or poisonous?) one? I grasp the bowl of my red spring, my white spring, my black spring, when I cool its force (or pain). Oh, I grasp the bowl of my red cenote, my white cenote, my black cenote, when I cool its force (or pain). I grasp the bowl of my red forest-pond (*kaxek*), oh, my black forest-pond, when I cool its

106 force (or pain)./ I grasp the bowl of my white hail, my black hail, when I cool its force, alas. Amen.

---

85 The *ppocinbe* is possibly the *pot-zinic* ant, but we should expect the name of a bird or flying insect.

The *chacah* [*chacau*, chocolate?] is to be drunk with two peppers, a little honey, and a little tobacco-juice. It is to be drunk.

XV

The incantation for red anal-kak *ulcers*

4 Ahau on earth, 4 Ahau on high, is when his birth occurs, when his creation occurs. Who was his creator? Who was his darkness? He created him, did Kin Chac Ahau, Kolop-u-uich-kin ("sun-great-lord, wounder-of-the-eye-of-the-sun").

His red eruption (*ḳaḳ*) would be the *Ḳaḳ-tamay*-monster, 107 the Kak-ne-chapat ("fire-tailed-centipede"),[86]/ the Uuc-ne-chapat ("seven-tailed-centipede"), the offspring of Ix Chante-kak ("lady notable-fire"), Ix Chante-oyoch ("lady notable-timid-pauper"), the offspring of Ix Ho [Ko] in the Tzab ("rattles-constellation"), Ix Ho [ko] in the clouds, the offspring of Ix Kantanen-u ("lady yellow-moon-insect"?), the offspring of Ix Hom-ti-tzab ("she who-sinks-into-the-rattles-constellation"), the offspring of Ix Culum-chacah, the offspring of Ix Meklah ("lady embracer").

He was born to be chopped down violently by Ah Tabay at the place of Uuc-yol-sip, Can-yah-ual-kak ("vigorous-enemy-of-erup-tion"). He substituted at the place of Ti-cah-puc, at the place of Ix Moson-cuc ("lady whirling-squirrel"?), at the place of Ix U-sihnal ("lady moon-birth"?), at the place of Bolon-puc. The second offspring at [the place of] Som-ch'in ("sudden-hurling"), Som-pul("sudden-108 casting"),/ to be slapped by the heavenly fan, by the heavenly staff.[87]

He would go to the place of Ix Cocoyol-cab ("lady abstinence"), to the place of Ix ..., to the place of Ix Ch'ich'cit ("lady bird-father"), Palum-cit, ... -lum-kik. About to come, about to arrive, is the erup-tion, speckled [like a turkey], from the thirteenth layer of the earth.[88]

---

[86] These monsters are apparently cited because of the syllable *ḳaḳ* in their names. It can mean "fire" or "eruption," and an eruption is the complaint here. This would also apply to the repeated mention of "burning" on MS p. 110 below.

[87] In an early colonial drawing we see a ruler holding a fan with a handle ending in a snake. Here the expression *canil ual* could mean either "heavenly-" or "snaky-fan."

[88] The thirteenth layer of the earth is probably an error. There were thirteen heavens, but only nine layers of the underworld. Mention of Ix Hun Ahau indicates that the underworld was meant.

... at the place of Ix Hun Ahau, at the place of ... ye who are about to arrive.

Who created him? He created him, did his father, Kin Chac Ahau, Colop-u-uich-kin. He created my fire (or eruption) in the bowl/ of the Kak-tamay-monster, Kak-na-chacpat [Kak-ne-chapat] ("fire-tailed-centipede"), the offspring of Ix Chante-oyoch, the offspring of Ix Hom-ti-tzab, the offspring of Ix Hom-ti-muyal, the offspring of Ix-Kak-tachel, the offspring of Ix Culum-chacah, the offspring of Ix Meklah-oyte, the offspring of Ix Meklah-u-sip.

He walks, he turns back, he arrives. Ix Ahau-na ("palace-lady") came into the heart of the sky. The offspring of the lady of the sea, the offspring of the lady of the cenote, the offspring of her who sits in the mud, the offspring of her who emerges from the sand. Then he was born to be slapped by the heavenly/ fan, the heavenly staff.

He would go to the place of Ah Nohol ("lord of the south"), to the place of the dweller in the hills, to the place of her between the hills. The offspring of Ix Chi-ticil Uaclahun. The offspring of her on the hillside, her on the low hill. He would take him who has chills and fever on the hill.[89]

Thus was he created, thus was he darkened [in the womb?]. For four days burns the hill; then Uuc-calam burns; then Ix Ma-ul burns; then Ix Co-ti-pan burns. Then the *kuk* ("quetzal") would burn; the *yaxum*-bird would burn. This is when the eruption (or fire) would burn. Shortened is the tip of the red-flowering, the red-budding eruption (or fire)./

Then it was born. It progresses, it turns back, the red-extractor (or unraveler), the white extractor, the red joiner, the white joiner;[90] it turns back, it progresses. Then he was born to be slapped by the heavenly fan, by the heavenly staff. He would fall among the trees, among the bushes.

Who was his mother? Who held him in her arms? The offspring of Ix Kin-sutnal ("lady sun-turns-back"). Then he was born to be

109

110

111

---

89 Chills and fever are especially prevalent in the southern hilly region known to archaeologists as the Puuc. The Maya call is the Uitz country.

90 Pairing of words with contrary meanings appears to be a favorite rhetorical device in this manuscript.

slapped by the heavenly fan, by the heavenly staff. He would go on to the bright savanna, to the place of Ix Chac-lah-yeeb ("lady rain-faced-dew").

112   He would be thrown behind his arbor. There the wooden/ trough (*tem-te* [*chem-te*]) would burn; the red stone trough of water [*chem-tun hai*] would burn; the red pitted water (*muzen-hai*) would burn. There the *acantun* was cast down to break, when its burning occurred, when the force (or pain) of the fire (or eruption) occurred. Bound is the precious stone of the fire (or eruption).

Then it was born; it progresses; it turns back, the red extractor, the red joiner, to be slapped by the heavenly fan, by the heavenly staff. He would fall to the east sea. The edge of the sand would burn; the

113   seashore would burn;[91] the source would burn;/ the spring would burn; the *puhi*-rush would burn; the water-lily (*nab*) would burn; the reed (*halal*) would burn. The filling (or stuffing) would cease, when the force of the fire (or eruption) occurs. Bound is the jewel (*tun*) of the fire, red-budding, red-flowering fire.

Then he was born, he progresses, the red extractor, the white extractor, the red joiner. Who created him? He created him, did Chac-uayab-xoc ("red-ominous-shark"), Chac-mumul-ain ("red-muddy-crocodile"). Red would be the bowl[92] of her offspring. Amen./

114   XVI
This is for cooling a high fever and for cooling an eruption ("fire").
                An eruption on sick people

The coolness of my foot, the coolness of my hand, when I cooled the eruption! Five are my white hail-stones, my black hail-stones, [my] yellow hail-stones. Then I cooled the eruption. Thirteen are the layers of my red dressing, my white dressing, [my] black dressing, [my] yellow dressing, when I received the force of the eruption. A black fan was my symbol, when I received the force of the eruption./

115   With me comes the white [aquatic] *ixim-ha*-plant, when I received

---

[91] These words, "the edge of the sand would burn, the seashore would burn," are quoted almost verbally from a prophecy ascribed to Chilam Balam (Tizimin MS, p. 19).

[92] The *lac* ("bowl") was an effigy-bowl, which the Spaniards called an idol.

the force of the eruption. With me comes the white *nab*-water-lily, when I received the force of the eruption. Shortly ago I applied [to it] the coolness of my foot, the coolness of my hand. Amen.

XVII

Snake-pulsation of the abdomen (cantippte); *the words for it*

Curses upon you! Who was your creator? He created you, did the father of Ah Uuc-yol-sip.[93] Shortly ago, how? was the birth of the red loosener, the white loosener, the black loosener, the yellow loosener. [There was] his necklace, there was/ his fastener, when he was born. Shortly ago originated the cord, the sack, of Ah Uuc-yol-sip, when it originated.

116

When he was born, who was his mother? [He was] the offspring of Ix Hun-tipplah-can ("lady unique-pulsator-of-the-sky"). Then he caused the sun to pulsate; then he caused the moon to pulsate; then he caused the stars to pulsate (or twinkle): the great mover, the great turner.

Chop ye his neck, ye four Bacabs. Four are my red husking tools. So I chopped his neck; so I husked his surplus part (*holmal*).

117

This is the lust of creation, the lust/ of darkness. He does not sleep, he does not curl up, over the wooden man, the stone man, because of it.

I cast you, slap you,[94] with the power of the fan, with the power of the staff, ye four gods, ye four Bacabs. The submerged stone [or "stone throne," a pun] is my symbol, of which I speak. Then I plunged you into the genitals of your mother, into the genitals of your father

Rise up to see it! Rise up to declare it! *Cuyum*-snake-blood are you; *ḳanch'ah*-snake-blood are you. How? *Koḳob*-snake-blood are you.

118

How?/ *Calam*-snake-blood are you. How?

Cut ye his neck! Husk ye his surplus (or slippery?) part! Four are my husking tools. Lo, I chop the neck of the lust of creation, the lust of darkness. He does not sleep, he does not curl up, the wooden man, the stone man, because of it.

[93] Ah Uuc-yol-sip was a hunters' god, and the pulsation implied in the name of the complaint is associated with the vibration of a bow-string.

[94] Note the disrespectful manner in which the Bacabs are addressed. The pronoun "you" is in the plural.

He is cast down by Hun-sip-can ("unique-Sip-in-the-sky"), Hun-sip-muyal ("unique-Sip-in-the-clouds"). He would fall behind the east sky. There he caused the waves to pulsate. He caused the sand to pulsate. He caused the top of the red broth (*ḳabal*) to pulsate. He caused the red beaten water to pulsate. He caused the red wooden trough (*temte* [*chemte*]) to pulsate. He does not sleep, he does not
119 curl up, because of it, the wooden/ man, the stone man.

I cast you down, I slap you, by the power of the fan, by the power of the staff, ye four gods, ye four Bacabs!

He would fall to his tree, to his bush, the red *paḳam*-cactus, where he breakfasted [*tu ḳam-ci u chi*, a bad pun]. Who are the wooden man, the stone man, where he breakfasted? The red *culix*-(bird or insect), the *chac-eḳ* [*chac-ec*-wasp],[95] the *ix uixum*-(bird or insect), the red *ix uixum*. These are his birds (*ch'ich'il*), these are his birds of tidings (*mutil*).

He would fall to the place of Sintun-bul Ahau ("flat-stone-game lord"). I cast you down; I slap you with the power of the fan, with
120 the power of the staff./ He would fall to the place of Ix Kan-kinib-te ("lady yellow-wooden-heater"), [Ix] Kan-kinib-tun ([lady] yellow-stone-heater").

Then he took his force with the pack-net of pain, when he was seized. Then he enters to the bound-burial.[96] He would fall to the place of Ix Kak-yol-mat, the lust of creation, the lust of darkness. He does not sleep, he does not curl up, the wooden man, the stone man, because of it.

I cast you out, [I] slap you, by the power of the fan, by the power of the staff. Behead him, ye four gods, ye four Bacabs. He would fall to the place of Som-ch'in ("sudden casting"), Som-pul ("sudden
121 hurling"),/ to the place of Can-yah-ual-kak ("vigorous-enemy-of-fire" or "eruption").

Then he took the bitter of his mouth, the sour of his mouth. Then he spoiled the virgin *op*-tree. Then he spoiled Ix Bolon-puc ("lady

---

[95] Here the name of the *chac-ec*-wasp has been turned into *chac-eḳ* ("red-" or "great-star"), the name of the planet Venus (Motul Dictionary; Dresden Codex, pp. 24, 46–50; Thompson, *Maya Hieroglyphic Writing: An Introduction*, 220–21).

[96] The "bound burial" may refer to a mummy bundle.

nine," or "many-hills"), when it pained, when it was seized. Then he was beheaded by Bolon-ti-ku, [by] Oxlahun-ti-ku. Then he does not sleep, he does not curl up, the wooden man, the stone man, because of it.

He falls to the place of flatulence ("white-cramming-breath" or "wind"), there he took his fainting ("white-death"), his morbid ("white") sweating, his morbid ("white") yawning. He would fall to the place of hiccough-sighing. There he licked the froth from his groaning (*acan*), there he took his short breathing (*tus-ik*). Four are 122 my red/ husking tools, when I forcibly bruised the lust of creation, the lust of darkness. He does not sleep, he does not curl up, the wooden man, the stone man, because of it.

I cast you out, [I] slap you, by the power of the fan, by the power of the staff, ye four gods, ye four Bacabs! A stone throne [or "submerged precious stone," a pun] was my symbol, when I trampled you down [a pun] into the genitals of your mother, into the genitals of your father. You, lust of birth, lust of begetting. Amen.

XVIII
Rattlesnake (ahau-can) *in the abdomen of a man*

Shortly ago, how? there was born the snake (*canil*) of creation, 123 the snake of darkness./ Shortly ago was born the red Uba Ahau. Shortly ago, how? was born the white Uba Ahau. Shortly ago was born the black Uba Ahau. Shortly ago was born the yellow Uba Ahau.

Four are the arbors, four are the *acantuns of Hun-yah-ual-*cab ("unique-enemy-of-the-world"), Hun-yah-ual-Anom ("unique-enemy-of-Anom" or "-humanity."). He would be be beheaded by his mother, by his progenitress (*cool*). *Uidzil* (fauna?) would be his blood, *uixum* (fauna?) blood. There would enter the *buhum*-snake, 124 the *cuyum*-snake/ of the grassy place, the *cuyum* of the savanna. Ix Ko-ti-tzab ("*ko*-bird-in-the-Rattles-constellation"), the offspring of the male slave (*pentac*), the offspring of the female slave (*munach*). Ix Catil Ahau, Ix Madzil Ahau, Ix Pokol-pic, Ix Hun-pudzub-kik ("lady blood-drawing-needle").

Now he falls at the place of Kin-patax-uinic ("fevering-pimple-man"?). He licks the froth of the *too*-plant, the froth of the *acan*-plant. He would fall at the place of Bolon-hobon ("many-colored-one"); he would fall at the place of the white Som-pul-acat ("suddenly-cast-seed-capsule"); he would fall at the place of Ix Bolon-sut-ni-cal ("lady many-neck-turns"). He would suck the *ich-can* [*ich'-can*-plant.]. He would enter the metal horn (*xulub* mascabil)./ He would enter into the virgin needle, its sharp point. He would enter into the pruned *sahum*-plant, the tongue of the narrow spindle, the tail of the thimble (or ring?) of Ix Hun Ahau. She aids his entrance to the covered oyster [or odor? a pun]. The bowl of the bright cochineal would be his blood.

This is his heart, a red bead. This would be his gall. He would enter to the crest of the verdure. Then he is bound at the top of the hill, at the top of the high fertile land (*cacab*). The hill would rise aloft, when the loosening of creation is bound. He turned his neck. Cast ye him behind the east sky, behind the west sky.

He would be bound on the seashore./ Raised would be the estuary, raised would be the *suc*-grass to bind the loosening (or lust?) of birth, the loosening [or lust, a pun] of creation, the loosening (or lust) of darkness. He would fall behind the south sky. The evil one (*dzidzic*) would burn; the winking one (*mudzuy*) would burn. Raised aloft would be the post of the canopy; raised aloft would be the post of the arbor.

Seven! Can Ahau! Hun Ahau! Amen.

XIX

Kanch'ah-*snake in the abdomen of a man*

Unique 4 Ahau, [the day], 4 Ahau [1 Ahau], the night. Shortly ago, how? I received your force (or poison), red *kanch-ah*-snake. Shortly ago, how? I vigorously bruised you,/ white *kanch'ah*-snake. Shortly ago, how? I beheaded you, red *cuyum*-snake, white *cuyum*-snake. Shortly ago, how? I vigorously bruised you over the green wooden man, the green stone man. Shortly ago, then, how? I coiled you. Shortly ago, how? I stretched you out.

What, then, how? is the symbol of the opening in your neck? The

43

green neck of the hollow cord, with which you turn in the virgin jar. Then you took your force (or poison), when you licked the chocolate in the virgin jar, when, moreover, you licked the froth of the chocolate, 128 when,/ moreover, you took your force (or poison). Then you removed (or swallowed) the white flat stone. Then you took your force (or poison).

Curses upon you! Shortly ago, how? I cut you over the green wooden man, over the green stone man. What, then, how? is my symbol? I, when it arrived, I curled you up, red *ḳanch'ah*-snake.

You shall see my coming; you shall not see my going. Shortly ago I demolished (*puch'ub*) your face, white diarrhea (*puch*), red pus (*pudz*).[97] Amen.

XX
Snake in the abdomen of a man/

129 First Hun Ahau! I stand erect ready to trap (*pedzeb*[98]) you, lust of birth, ready for four days for you to turn, for four days ready for you to move about, by means of your mother, by means of your father. You, lust of birth, lust of darkness!

Shortly ago, then, I vigorously bruised you, you red tainted bowel, you red rattlesnake. Thus, then, you descend to the place of the white Anom, the white man.

130 Who is my symbol, when I vigorously bruise you?/ The great setter-up (*ah thalcunah*) am I; the great stretcher-out (*ah chelcunah*), the great curler-up (*ah copcunah*) am I.

Unique 4 Ahau was the day when you were born, lust of creation, lust of darkness. Amen.

XXI
Can-tippte (*"snake-pulsation"* or *tapeworms?*) *in the abdomen of a man. Very good*

Shortly ago, how? I seized you. I am your mother; I am your father. You are white snake-pulsation, alas. You are red snake-pulsa-

----
[97] The Maya words for "demolish," "diarrhea," and "pus" are assonants and probably employed for the rhetorical effect.

[98] *Pedzeb*, "to trap," is a pun on *pedz*, "incantation."

131 tion, alas. Oh, who would you be at sunset? Who, alas, at dawn? You are the lewdness (*coil*) of birth,/ alas. You are the lewdness of creation, alas.

Shortly ago I stretched you out. I am your mother, I am your father, white snake-pulsation. Turn about vigorously, when I suck you out. White snake-pulsation are you. Be suspended! I cast you into the heart of the sea.

Then, how? you enter the place of great putrefaction (*can ch'ocilil*).[99] Then, how? you enter the place of great (*can*) fish. Then, how? you enter among the tall (*can*) *hulub*-bushes. Then, how? you enter the place of the high (*can*) *suc*-grass.

132 Who, then, how? is your symbol? The white *ḵanch'ah*-snake. Cum Ahau[100] by day. Who, then, are you?/ Suspended are you, white snake-pulsation.

Who, then, is your bird of tidings (*mutil*)? Oh, the white *eḵ-pip*-hawk. Oh, the white *uaḵeh*(-bird?). Oh, the white *ah ii*-hawk. Oh, then, how? I bind you to his foot. Then you ascend to the heart of the sky.

Shortly ago I committed you to Ku-ah-tepal ("God the ruler"), alas. Oh, your born offspring, your begotten offspring, when my word is verified behind the east sky, alas. You fashioned the female human figure (*ix uinicil*), when you seated then your wooden image (*cul che*).

133 A paste/ of *ḵutz* (tobacco) is to be pressed on the abdomen of the man. Then he is to be anointed with the juice of the *ḵutz* on his abdomen. This is the drink to be given for snake-pulsation. Shortly ago, how? I created the *can-chac-che*-shrub, its stalk. Shortly ago, how? I created the *ḵutz-aban* ("tobacco-bush"), its wine. Shortly ago, how? the white *can-tiplah* (fl.?). It is to be drunk, its wine. Well steeped is its wine. Then I stretch you out, white snake-pulsation, red snake-pulsation. Amen./

99 The "place of putrefaction" might be a reference to the lower intestine and *suc*-grass, to pubic hair.

100 Cum Ahau ("seated lord") is apparently the same as *Cum hau*, explained in the Motul Dictionary as "Lucifer, the prince of the devils." I have not encountered it elsewhere in the literature of the colonial Maya.

XXII

134   Kanpedzkin (*wasp?*) on (*or in?*) *the head of a man*

The yellow *dzuto* (fl.) is to be heated with four peppers (*ic*) and drunk.

1 Ahau, 4 Ahau, during his birth, while he was being created! Snake (or shoot?) of creation, snake of darkness!

Who was his creator? Who was his darkness? He created him, did Kin Chac Ahau, Colop-u-uich-kin, Colop-u-uich-akab ("snatcher-of-the-eye-of-the-sun, . . . -of-darkness"), in the heart of the sky, in the heart of Metnal,[101] during his birth, during his creation.

Who was his mother? Who was his lustful one (*col*)? [He was] the offspring of Ix Hun-acay-kik [Ix Hun-hacay-kik, "lady unique-
135 slippery-blood"?], the offspring of Ix Hun-acay-olom,/ in the heart of the sky.

Curses on the snake (*can*) of creation, the snake of darkness,[102] the unique enemy of man, the unique enemy of Anom, when he was awakened! Behead him, scratch him, ye Bolon-ti-ku, Oxlahun-ti-ku! Let there be an end to his career! Let there be an end [to the] advantage of the lust of creation, the lust of darkness.

Shortly ago he injured the wooden man, the stone man.[103] Curses upon him! Directly he is to be cut. Oh, the offspring of Ix Hun-tah-kik, Ix Hun-tah-olom! This would be the his mother; this would be the lustful creation by his father, Kin Colop-u-uich-kin, Colop-u-
136 uich-akab. How? Fire (or anger?) is his heart;/ fire is his chiseled flint.

Ye Bolon-ti-ku! Slap ye him; clasp ye him violently, the lust [*col*, a pun on *colop*] of creation, the lust of darkness. [He is] directly to be cut off, mostly his force (or pain), mostly his fever. Curses upon him!

Shortly ago he burned the arbor; shortly ago he burned the genitals (*ton*). Then flamed the red lancet (*ta*), the white lancet, by his means;

---

101 It is of interest to find these deities, apparently eclipse gods, associated both with the sky and with Metnal, the underworld.

102 Possibly the mention of this snake is a reference to the wasp grub, though the usual term for the latter is *yikel*.

103 Here again is a suggestion that the "stone man" and "wooden man" represent the patient.

then flamed the red genitals, the white genitals by his means;[104] the red *ḳanal*-wasp by his means, the white *ḳanal* by his means.

The offspring of Ix Hun-petah-kin ("lady unique-circular-sun"), Ix Hun-petah-akab ("lady unique-circular-darkness"), Kin Chac Ahau Canal.

137 Then he took what he needed. How? Then he licked the red/ bezoar, the white bezoar. Then he licked the red *pay* ("skunk") [*ppay*, "powder"?]. Then he took the opening of his throat; then he took his white vomit; then he took his white death ("fainting"); then he took the narrow part of his neck, the interior of his throat. Curses upon him!

Then burned the fever (*chac-uil*, "red-*uil*"), the *sac-uil* ("white-*uil*")[105] because of him. The piercing *soh*-plant, the piercing *aḳab-toḳ* ("dark-flint," fl.?), the piercing *holom-ḳaḳ* (fl.?), the *chac-topplah-ḳaḳ* ("red-budding-fire," fl.?), because of him. The snake (*can*) of creation, the snake of darkness. For four (*can*) days is his fever. Curses upon him! Cut ye his outer covering. Scratch it off.

138 These things are to be said. Red *ḳanal*-wasp,/ red *ḳanpetḳin*-wasp, white *ḳanpetḳin*, red *tupchac*-wasp, white *tupchac*. They are to be dragged along, the red *hol* [*holom*-wasp], the white *hol*. This would enter into your force, not to be roasted, not to be cut.

Who was his mother? Who was his progenitress (*col*)? The offspring of Ix Hun-petah-kin, Ix Hun-petah-akab. Who is his bird? Who is his bird of tidings? The Sac Pauahtun.[106]

I stand erect. I am your mother; I am your father. I consign you to the evils (*ḳasal*) of Metnal.

139 Shortly ago I disparaged you to your tree,[107] to your bush./ You, red *ḳanal*-wasp! You, red *ḳanpetḳin*-wasp, white *ḳanpetḳin*! You, red *tupchac*-wasp, white *tupchac*! Ye, his tree! Ye, his bush! The red *dzoc* [*dzocob*-palm?], the white *dzoc*, are your tree, your bush. There

104 For this association of a flint-lancet with the male genital organ, see MS p. 4 above and n.

105 I suggest that *sac-uil* is an improvised word.

106 It is difficult to understand how one of the Pauahtuns could be considered to be a bird (or an insect), even ritually.

107 This threat to disparage the evil spirit to his tree is interesting, because we do not know just what was the relationship of a person to his tree.

47

you were when he slept; there you were when he curled up, over the wooden man, the stone man.

Here, then, are thirteen jars of my cold water, my cooled water, my cold hail, my red hail, my white hail, my white overflow (*tulub*, also "lizard"), my coolness, my chill.

I am your mother; I am your father. Kin Chac Ahau Canal ("sun-
140   -great-lord-/on-high"). Thirteen are my low waters, my high waters, my hail-water, with which I cool his force (or pain). Lust of creation! Lust of darkness! Amen.

XXIII
The words for kanpetkin-*wasp poisoning*

When the Chacal ("red") Bacab resounds, he immerses himself in his small jar; he immerses himself in his large jar. I take your place, you, red *paap*-jay, white *paap*. This is on the strand; this is on the shore. I take your place, you, red *chahum*-woodpecker. I take your
141   place, red *colonte*-woodpecker.[108]/ This is the strand; this is the shore. Four are my red drills, with which I drill [for] the worm of the food, the worm of the bread-stuff on the metate.

Then they continued to arrive, where? how? the snake of the day, the snake of the night. Then arrived the red oscillator (or leveler), with which the fire is flattened. [The fire] of the red heart of the *habin*-tree, when my red stone *comal* (*xamach-tun*)[109] is set up, where I roast the red wasp-larvae, seventeen four-hundreds of them, where I roast the flea-larvae then. How?/

142   Then it came about that my red stone *comal* was set up. Then I roasted you, the buried (or hidden) worm, the neck-cord-worm (*ix tab-cal-nok*), the deadly poisonous worm, the son[110] then, how? of the Chacal Bacab.

I take your place, red *uakeh*-bird; I take your place, red *pap*-jay. This is on the strand, on the shore. Lo, how? Oh! Shred ye him there. Bat him about [like a ball] there./

---

[108] Here the reciter assumes the role of the birds who feed on grubs or wasps.
[109] The *comal* (*xamach*) is the flat pan on which *tortillas* are cooked. *Xamach-tun* can mean either a stone *comal* or a potsherd.
[110] The term *mehen* ("begotten son") is extremely rare in this manuscript.

143   Set it up firmly, my virgin *luch* ("tree-gourd"). Then I tore loose the red deadly poisonous, the white deadly poisonous, *kanpetkin*-wasp-infection. Amen.

XXIV

This is when a seizure shall fall upon a man

Let there be taken the spine of the maguey (*ci*); it is deep in the ground. Then bleed him with four spines at the corner of his mouth, along his backbone, from his hip, from his heart, from the tip of his foot.

144   After bleeding him, then pour over him one jar of heated water and one jar of cold/ water. First the water must be tested on the man's foot.

These are the words: Thus, then, how? did the blow fall [on] the head of seizure. It fell over the white stone man. Short ("white") breath is his breathing, when it falls. Give your command over him. Trim ye him, ye four gods, ye four Bacabs!

The black breath was his symbol, when it came over the black stone man.[111] So it is, alas. Four times I spoke, when I beat him. Who is his tree? Who is his bush? The white *copo*-tree is his bush, the red *copo* is his bush.

145   Then, how? I declare his fasting:/ One time he is to eat, during the entire day; one time he is to drink, suitably, during the entire night also. Amen.

XXV

The words for cooling water, when it is on the fire

Nine-stick-fire! I chop [off?] the head of Itzam-cab ("earth-lizard"), the symbol of the pot on my fire, I say, when he stands erect over it. Curses upon him!

This, then, how? is the liver of Itzam-cab, the symbol of his hearth. This, then, how? is the thigh of Itzam-cab, the symbol of the wood on my fire, I say, when he stood erect over it.

146   The licking/ tongue, how? of Itzam-cab is the symbol of the licking of the fire. A three-year-old hoof (*ox haben dzidz*), how? is

[111] It is unusual to find any mention of a white or black stone man or wooden man.

49

the symbol of the coals, when I trampled it down. The red *cocay* ("firefly"), the white *cocay*, are the symbol of the spark of the fire. Many small heaps of sand, how? are the symbol of its ashes. The red *bubul-can* ("frog-spawn-shoot," fl.?), the white *bubuy-can* [*buy-can*, "foggy" or "filmy shoot," fl.?] are the symbol of the smoke of the slender sticks.

What then, how? oh! are the thirteen jars of my cold hail, with which I extinguished its force over the wooden man, the stone man?/

147 These, then, how? oh! are the thirteen jars of my hail-water, when I extinguished it, when I cooled it.

This, then, how? oh! is the liver, how? of Itzam-cab, the symbol of his pot.

This, then, how? oh! is the head, how? of Itzam-cab, the symbol of the stones of his hearth (*koben*).

This, then, how? oh! is the symbol of the stones of his hearth (*koben*).

This, then, how? oh! is the thigh of Itzam-cab, the symbol of the sticks of his firewood.

148 This, then, how? oh!/ is the tongue, how? of Itzam-cab, the symbol of the blaze of its fire.

This, then, how? oh! is the red sand, the symbol of its ashes.

This, then, how? oh! is a single measure of its wine (*ci*); and then I cooled the red *cocay*-firefly, the white *cocay*.

Unique Can Ahau. Amen.

XXVI

To cool what has been heated by drilling

Thirteen jars of water from the heart of my red overflowing spring of water./

149 Thirteen turns I gave it, when I turned it. I am the red-seated one, the white-seated one. Thirteen turns, when I turned it at the place of the maternal grandmother (*chich*) of Ix Bolon-puc.

Then I put it to sleep over the green wooden man, the green stone man, from the sky.

Four are the arbors of the red kiln, the white kiln. Thirteen are the divisions of the white kiln (*mucab*) for raising the red stone raiser (or joiner), the white stone raiser. Amen./

XXVII

150

The words for fire biting on wood

To be charmed, the fire is always kindled with a fire-drill.

Unique Can Ahau! Where? How? Where did it enter into the symbol of your fire? You, green wooden man! The pot of Ix Bolon-puc. That entered into the symbol of the [three-stone] hearth of your fire. You, green wooden man!

The thigh of Ix Hun-itzam-na ("lady unique-lizard-house"). That entered into the symbol of the biting on wood by your fire. You, green wooden man!

Oxlahun-tun-muyal ("thirteen-jewel-cloud").

Where, then, how? did it enter into the symbol of the smoke of 151 the fire?/ You green wooden man!

Oxlahun-caan ("thirteen-sky").

Where, how? did it enter into the symbol of the blaze of your fire? You, green wooden man!

The stones of the spring entered into the symbol of the coals of your fire. You, green wooden man!

Three small heaps of sand, where? how? entered into the symbol of the ashes of your fire. You, green wooden man!

Shortly ago, then, how? I set you firmly [in?] the spring (*sayab*). V. V. V. V. V. I set you firmly in the midst of your fire. You, green/ 152 wooden man!

Red forest-pond (*kax-ek*),[112] white forest-pond, black, yellow forest-pond. I set [you] firmly in the midst of your fire. You, green wooden man!

Shortly ago, how? I arrived. Oh! The red wind, the white wind,

---

[112] I have found the term *kax-ek* ("forest-pond") elsewhere only in Avendaño's account of his journey to Tayasal (P. A. Means, "History of the Spanish Conquest of Yucatán and of the Itzas," *Papers* of the Peabody Museum, VII, 159).

the black wind (or breath?) am I, then, when I arrive. The great loser (or waster?), then, how? am I, when I arrive.

Oh! The red *copo*-tree, the white *copo*, the black *copo*, the yellow
153 *copo*, the red *chacah*-tree, the white *chacah*, the black,/ the yellow *ix kanan*-shrub, the red *puc-ak*-vine, the white *puc-ak*, the black, the yellow *puc-ak*. These, then, how? all receive your fire. You, green wooden man!

Thirteen (or supreme) are my cold hailstones, when I receive your force. This is the great forceful one. Curses upon you! Amen.

XXVIII
The words for a burn; the charm for fire biting on wood

The *kak-chacah* is its plant. The white of a hen's egg is to be anointed on the sore, over the burn.

Unique 4 Ahau was the day of your birth. You, *yax-cab* ("green-
154 earth" or "-honey," fl.?)!/ Chac-petan-kin ("red-rounded-sun") is your father there in the sky. Ix Hochan-ek ("lady scraped-clean-star"?) there in the sky is your mother. Ix Pic-tzab ("lady countless-rattles") is your mother there in the sky. Ix Hun-tip-tzab is your mother there in the sky.

What, then, how? is my symbol, when I stand erect to extinguish your force. Yax-hal Chac ("green-water-rain-god"), then, is my symbol, when I stand erect to extinguish your force.

What enters into your head? *Holom-kak* ("*holom*-wasp-eruption") enters your head. What enters into your face (or eye)? Eruption (or fire) enters your face. What enters your arm (or hand)? Eruption (or fire) enters your arm. What enters your bowels? *Kakal-cab* ("fired" or dried "honey" or earth) enters your bowels. What enters your foot? The thigh of Hun-itzam-na ("unique-lizard-
155 house") enters your foot./ You, green wooden man!

Paklah-sus ("slapped-sand") is his name. He would go along in company with his mother, Ix Ppohal-mum ("lady rubbed-in-the-mud"), when he was born (*sihi*). He would go along in company with his mother, Ix Muk-yah-kutz ("she-who-strengthens-the-tobacco"), when his force was cooled (*sishi*). Amen.

XXIX

The words to dry a running sore, whatever the injury on a man may be

Hun Ahau! Dried one of wood! Dried one of stone!

156   With me arrives, how? my red *chacah*-tree; with me arrives,/ how? my white *chacah*; with me arrives, how? my red flood of saliva, my white flood of saliva. The great exuder am I; the great stancher am I. How?

So this is my behest, when I arrive to break your force, to disperse your force. The great exuder am I; the great stancher am I. Dry one of wood! Dry one of stone!

With me arrives my red *copo*-tree, my white *copo*. With me arrives
157   my red flood of saliva, my white flood of saliva./ The great exuder am I. How?

So this is my behest, when I arrive to break your force, to disperse your force. The great exuder am I. Dry one of wood! Dry one of stone! Amen.

XXX

The words of the incantation (siyan) *of the spider*[113]

First spider, second spider, third spider, fourth spider! Green spider of wood (*am-te*), green spider of stone (*am-tun*)! Three days were you apart in the trough of the earth (*cab*). Ah Uuc-ti-cab ("lord seven-earth"). Then, how? you took the viscous poison (*cabil*) of your back.

158   Four days were you beneath the garden-plot/ [*am-tun*, a pun[114]]. The cochineal of your grandmother, the virgin Ix Chel, Chacal ("red") Ix Chel, Sacal ("white") Ix Chel, is the symbol of the back of the green spider of wood (*am-te*), the green spider of stone (*am-tun*).

This, then, is the virgin stone needle (or bodkin) of the virgin Ix Chel, Sacal Ix Chel, Chacal Ix Chel. This is the symbol of your sting. Thirteen balls of the dyed thread of the virgin Ix Chel, Chacal

---

[113] This incantation for the spider has already been published (Thompson, "The Moon Goddess in Central America," Carnegie Institution of Washington *Publication 509*, Contribution 29, 148.

[114] *Am-tun* can mean either "stone-spider" or "garden-plot."

159 Ix Chel,/ Sacal Ix Chel. This, then, how? is the symbol of your gall (or bitterness, *ka*).

Shortly ago I snatched it away; shortly ago I removed it; shortly ago I untied it. Curses upon you, green spider of wood, green spider of stone.

Of four breadths is my black mantle. Thus, then, I [spread it]. These, now, are my fourteen jars, then, of my hail-water; thirteen jars of my cold water, with which, how? I cool the force (or poison)

160 of the green/ spider of wood, the green spider of stone.

Spider, spider, spider! Amen.

XXXI

The words for the scorpion (sinan), *when it stings*

Sting, sting, sting!

Fully jointed is your tail; successively jointed is your middle part, like a dragonfly (*tulix*); a *mo*-macaw is your head.

You were cast on the seashore. There you fell to the pit of plucked produce (*y-uxi*); there you took your whetstone (*u yuxil kabi* [*u huxil kab?*]). You were cast to the place of Saba-yol in the Chuen [constellation]. There you fell with arms extended (*sinan*); there you

161 took your name,/ *sinan* ("scorpion"). Curses on your sting (*fe luna ta uach*).

The virgin needle would be your strength, which you took to enter into your sting. Suhuy-kak ("virgin-fire" [goddess]) would be your strength, which you took to enter into the venom (or force, *kinam*) of your sting. Finally the *sisbic* ("vanilla-bean") is in your sting.

You were cast into the midst of the *kula*.[115] There you took the undulations of your back. You were cast into the heart of the trees (*che*). There you took the *yax-cheil* ("hard tissue"?) of your back,

162 of your belly./ Curses upon you! Sting! Sting!

Entirely jointed is your tail. You, offspring of the cave! You, offspring of the watering trough! You, curses on your sting [or genitals,

---

115 I can find *kula* only as the name of a cenote on the road from Chankom to Tekom.

54

a pun],[116] upon your lineage, because of your mother, because of your father.

XXXII

A worm in the tooth, a fiery worm

Now, oh how is it with you? How about you?

Red is my breath; white is my breath, black is my breath; yellow is my breath.

Shortly ago, how? did you trim to its heart the red *chulul*-tree, 163 the *tuncuy*-tree,/ the *chac-toķ*-tree,[117] the red *eķ-hub* [*eķ-huleb?*], the red *ķanpoc* [*ķanpocolche?*], the red *ix malau*.

You, then, how? Take the heart of the food. What gave pain? The red needle. What is the symbol of the saliva of your mouth? The white *hol*-tree, the red *hol*.

The great fiery worm are you, the *nabal-bacte*-worm. Who, then, was your mother? Who also was your father, when you were born? Ix Hun-tah-dzib ("lady unique-splotch-paint"?), Ix Hun-tah-nok ("lady unique-splotch-worm"). Shortly ago you painted the red earth [a type of soil].

164 Where did you get/ the brush with which you painted it? The red brush. There you got it, in the Chuen [constellation]. Indeed, you painted it, the leaf of the red *tudzi* [*tadzi*-tree?], the red *chacah*-tree, the *habin*-tree, the red *yax-cab* (fl.?). Indeed, you painted the leaf of the red *chacah*, the red (*chac tan*) *ch'ahum*-woodpecker. Indeed he was seized in the heart of the food. Indeed, I dragged along the red (*chac tan*) *uaķeh* [bird?].

I stand ready to take his fire. I roast him in the heart of the food, in 165 the tooth of the green wooden man, the green/ stone man.[118] Red is my breath, white is my breath, black is my breath, yellow is my breath.

What tree is his tree? The red *chacah*-tree, the white *chacah*, the black *chacah*, the yellow *chacah*.

---

[116] Maya, *ach*, which can mean either "sting" or "male genitals"; hence the following reference to lineage (*sian*).

[117] The hard wood of these trees is likened to the hardness of the tooth.

[118] Here again the wooden and stone man appear to represent the patient.

Oh, what are his birds? The red *colonte*-woodpecker, the white *colonte*, the black *colonte*, the yellow *colonte*. These are his birds.[119]

Thus they are set up, my red stone *comal* ("griddle"), my white, my black, my yellow stone *comal*; and then I roasted your face (or 166 eye); you, my red breath,/ my white breath, my black breath, my yellow breath.

Be you cast into the red flint, the white flint, the black, the yellow flint. Be you cast into the red conch, the white conch, the black, the yellow conch.[120]

Be you set up, my red *tuncuy*-tree, [my] white *tuncuy*, my black, [my] yellow *tuncuy*, that I may roast your face (or eye), your mouth.

Be set up, my red *comal*, my black, [my] yellow *comal*. Be set up,/ 167 my red *kankilis-che*-tree.

This is the fierce fire, where I roast your face (or eye). Then I roast you, tooth. Curses upon you! Tooth, tooth, tooth, tooth!

XXXIII

This is also a worm, in the tooth also

Unique Can Ahau! Curses upon you! [*Ten ch'ub a chuc*; addressed to the worm in the tooth.]

Shortly ago, how? a new worm was born, a night worm, a deadly poisonous worm, a fiery worm, an awakening worm, a *sibis*-worm. I curse you!

Hollowly resounding in the *copo*-tree, hollowly resounding in the *tzalam*-tree, hollowly resounding in the *yaxnic*-tree, hollowly resound-168 ing in the *kulimche*-tree,/ hollowly resounding in the *kan-toppol-can* ("yellow-budding-shoot"), hollowly resounding in the *chacah*-tree.

Spread about, they [the worms] move, to be seen by the red *ch'ahum*-woodpecker, the white *colonte*-woodpecker. Oh, this would be sudden forcible biting. This would be seen by the *ek-u-ne* ("black-tail-snake");[121] this would be seen by the *ah tan-xot* ["he-who-cleaves-in-the-middle," snake?]. He would arrive in the midst of the foliage.

119 I infer that the worm is to be extracted from the tooth, just as the woodpecker extracts the worm from a tree.

120 The flint and the conch are compared with the hard tooth.

121 It is hard to tell what part the *ek-u-ne*-snake plays here. Since it is reported to

169 The *yaxche*-tree is its sign to release what is known. It would not come to pass, it would not ascend, its sign. It would be on/ the *aklis-bul* ("bean-vine"). These, then, are corded faggots to be dragged in because of the food.

Four days, and he would return shortly to the forest, to the belly of the food, to the forest, to the heart of the food. *Uakeh*[-bird?], *uakeh*! What *uakeh*! The paternal *uakeh*, the father *uakeh*, the *uakeh*. The unripe food, the unripe breadstuff. Oh, not pleasing is his command to my heart.

What do ye still cut? [What] do ye still husk? [What] do ye still mangle?

170 He does not sleep, he does not curl up. The lust (*cool*) of birth, the lust (*col*) of/ creation. *Untzil, untzil* ("so it is"). *Uakeh* of the water.

Now he goes. He would ascend to the sky, to the place of his father, the thirteen[-gods].

Firmly set would be the virgin dry-stone wall; and then he goes to the door of the wasps' nest. There his evil would be shut in. He is thrown, to be crammed into the interior of the conch-shell (*hub*), the place of Hub-tun Ahau.

171 Set up, then, is my red *comal*, where I roast him. Then I roast my red breath,/ my white breath, my black breath, my yellow breath.

Then, how? I drag in my red *tuncuy*-tree, my white *tuncuy*. This, then, is to kindle the fire, where I roast my red breath, my white breath.

What is his bush? The red *chacah*-tree, the red *kutz*-tobacco, the white *kutz*.

This was his mother, the *ul*-snail, in a way, your father. You are the great substitute (or mask, *koh*). I bite you; I bite the back of your claw. Hun Ahau. I curse you, seizure!

First scattered there, first scattered then!

172 On unique 4 Ahau was he born,/ was he created, by his mother, by his father, Kin Colop-u-uich-kin.

I curse you, seizure! It ends now, finally.

eat small birds, it may be watching the woodpeckers, for it is quite a large snake. But possibly the snake might be feeling a relationship with the worm that the bird is eating.

XXXIV

The words for inflamed gums ("red monkey-gums")

Red clotted blood on the red . . . , on the red *uakeh*-[bird?], the red *pipican* [fauna], the white *pipican*. Their blood continually flows together on the ground to me, how? These join one another, their eruptions (or fires?). You, black clotted blood, red clotted blood, 173   yellow clotted blood,/ white clotted blood!

You, black *pipican*, red *pipican*, white *pipican*! That was their symbol, when I extinguished their fire (or eruption).

I call the great sleeper. Come, yawning; come, blinking!

What, then, is the new bed-cover? Its green cover is the tail of the *kubul*-oriole, when I change his bed-cover.

I call the great sleeper. I remove the great stinger (or biter). Come, nodding; come, yawning; come, blinking; come, sinking [into sleep]; come, [sensation of] pressure; come, snoring!

Great Can Ahau!/

XXXV

174   *Incantation for the placenta*[122]

This, then, is when you encounter it bursting open [like a bud].

Who, then, is the lust of the sire (*cit*[123]), the lust of darkness? Ix Hun-dzit-balche ("single slim *balche*-tree")[124] is the lust of the sire, the lust of darkness.

The platform-shelf (*canchelic*) is my red *tuncuy*-tree. Thus I placed it beneath [on?] the bowels of Itzam-cab ("earth-lizard"). The platform-shelf, then, is my round [wicker] stand, the stand for the bottom of my jar also./

---

[122] Among people of Maya stock in Chiapas at the present time a normal birth is attended by the husband and a midwife. In case of the retention of the placenta, a "man who knows" is called in. In addition to his manipulations he "combats" the powers of death and causes them to flee (C. Guiteras Holmes, *"La magia en la crisis del embarazo y parto en los actuales grupos mayances de* Chiapas," *Estudios de cultura Maya,* I, 164–65.

[123] The word *cit* ("sire") has survived only in the terms *citbil,* applied to God the Father, and *ix cit,* "paternal aunt."

[124] Maya, *ix hun-dzit-balche,* possibly a proper name. There is a well-known town in Campeche named Dzitbalche.

175   Great movement, great pain! Now he is cast into his arbor, his *acantun* by his mother, to the base of the *ƙinim*-tree.

Four days would he be stretched out at the base of the heater (*ƙinib*), where he took his force (*ƙinam*) also.[125] He is cast down, how? to the place of his father, the red *ƙul-sinic*-ant. There he took his pain (or stinging).

What then is the symbol of the honey of Chac-uayab-cab ("great-
176 supernatural-bee")?/ Its symbol is the honey of my maguey (or wine?).

Chac Bolay! Where is my symbol, when I arise to lay my hand on the bowels of Itzam-cab? My supreme belly are you [*oxlahun tzuc*, "thirteen divisions," a pun].

Bed-soiled are you [or "Where are you?" a pun]. Covered tobacco (*ƙutz*) are you then. The lust of the sire (*cit*), the lust of darkness [the womb?] are you.

Shortly ago was the biting (or stinging) of Hun-yah-ual-uinicob ("unique-enemy-of-men"), Hun-yah-ual-anomob ("unique-enemy-of-the-Anoms").[126] Completely ruined would be the sky; completely
177 ruined would be the earth,/ for them. Hun-yah-ual-uinicob, Hun-yah-ual-anomob. Supreme belly are you.

Where are you? The great causer of pain are you, the great biter (or stinger). Then I cast you into the bowels of Itzam-cab.[127] Supreme belly are you.

Where are you? Red *ƙanal*-wasp, white *ƙanal*! Supreme belly are you. Where are you? Red seizer of the *ti*-[insect?], white seizer of the *ti*, you, seizer of the *uƙ*-louse. Red *tupchac*-wasp, white *tupchac*./
178   Shortly ago you stung, Hun-yah-ual-uinicob, you great causer of pain, you, great stinger (or biter). Completely ruined is the sky, completely ruined is the earth, in the face of Hun-yah-ual-uinicob.

Shortly ago, how? [there was] great Hun-pic-ti-uoh ("8,000 *uooh*-

[125] *Kinib* ("heater") and *ƙinim* (a fruit tree) seem to be merely puns on *ƙinam* ("force" or "pain").

[126] Here, perhaps, the placenta may be personified and considered to be an enemy of the foetus. I take the name Anom to mean humanity in general.

[127] Casting the placenta into the bowels of Itzam-cab may well mean burying it in the earth. Today it is customary to bury the placenta under the hearthstones (Robert Redfield and Alfonso Villa R., *Chan Kom, a Maya Village*, 359).

creatures")[128] also. Shortly ago [there was] the great *pap*-jay also, on the head (or top) of Itzam-cab. [There was] your supreme (*oxlahun*, "thirteen") crossing of the fountain (or urethra?).

179 My seat [or incantation, a pun, *cuntanma*[129]] is my red stone seat (*culub*), my symbol of my/ sitting on it (*culic*) also. Here would be his bird of tidings, because of his mother, because of his father. The red *tacay*-bird would be his bird, his bird of tidings.

Vigorously slapped then, how? is my fire, when I descend. What is the fire-colored (*ḳaḳ-tan*) *mucuy*-dove? Shortly ago I set Can-yah-ual-kak ("vigorous enemy of fire") beneath the bowels of Itzam-cab ("earth-lizard") also. Supreme (*oxlahun*) belly are you.

Where, then, how? are you? Covered *ḳutz* ("tobacco") are you, when I cast it in the bowels of Itzam-cab.

180 My red furrow [vulva?]. my white furrow,/ are its symbol. [Now present] is my seated thing (*culic*); there is my thing which suddenly bursts forth [the placenta]. Amen.

XXXVI
The words for cooling a pit-oven

Shortly ago I stood above the red circular thing;[130] shortly ago I stood above the white circular thing; shortly ago I stood above the black circular thing; shortly ago I stood above the yellow circular thing.

181 Thirteen jars are of my cenote-water; thirteen measures are of my/ hail-water. It [the water] falls on the flat heating stone. Shortly ago I stood erect behind the red cloud-wind; shortly ago I stood in the face of the white cloud-wind; shortly ago I stood in the face of the black cloud-wind; shortly ago I stood in the face of the yellow cloud-wind.[131]

---

[128] Hun-pic-ti-uoh, see Glossary of Proper Names. Here is a possible indication that the unidentified *uooh* may be a bird, albeit a fabulous one, but its identity remains doubtful.

[129] *Cuntanma*, or *cumtanma* ("being seated"), may well be a pun on *cunthanma* ("incantation").

[130] From the context I would take the "circular thing" (*petay*) to mean the pit-oven. The modern pit-oven, however, is described as a shallow rectangular excavation (Redfield and Villa, *Chan Kom, a Maya Village*, 41).

[131] The "cloud-wind" would seem to refer to the steam or smoke from the pit-oven.

Shortly ago, how? I loosened the red circle;[132] shortly ago I loosened the black circle; shortly ago I loosened the yellow circle. The great loosener am I.

Shortly ago I loosened the yellow *anicab*-vine; shortly ago I

182   loosened the/ black *cibix*-shrub; shortly ago, how? I loosened[133] the red *dzoy* (fl.?), the white *dzoy*. Shortly ago I loosened the red *chunup*-tree. The great loosener am I, the great husker am I, when [I] stand erect

Shortly ago I loosened the *sac-chuen-che*-shrub. Shortly ago I loosened the white *ḳablam* (fl.?), I loosened the red *boḳen-ha*

183   ("beaten water"). I pull out/ the *tix-um-xuchit* (fl.?).

Open your mouth, *itzam*-lizard [Itzam-cab?]! Lo, it is broken apart. Amen.

XXXVII
The birth of the flint

Four days it turns. This rock is its mother. Her offspring are you, small fragment of flint.

Curses upon you, genitals (*ton*)![134] You, the red Bacab! By day, by night, ye four Bacabs!

Here, then, how? are four furrows to the horizon ("belly of the sky"). I curse you. Ye gods, ye Bacabs, create ye excellently the son.[135] It would be good that he understand. Alive are we./

184   Receive ye the creation, the descent, then, of its creation on earth. The *chim-toḳ-*("flint-capsule-") tree. How then did I not trust? I did not understand your divinity also.

For this I curse you. Ye Bacabs! I created it. How, ye gods, ye Bacabs, did I create it? It passed, it is to pass, what you permit, there where it passed also.

---

132 The red, black, and yellow circles might refer to the live coals, the black ashes, and some yellow burned earth in the pit-oven.

133 I can only conjecture that the "loosening" refers to pulling away the remains of the partly burned fuel.

134 Elsewhere in this manuscript and in the katun prophecies the flint-lancet (*ta*) is associated with the male genitals (*ton*). (See MS p. 4 above and n.)

135 Possibly the small piece of flint which is chipped into a tool is considered a "son" (*mehen*) of one of the Bacabs, but it is hard to see why the latter should be cursed. Later the reciter seems to claim to be the creator.

Have I not trusted you [plural] always? How then did I trust you in my heart. Four days it turned in the heart of the water, the lewdness (*coil*) of the small flesh (*ix mehen bak*) of your face./

185   1 Ahau was its day.[136] Split off, it comes. Pleasant is the vigor of its body. It is at the place of its mother. Ye are the shoots (or snakes?) of creation.

Shortly ago I received its force. Ye four gods, ye four Bacabs! Shortly ago I threw you about [like a ball], ye four Bacabs, four by yourselves, when he was created. How?

Who is his tree? The red *tok-aban* ("flint-bush"), the *dzulub-tok* ("festooned-" or "arbor-flint"). Ye four gods, ye four Bacabs! Four by yourselves, gods./

186   1 Ahau would be its day, ye four gods, ye four Bacabs. Shortly ago I received its force. Four alone. My red Bacab. Four gods are ye, four Bacabs.

Shortly ago I stood erect to suck hard, to receive its force. How? Behold, I stand erect to receive the force of the red *chim-tok* ("flint-capsule-tree").

Shortly ago I received the force of the white *dzulub-tok*-shrub. Ye gods, ye Bacabs!/

187   Shortly ago I received the force of the red *chuc-tok* ("charcoal-flint," fl.?), the white *chuc-tok*. Shortly ago I received the force of the black *chuc-tok*; shortly ago I received the force of the yellow *chuc-tok*.

Shortly ago its force was taken, ye gods, ye Bacabs. What is its symbol? The red *pepem*-butterfly,[137] the white *pepem*, the black *pepem*, the yellow *pepem* are its symbols. These then are the four by themselves.

---

[136] Since the flint comes from beneath the earth, it is logical that 1 Ahau should be its day.

[137] This association of the flint with the butterfly reminds us of the Itz-papalotl ("obsidian butterfly"), an insect monster of Mexican mythology. Seler (*Gesammelte Abhandlungen zur amerikanischen Sprach-und Alterthumskunde*, IV, 717, 727) sees the butterfly as a star deity portrayed in two of the Maya codices (Madrid Codex, pp. 8, 55; Paris Codex, p. 24). In the Chumayel manuscript we find the butterfly associated with human slaughter (Roys, *The Book of Chilam Balam of Chumayel*, 103); and the Motul Dictionary gives it as the name of a dance. For the Itz-papalotl see also Thompson, *Maya Hieroglyphic Writing: An Introduction*, 85.

Shortly ago I stood erect. This is his breakfast (*u kam u chi*), the
188 red *pakam*-cactus ("prickley pear"). Shortly ago his breakfast/ was
the red *chacah*-tree. Shortly ago his breakfast was the red *op*-anona.
This red *sicil* ("squash-seed") is its symbol. Ye gods, ye Bacabs! How?
Who created him at birth? Ye four Bacabs.

Shortly ago I received its force. 1 Ahau was the day when he was
born. Ye gods, ye Bacabs!

197 On 1 Ahau was the birth/ of the flint [point]. Unique 4 Ahau
[1 Ahau?] was the darkness.

Shortly ago, how? I received the white *pepem*-butterfly, the red
pepem.

What, then, how? is the symbol of the binding of his flint? The
white *lucum-can*-worm. What then is its symbol? The red *lucum-can*.

What then, how? is my arrow? The *yax-kam* [*yax-kanan*-shrub?].
This, then, is the symbol of my arrow.

198 What then is the symbol of its wooden warping-frame?/ The
tongs (*nathab*) of my Ix Bolon-puc[138] are the symbol of its warping-
frame.

What then, how? is the symbol of the cord of my bow? The white
lucum-can ("angleworm") is the symbol of the cord of my bow. A
curved snake is his [my] bow. What then, how? is the symbol of my
stringing my bow? *Sin-ni-ni-ni, tzi-ni-ni-ni, tzin*! [The twanging of
my bow-string.]

What then, how? is my symbol? The white *ah-bab*-frog,[139]
stretched on the ground, the red Bacab. What then, how? is my symbol? Oh, the red *dzulub-tok*-bush, the white *dzulub-tok*, are my
189 symbol,/ with which I am conjuring (*tin pedzci*).

Shortly ago you saw my coming; you did not see my going. Shortly
ago descended the resin of the white *kik-che*-tree,[140] the red *kik-che*.
Amen.

[138] I can make nothing of the reference to Ix Bolon-puc.

[139] Boys impersonating frogs take a part in the modern rain-making ceremonies
(Redfield and Villa, *Chan Kom, a Maya Village*, 142, pl. 13).

[140] I can only surmise that the *kik-che* (rubber tree) is cited because its sap was
employed in attaching the flint point to the arrow-shaft, although I do not know that
it was so used.

XXXVIII

The words for an obstruction of the breathing passages

Red Itzam-kan, *ta te no*! [*tal ten-o*, "come to me, hallo"?] Thirteen ("supreme") are the waters of my red gutter (*chulul*[141]), when I guard my rear behind the east sky.

White Itzam-kan, *ta te no*! Thirteen are the waters of my white gutter, when I guard my rear behind the north sky.

190 Black Itzam-kan, *ta te no*! Thirteen are the waters of my black gutter,/ when I guard my rear behind the west sky.

Yellow Itzam-kan, *ta te no*! Thirteen are the waters of my yellow gutter, when I guard my rear behind the south sky.

Red Itzam-kan, *ta te no*! Thirteen are the waters of my red rock tank, when I guard my rear behind the east sky.

White Itzam-kan, *ta te no*! Thirteen are the waters of my white rock tank, when I guard my rear behind the north sky.

191 Black Itzam-kan, *ta te no*! Thirteen are the waters of my black rock-tank/ when I guard my rear behind the west sky.

Yellow Itzam-kan, *ta te no*! Thirteen are the waters of my yellow rock-tank, when I guard my rear behind the south sky.

Red Itzam-kan, *ta te no*! Thirteen are the waters of my red sea, when I guard my rear behind the east sky.

White Itzam-kan, *ta te no*! Thirteen are the waters of my white sea, when I guard my rear behind the north sky.

192 Black Itzam-kan, *ta te no*!/ Thirteen are the waters of my black sea, when I guard my rear behind the west sky.

Yellow Itzam-kan, *ta te no*! Thirteen are the waters of my yellow sea, when I guard my rear behind the south sky.

Red Itzam-kan, *ta te no*! Thirteen are the layers [*yal*, a pun on *yaal*, "waters of"] of my red wind (or breath), when I guard my rear behind the east sky.

White Itzam-kan, *ta te no*! Thirteen are the layers of my white wind, when I guard my rear behind the north sky.

193 Black Itzam-kan, *ta te no*!/ Thirteen are the layers of my black wind, when I guard my rear behind the west sky.

[141] *Chulul* usually means either "bow" or the tree of that name, but here the con-

64

Yellow Itzam-kan, *ta te no!* Thirteen are the layers of my yellow wind, when I guard my rear behind the south sky.

Red Itzam-kan, *ta te no!* Red Itzam-kan, *ta te no!* Thirteen are the layers (*yal*) of my red web (*ƙan*) [of] the red *leum*-spider, the yellow (*ƙanal*) *leum*, the black *leum*, the white *leum*, when I guard my rear in the heart of the sky. Spread out is their stick poison.

Thirteen ("supremely") dry was I, when it was erected, the red bow [*chulul*, a pun on *chulul*, "gutter"], when I guard [my rear]/

194 in the heart of Metnal, the underworld, over the wooden man, the stone man.[142]

Who obstructed him there? Who obstructed your father, when I requited your offspring?

Where would I better address them? Chacal Ahau ("red lord"), Sacal Ahau ("white lord"), Ekel Ahau ("black lord"), Kanal Ahau ("yellow lord").

Cut off, how? is the mucus of his throat. Where, how? is the *sahom*-herb for his mouth? The *chac-ya* ("red sapote") is [for] the excessive blood in his mouth. Amen.

XXXIX
Obstruction of the breathing passages also

[This includes] stoppage of the breath: above, below, in beds, *xanab pasmo* ("sandal-seizure"), *ƙax-naƙ* ("abdominal pressure"), *mazcab-ppoc* ("metal cap"), the incantations (*sian*) to call it./

195 It continually chokes you, it continually obstructs you, [like] fresh fire-smoke in your face. Then you curl up; you [seem to] hang suspended . . . .

My command falls on the *yuyum-acan* ("oriole-*acan*," fl.?). I shake (*yumtic*) thirteen [of them] alone, the *bub-tun-uitz* (fl.?), over the *ueyulal*.[143] I set over the pictured Sip; I set over the *boboch* (fabulous fauna?). Paramount (*oxlahun*) is the command, when it is established (*hedzeb tun*).

text indicates plainly that the word is derived from *chul* ("to drip"). The usual word for gutter is *chul-ha* ("water-drip").

142 Here, I infer, the reciter means that he is protecting his patient, symbolized by the wooden and stone man, from dying and going to Metnal.

143 I can find no meaning for *ueyulal*.

Then I tied you down with a virgin hair, with a virgin *cibix*-plant, with a virgin *dzoy* (fl.?), a virgin *tab-can* ("cord-shoot-vine"), the

196   *chac-anicab*-vine, the *ƙaxab-yuc* ("antelope-binder-vine")./ I bind you. So with what are you suspended? With the virgin bark bast.

What enters into the tendon of the back of the spoiled one of creation? The virgin carded fiber, the shredded bast, enters into the tendons of his back, presses against it.

What enters into the small tendons of his heart, extending to his leg, to his arm? So what enters to his heart? The stripped shredded bast. It falls behind; it falls in front, to be established at the front./

199   Chac Ahau ("great lord") there on high! Chac Ahau on earth! So what was my symbol, when I stood erect on the road of fallen bones (*hom bac*), on the road of fallen skulls (*hom tzeƙel*)?[144]

In the light, in the dark, fire was I below; smoke was I above. Then I stood erect before the lust of creation, the lust of begetting (*mehen*).

So who was your father? So, in front of your father is the lust of begetting. Bread is your strength; oh, twice as much honey am I one night. Then you spoil (*ƙasic*) your father, oh, on the seventh day, on

200   the seventh night.[145]/ Then we meet outside. There am I. So you join me, spoiled one of creation, spoiled one of darkness.

Who obstructed me? Oh, unique stopper (*mac*) on high, unique stopper on earth! I stopped (*maci*) your breath with an earth-stopper (*macapil-lum*), when I spread it on your breast, when you joined me.

So what pressed upon your breath? The spoiled one (*ƙasul*) of creation. So what adhered to your foot? Red-earth-mud. It adhered to your wooden prop. What is your symbol, when I establish you, when I seat you on your seat? Chuen.[146]/

201   An enormous flint (*chac ahau toƙ*) enters into your bowels, while I suspend you there one day. Then struggle for seven nights, for seven days, when we make the encounter. I cast you away, spoiled one of creation.

144 I can interpret the road of fallen bones and skulls only as the path to Metnal, the realm of the dead, which is frequently symbolized in the Maya picture-manuscripts by skulls and cross-bones. The reciter is guarding his patient from taking that road.

145 I can find no evidence of a seven-day period among the pre-Spanish Maya, although *uuc* ("seven") is not an unusual element of Maya names.

146 For Chuen, see Glossary of Proper Names. It is hard to see its relevance in the

A Maya drawing entitled Spider-snake-macaw-wind seizure
(am-can-mo-ik-tankas)—Book of Chilam Balam of Kaua.

Benito Cauich, *yerbatero* of Pisté.

Photograph by Morris Steggerda

So what is my symbol, when I encounter you? The red *leum*-spider, the white *leum*, the black *leum*, the yellow-red *leum*. These are my symbol, when we meet in front, when we meet behind, when I firmly establish you.

So, where came you, when you came? In the heart of the *yaxche*-tree, in the heart of the east./ There you took your force; there you took your breath. Four palms [deep] in the ground did I stop your breath. Right inside did I stop your breath, did I hold you down, did I choke you. . . .

Where came you, when you came? In the heart of the *yaxche*-tree, in the heart of the north. There you took your force; there you took your breath. I put an end to your force; I put an end to your breath.

The offspring are you of the female person (*ix uinic*); the offspring are you of the mother.

Where came you, when you came? In the heart of the/ *yaxche*-tree, in the heart of the south. There you took your force; there you took your breath. I put an end to your breath. So with sudden force I put an end to your breath; I seized you. Frightened is creation; frightened is the *yche*-man (*yche uinic*); frightened is the portrayed figure (*tii-uinclis*); frightened is the *bob-och*-brute.[147] Frightened is the *bob-och* in Metnal; frightened is the *bob-och* on earth. He falls into Suyua, my house of command, Kukulcan. Four divisions of equipment. Frightened is the *bob-och* in the sky; frightened is the *bob-och* in Metnal; frightened is the *bob-och* on earth. But my heart was not frightened, when your heart was frightened. Once only, the *bob*-brute; once only the portrayed figure (*uinclis*)./

Thus is your incantation (or birth? *sian*). The virgin blood (or sperm, *kikel*) of shredded bast. This seizes you, once only, the portrayed figure. This enters into your blood (or sperm), and then your strength fell.

present context. Possibly any association with the north might be considered unfavorable to a patient suffering from an obstruction of the breathing passages.

147 I can make little of the *yche*-man, the *tii-uinclis*, and the *bob-och* except that they appear to be frightening figures that cause a person to lose his breath. Very possibly the phrase *oy ta* should be translated "frightening," not "frightened." Today in Quintana Roo the *bob* is believed to be a mythical animal covered with shaggy hair. It has the body of a horse and the head of a lion and eats men (A. Villa Rojas, *The Maya of East Central Quintana Roo*, 104).

Where came you, when you came? From the heart of Metnal, from the heart of the water. Where came you forth? From the mouth of the dark cave.

There came your cry from Metnal; there came your cry from the horizon [*u nak caan*, "the belly of the sky"]. Then you hung there, the spoiled one (or sperm, *kasul*) of creation, the *kasul* of bursting into flower, the *kasul* of birth./

205 What seized you? The shredded bast (*yx hob hol*) .... This puts you erect. Firmly fixed is the *kasul* of creation. It fell ... over him. Oh, stunned were his ears. Suddenly they were suspended from the sky, amid the groans, oh, cries, oh!

So what is the symbol of my dart (*nabte*), my aid (*anate*)? My *sahum*-plant, the virgin *op*-tree, are its symbol. My *sahum*-plant is my dart.

Then I pried out his heart. There came forth then, how? a *yax-ci-*agave [from] the breast to stanch his blood.[148] Frightened, oh, is your vigor, when it falls.

Jesus Mary![149] Your breath, when it is taken away! Oh, your vigor, when it falls! To the east is your breath stopped. xx xx.

Jesus Mary! Your breath, when it is taken away! Oh, your vigor, when it falls also! Stopped is your breath, oh! xx xx/

206 Jesus Mary! Your breath, which is taken away! Oh, your vigor which falls! To the south is your breath stopped.

The spoiled one (or sperm?) of creation, the spoiled one (or sperm?) of birth, is forcibly extended then. How? I do not move it.

Repeatedly stopped in the Chuen[-constellation?], repeatedly stopped in the clouds, stopped on the ground, stopped in the wind (or in his breath?), stopped by day, stopped by night, stopped before me, stopped behind me, stopped all around! It stops, oh, it ends. Amen. xxxxxx

148 On page 3 of the Dresden Codex we see the corpse of a bound female victim lying on a sacrificial stone. From her opened breast arises a tree. On it is perched a vulture holding in its beak an eye, which it has plucked from the victim.

149 "Jesus Mary" is one of the very few expressions relating to Christianity in this manuscript; the only frequent one is "Amen," which ends almost every incantation.

68

There, then, it is broken. Broken open is the breath, then. Repeatedly broken, then, is the groaning. It ends./

XL

207   *The words for the bones* (bac); *one-day* [*debility*]

Shortly ago I stood erect (or ready). I am your father; I am your mother. Ix Bolon Dzacab ("lady eternal-one") is my symbol, when I stand erect. I am your mother. Let me plant (or join together) the *yax-che*-tree (*yax u che*), the fresh fold (*yax uudze*).

Shortly ago I stood up to red bone[-debility]; shortly ago I stood up to white bone[-debility]; shortly ago I stood up to black bone-debility; shortly ago I stood up to yellow *chay-chi* [*ch'ay-chi*, "mouth-debility"?].

Shortly ago I stood up to my red confronter (*ah tan*); shortly ago I stood up to my black confronter; shortly ago I stood up to my yellow confronter.

Shortly ago was created the red binder, the *yax-che* ("fresh-tree"), the fresh fold (*uudze*).

208   I am standing erect, where?/ to pull the red dislocator there, the red dislocator, the black dislocator....

Shortly ago, where? how? I bound the red fold (*uudze*), the white fold, the black fold, Uuc-seye ("seven-beater"). Amen.

XLI

The words for the bones; *three day bone*[*-debility*] *also*

4 Ahau is the day; Can Ahau is the creation.

What enters into the bones? Oh, the red peg, the white peg, the yellow peg,[150] fresh clotted (?) blood (*olom*).

What enters to the tendons? The red *say*-ant, the white *say*-ant,[151] the yellow *say*-ant, fresh vigor, fresh clotted(?) blood./

209   The red sprinkler-gourd, the white sprinkler-gourd, the black sprinkler-gourd, the yellow sprinkler-gourd [for cement]. The great

---

150 In this complaint it would appear that the bones feel loosely knit, and here the incantation has the effect of attaching them together more firmly, as though with a peg.

151 The name of the *say*-ant is a partial pun on the term for dislocation of the bones, *zayal-bac*. *Say*, or *zay*, however, also has other meanings, such as to scarf or dovetail, and is the part of a rush used in making mats.

closer, the great assembler. Come then to mend (or cement together) the opening in his bone.

My red confronter, my white confronter, my black confronter, my yellow confronter!

Red nest-descender ("chimney swift"),[152] white nest-descender, black nest-descender, yellow nest-descender! Great cementer, great joiner, great assembler, come, then, to cement his bones.

My red alleviator, my white alleviator, my black alleviator, my yellow alleviator!

210 Red nest-descender,/ my white alleviator, my red alleviator, red-winged one, white-tendoned one, great joiner, great cementer, great assembler, go then to fasten the cartilege of my red alleviator.

What, how, is his bird? What, how, is his bird of tidings? The red *bac-hol*, the *bacen-chulul*, are his birds. What is his tree? What is his bush? The *dzacal-bac*-("bone-cure-")shrub. What is his tree. The *bacel-ac*-tree, the *bacal-che*-tree.

Who was his tree, what was his symbol, when I bound (*ḳaxtah*)
211 him lightly,/ when I bound him tightly? The red *ḳax-ix-chel*-vine, the white *ḳax-ix-chel*, the red *ḳax-ix-ḳu*-vine,[153] the white *ḳax-ix-ḳu*.

The supreme (*oxlahun*, "thirteen") resin am I. My red cenote where I tightly bound the forceful one, the great steamy one (*ah oxou*), the great resounder. . . .

Who created him? He created him, did Colop-u-uich-kin, Colop-u-uich-akab.

Awaken, bone! Awaken, clotted blood! This then is the hand of God the Father, God the Son, and God the Holy Spirit. Amen./

XLII
212 *The words for calling a deer* [untranslated][154]

152 Although its actual name, *cuzam*, or *cozon*, is not employed, it is plain that the chimney swift is meant here. Swifts are a familiar sight at sunset, when large numbers of them are to be seen descending into the same well. Several hearts of swifts are strung on a cord and bound on a patient's arm to prevent the recurrence of nightmare, depression, or epilepsy (Roys, *The Book of Chilam Balam of Chumayel*, 85, 88).

153 Here apparently we have a pun on the word *ḳax*, which can mean either "to bind" or "forest" and "wild," referring to a plant.

154 Although it is legible, this incantation appears to be written in a mixture of Yucatecan Maya and some other language of the Maya stock.

TRANSCRIPTION OF THE MAYA TEXT

N TRANSCRIBING THE MAYA TEXT of the "Ritual of the Bacabs" the notation found in the manuscript has been followed as far as possible; but to avoid difficulties in printing, the following changes have been made.

Maya text	Substitutions
ch *with a bar crossing the shaft of the* h	ch'
p *with a bar crossing the shaft*	pp, *which is also frequent in colonial Maya manuscripts*
y *with a bar crossing the tail, the usual Maya abbreviation of* yetel ("and" or "with")	y

In the present manuscript "s" is almost always employed to express approximately the sound of English "s." In Maya manuscripts generally, however, "z," "s," and "ç" are used indifferently to record this sound. The Motul Dictionary uses "ç," but in the published edition it is changed to "z." The unpublished Vienna Dictionary also gives "ç." Pío Pérez employs "z," as does our copy of the San Francisco Dictionary, the manuscript of which is lost. Beltrán's grammar has "z." That of San Buenaventura gives both "ç" and "z," perhaps preferring the former.

As in the case of the preceding translation, the paragraphing is my own and does not appear in the Maya manuscript. The incantations, however, are usually separated from each other in the manuscript by a horizontal line.

One liberty has been taken in the transcription of the Maya text. Here, as elsewhere in colonial Maya manuscripts, a multisyllabic word is sometimes, though by no means always, divided into syllables and written as though it were a succession of monosyllabic words. For

example, the name of a species of acacia is *ḳantemo,* but we also find
it written *ḳan te mo.* In such a case I have transcribed it *ḳantemo.*

I

4 U thanil balam mo tancase u coil tancase lae

Hun Ahau hunuc can ahau can ahau bin ch'ab can ahau bin akab
ca sih ech

mac cech tah ch'ab mac cech tah akab u ch'ab bech kin chac ahau
colop u uich kin ca sih ech

max a na max a coob cit ca ch'abtab ech chacal lix chel sacal ix
5 chel yx hun ye ta yx hun ye toon la a na la a cob a cit can ci/ tu pache
can ci tu pach che max cal sih cech u cool ch'abe u cool akabe can cha
lo che can chahlo tunich ca sih ech u cool akab

ah ci tancase cech u cool ch'abe ce ech ah co tancase cech nicte
tancase cech balam tancase cech ah mo tancase cech ceh tancase

6 max a che . . . [max] a uaban bax a [dzul]bal ca sih ech/ chacal
tancasche sacal tancasche ekel tancasche kanal tancasche [cha]cal
kantemo sacal kantemo ekel kantemo kanal kantemo a che la a che
cech mo tancase chacal has max sacal hasmax ekel hasmax kanal
hasmax chacal kokob max y. y. y. chacal nicte max y. y. y. la a che ci
nicte tancase max tancase cech co tancase . . ./

7 bin ycnal yx hun pudzub kik yx hun pudzub olom u col ba ch'ab
u cool ba akab ti t kax u kinam ycnal ix hun pudzub kik yx hun
pudzub olom ti tu ch'aah u kinam ycnal tu xeah haa ma bacan hai
olom bacan ah oc tancas ah ci mo tancas he bacan . . . ch'ab can
tancas bacin

pichint ex to cech cantul ti ku cex cantul ti bacab u lubul bin ycnal/
8 ix kan kinich ix kan ch'aah olom ycnal ix hun tah acay olom pich'int
ex to ycnal ix hun tah acay olon pich'int ex to cex cantu[l] ti ku cex
cantul ti bacabe u lubul bin ycnal yx co tancas ek can kin chilan ycnal
yx co tancas ek tu chiah u kab u col ba ch'ab u col ba akab tu ledzah
ix ti kik tii maxcal xan tu ledzah ix kihi [kik] ti acantun.

9 bla pul ex/ to u col ch'ab u col akabe cex cantul ti ku cex cantul ti
bacab u lubul bin tan yol metnal yicnal u yum can yah ual kak culic
yx ma uaye yx mac u hol cab

la baca u naa la baca u col cit cat kuch tan yol metnal humacnac
culucnac yauat u ch'ich'il bax ch'ab la cex cantul ti ku cex cantul ti
bacabe ci bin yalabal tumen can yah ual kak cantul ku cantul ti bacab

10   humucnac/ yauat u ch'ich'il u mutil tumen yx ma uaye ix mac u
hol cab chac tan chichi u mutil sac tan sisip chac tan sisip yx ko caan
yx ko munyal lob

in pul kin t a lubic tan yol metnal co tancas bacin mo tancas bacin
balam tancas bacin bla u col ch'ab c . . . i co cex cantul ti ku cex cantul
ti bacab oo tudz bal ix ha xan ma bacan lai kik bacan olom bacan/

11   tu che ah mo balam tancas

ci bin yalabal ca a thani cantul ti ku cantul ti bacab tumenel yx ma
uaye yx mac u hol cab

pul ex u noh [nah?] yetal [yetel?] u ba cex cantul ti ku cex cantul
ti bacab pul ex tu sac kahil ul col tulixe tu hol bal u nooke la baca oc
tu hol bal pichin [pich'in] suhuy cacaue la ba ca oc tu hol pichin bin

12   suhuy ne [nek?] la ba oc tu uich pichin chankala pichin suhuy/ yx
chankala u sol can yah ual kak la bin oc tu bal . . . u uich pichin bin
cumux can tii la bin cumlaci u bacel pichin bin saban ti la ba oc tu
yul tu pudz bah kik tu pudz bah olom pichin bin bat kan pichin halal
kan lae tu . . . pichin bin dzii kan la oc tu dziil u pach pichint kokob
tok la oc tu co pichin . . . chacal yx . . . u kas mukay yx balam pu . . .
la oc tu kil . . . ah ya . . . la ba . . ./

[*There is no page numbered 13, but page 14 is probably a continuation of page 12.*]

14   can yah ual kak lac tu homtanil ca bacin u nah u ba can heles kak
bin u pach mo pepen kan bin u tanel [tamnel?] mo sum . . .
[*interlined are the words*: "mo kas to . . . u . . ."] chebil kuch bin u
tuchil mo pixbil kuch bin u chochel mo dziuil [?] kab u hol u yit
mo . . . bil tok bin yichac [yich'ac] u misi[b?] bin can yah ual kak u
ne mo yal ix ko caan yx ko munyal ca sihi u coil akab u coil ch'ab lae

hunuc can ahau   Am[en]/

[*Page 14 is followed by a blank page.*]

II

15   U thanil ah oc tancas

lay xe u cahe huban ix u . . . [nak?] h xan chacaui xan lay ah oc
tancas lay u nunil xan tu kaba Dios yumbil

Can ahau bin ch'ab can ahau bin akab ca sihi ci u yol ch'ab u
yol akabe

Tal tu ho tas caan yal ix [ko] ti tzab ix ho [ko] ti munyal tan
chuch'uah ba tan tancase oc ci bin ca a nucah ca u . . . tah oc tancas
bacin

[*There is no page 16 but a blank page precedes page 17.*]

17   ci bin/ yalabal lae cu than ti yol caan uaye

bala sac tan oo bacan u ch'ich'il ix chac oo bacan u che tal tan
yol caan

macx u na yal bin ix kak tan chel yal bin yx kak te caan yal bin
ix kak te munyal [kak] bacin u kinam hax u [ti] ni kak ola u xe
kin chac ahau olac u xe x bolon can tumenel ten c lub a chu tancase

18   ci bin yalabal ci bin u kan [kam] ci tha[n]/ ci bin yalabal cu than ti
yol can uaye

bala sac oo bacan u ch'ich'il ix chac oo bacan u che tal tan yol can
macx u na yal bin ix kak tan chel yal bin yx kak te caan yal bin ix kak
te munyal kak bacin u kinam kax [hax?] u ti ni kak olac u xe kin
chac ahau tumenel olac u xe bolon can tumenel ten c lub a ch'u tancase
ci bin yalabal ci bin u kan [kam] ci than

19   chac hech bin tumenel ix chan/ hech bin tumenel chan kin chan
chan munyal

u lubul bin tu can be tu can lub ycnal ix ho can be yicnal cit ho
can lub ten c lub a chu tancase ci bin yalab tumenel ix ho can be ix
ho can lub

ci bin u kam than ah oc tancas bacin la ci bin u than ola[c] can uaye
yx chac oo la u mutil u pulul bin ti ykal ch'ab ykal xol ykal ual
u lubul bin pach caan . . . ycnal bolon choch ten c lub [a] ch'u tancase/

[*Pages 20–21 are in a different hand and evidently inserted from
another book of incantations; see Appendix A.*]

22.   oo ci bin u ci than uaye ola[c] u xe sac [ua]yab xoc sac mumul
lam [ain] olac u xe cantul ku cantul ti bacab tumenel puluc tok ti
yikal ual ti yikal chacal ual

u lubul bin pach can lakin ycnal bin kin popolal tun ycnal bin ix

ahau na ycnal bin yx kuknab olac bin u xeob olac bin yau[a]tob yal
bacin yx ti ho tzab tal tu ho tas can ah oc tancas bacin

ix chac oo bacan u che sac tan oo bacan u ch'ich'il u mutil cech ku

23   cech bacabe/ pul ex ti yikal ual ti yikal xol u lubul bin pach nohol
ycnal uuc chan chuc ah yk ycnal ah bolon yocte hun ni bin u tzotzel
pol cocob olac bin u xe tzotz ne pol cacab lubci kaxci u kinam ch'ab b
lae olac bin u xeob yx hun holte olac bin u xeob

ix malin cacau lubci kaxci sam cat thob dzul cacau tu cal cat thob

24   ix hun hol te tu cal ci bin u than ix hun hol te ta na/ tah tahlah ti
yikal ual ti ykal xol

ci bin yalabal u lubul bin ycnal u chikin dzulbal ix co ti pan ycnal
bin ix tah kab ser ycnal u lam tzim [olon tzin?] ten c lub a ch'u
tancase

ci bin yalabal tumenel ah olon tzin oo ci bin ca u kamah than mo
tancas bacin tu ho tas caan yal bacin ix [ko] ti tzab ix ho [ko] ti
muyal oo ci bin cantul ku cantul ti bacabe tumenel ah oc tancas bacin
ix chac oo bacin u che sac tan oo bacin u ch'ich'il u mutil puluc ti ykal

25   ual ti ykal xol u lubul bin/ ci chan kauil ycnal uaxac yol kauil ix can
[canan?] u hol cab olaci bin xhun ahau   Amen

III

U pedzil mo tancas y u nunil tancas y ah oc tancas y pencech
cha[c]uil

lac ix u chi ma u co lac ix tukalac yom u chi lay bin alahac lay
hunppel ti than cu hoppol ca alic lae u hach [u]tz[i]l than lae kutz
[utz?] bin pedzbal

Yax hun ahau hunuc can ahau bin kin hun ahau bin akab uchci

26   ch'ab/ uchci sihil tu can heb cannil uchci can heb u munyalil chab
[ch'ab] tamu[k] xan ci bin yalabal ten c lub a ch'u cex ku cex bacab
exe cat than ex ch'ab ci bin yalabal kuobe ci bin bacabobe bahun u
kan chi [kam chi] ca a thanab ci bin u than ku ci bin u than bacabbobe
uuc tuc ma chan ci bin yalabal ten c lub a ch'u tech ch'abe koko ci
bin u kam than ci bin u kam chi

27   bal a ya bacin xko ti caan ix ko ti munyal/ u mehen bacin kinich
kakmo yal bacin kak tan chel chac u petan kin chac u petan u. ca sihi

he ti ximni tu coo tu tan haulah u lac nockalac tu hol yacantun
uchic u sihil uchic ch'abtabal cen u dzulbal cen yaban uchic u sihil
uchic ch'ab

ci bin yalabal ek acal kantemo cech uohe . . . punab uchic u sihil
28   uchic ch'ab chac tan pul e u mutil bax u uayasba yak uchic/ bal hek u
xau bin yak chacal lukub tok bin u co sihom takin bin u uich hulbil
sac pet kin u mac u xicin saual kabil hool bin u chochel dzipit kab in yit

ti yilah sihil ti yilah ch'ab ci bin yalabal canchah [kanch'ah?] kik
canchah olom tu pach kab bal te kabal tun tu ledzah tu kam cu chi
chacal kuxub tu kam cu chi tu yilaah sihil tu yilah ch'ab tu chiah potz
29   uchic sihi tu ppeltah xol/ tu chiah kanche [kamchi?] uchic sihil

u picchintabal bin ycnal chac pauahtun chac ti tu ch'aah lotay kik
u kinamtei ti tu ch'aah molay kak u kinamtei uchic u toci uay yn kasic
ce uay yn xotic ce ci bin yalabal he bin u xiik uchic u kasale uch cu
xotole la bin oc tu ual ikil u chi na he bin u ch'ac pach uch cu xotole
la bin oc tu kax colox che [colol che?] abla ti dzoci yn ch'acyc y u
ba[c] ci bin yalabal/
30   u pic chin tabal bin ycnal yx hun ahau   Amen

IV

U thanil nicte tancas

coconac u than uinic tumenel chacuile tacitac yalcab uinic tumen u
coil xan

hunuc can ahau kin lic u ch'abtabal hunac ah kinam can u hol u
yax dzulbal uch cu sihil u cool al u cool ch'ab can edzlic u chacal
kabalil u sacal kabalil uchci u sihil ix on ix nicte uchci u sihil dzunun
nicte
31   tii tun bacin tu ch'ah u hol acan/ pudzbal yokol bax tun bacin u
uayasba tin chucci chacal patix uinic sacal patix uinic

oxlahun sut lic u sut tan yol caan tilic u kam chictic chac ix chichibe
chacal kutz sacal kutz tan bacin tin chuc ci he bacin u uayasba chacal
bacalche sacal bacalche u uayasba tin dzamah u ci yn te sac nicte
u tas u uay sabac nicte u tas u uay x kam [kan?] mukayche
32   [mucuyche?] u tas u uay/ utial bacin .y. u kab chichibe yetel u
kab sac nicte tin dzamah yuke

chee ten c lib [lub] a ch'u yum ac uinic yk yetel nicte tancas pakte
bin alabal yokol uinic hach co u than alcab u cah hadzaan tumen yk
lay bin alabac yokol caaten bin alabal

    ca tu hopoc [hoppoc] u tokol yak ti ye ci y chumuc u pach caa tun
ch'in ha tabac tii cho haa [choco haa?]:   Amen.

V

U thanil nicte tancas

33   Hun ahau hun can ahau can ahau bin ch'abe hun ahau/ bin akabe
    cante u hol u dzulbal cante u yacantun uchci u sihil can tah kik
can tah olom tu pach acantun acante cante u u tail cante u tonil cante
u dzulbal uchci u sihile

    bax u dzulbal chiuoh xiu sacal koch u dzulbal chac tan xacatbe
sac tan xacatbe u ch'ich'il

    macx u na yal bin x bolon che x bolon ch'och'ol yal bin ix paclah
actun yal bin ix yal hopoch' yal bin ix yal sik che ca sihi tan yol can

34   than ex/ ox tescun tancase ci bin yalabal uoh ci bin u nuc than yal
bin x uoh ti can x uoh tii munyal picchin bin pach can lakin tu hol
yotoch chac pauahtun max tah ch'ab lae u ch'ab colop u uich kin tu
kas hon [hom] to toc hon [hom]

    ci bin u thanob oxlahun ti kuob than ex to ox tescun tancase ci bin
yalabal uooh ci bin u nuc than tii ul bacin

    chac tan chiuooh sac tan chiuooh kik chiuoh kak chiuoh tancase
35   ti humni chac tan xacatbe u ch'ich'il chacal/ koch sacal koch u dzulbal
chiuooh xiu u dzulbal

    picchin tex pach can nohol tu hol yotoch kan pauah tun max
tah ch'ab lae u ch'ab colop u uich kin tan yol can

    than ex to oxtescun tancase ci bin yalabal uooh ci bin u nuc than
tii ul bacin

    chac tan chiuoh sac tan chiuoh kik chiuoh kak chiuoh tancase
ti humni u ch'ich'il chac tan xacatbe

36   kanal koch ekel koch/ chiuoh xiu u dzulbal kan ppulen bin u uich
put balam kuch ci la oc tu yit chiuoh kak chiuoh tancase ti u ch'aah
u tzapil u pach chi la u dzulbal ti u ch'aah u kinami

u picchintabal tu pach caan chikin tu hol yotoch ek pauahtun
ma[x] tah ch'ab lae tu kas hon [hom] to toc hon [hom]
 than ex ox texcun [tescun] tancase. ci bin yalabal uooh ci bin u nuc
than ti ul baci[n]

37 ek tan chiuooh chiuuoh kik chiuoh kak/ chiuoh tancas. ekel koch
u dzulbal chiuooh xiu u dzulbal ek tan xacatbe u ch'ich'il
 chiuoh kike chiuoh kake chiuoh tancase tah lah tex to cu kalic bin
u chi kaknab can kin cu tocic can kin cu kasic u chi kaknab humnahi
u ch'ich'il chac tan xacatbe sac tan xacatbe u ch'ich'il
 chacal koch sacal koch u dzulbal chiuooh xiu u dzulbal

38 than ex to ox tescun tancas ci bin yalabal/ uoh ci bin u nuc than
ti ul bacin
 chacal chiuoh sac tan chiuoh chiuoh kik chiuoh kak chiuoh tancase
can kin cu tocic can kin cu yelel tu chi kaknab el bin tabche el bin
yaxxun can kin cu tuhal cay tu dzulbal uchci u sihil
 tah lah tex to u lubul bin pach can xaman tu hol yotoch sac
pauahtun macx tah ch'ab lae u ch'ab kolop u uich kin tan yol caan/

39 tu toc hon ci bin u than oxlahun ti kuob ox tescun tancase ci bin
yalabal uoh ci u nuc than ti ul bacin
 sac tan chiuoh kan tan chiuoh chiuoh kak chiuoh tancase chacal
koch u dzulbal tii uoh xoc u dzulbal tu hol yotoch sac pauahtun
 tah lah tex to u lubul bin tan yol caan than ex u kasil ch'abe u
kasil akabe tu kas hon tu toc hon tu tocah u uich kin than ex to ci

40 bin yalabal tumen/ ox [tes] cun tancase uoh ci bin u nuc than
 ek tan chiuoh bacin ti hunni [humni] chac tan xacatbe sac tan
xacatbe u ch'ich'il
 chacal koch sacal koch chiuoh xiu u dzulbal tan yol caan dza ex
yetel a ba pichin u matz tab [matzab] kin ti tu ch'aah u kiname
chiuoh kik chiuoh kak chiuoh tancas pichin bin tan hom lah cab
pichin tex to

41 bax u ua[ya]sba ca luk tan/ yol caan u le bin koch u uayasba caa
luki tan yol caan yanhi bin u uohil xan kaxcie holmek t bin tumenel
x bolon che bolon ch'och'ol ix cucul patz kin ix yal hopoch can kin
kan pullen tu chun chacal koch yanhi u macapil halal yanhi u uohil
xan kaxcie lubcie ti tu ch'aah u mac yki ti tu ch'aah u mac tubi

42   can kin cu hun [hum] chac/ tan xacatbe sac tan xacatbe u kasic u
chi kaknab

macx tah ch'ab lae u ch'ab kolop u uich kin tan yol caan

than ex to oxtescun tancase ci bin yalabal uoh ci bin nuc than yal
bacin uoh ti caan uoh ti munyal ti ul bacin

chac tan chiuoh chiuoh kik chiuoh kak chiuoh tancas ti oc ti chiuoh
haail u chi kaknab el bin oppol el bin yaxun can kin cu tuhal cay ti u

43   ledzah yom haa la oc tu/ sac tub chiuoh tancase u lubul tan kakal
chakan tii chook chacal cus [sus?] tu cali

u lubul bin ycnal som chi [ch'in] som pul tii tu ch'aah u dzus u cali
u kasic chacal boken haa la oc tu sac tub chiuoh tancase hul lic chacal
kab bal [kabal] ti tu kas uinicil te uinicil tun uet u lac yn chacal toon
yn sacal toon uchic yn can maxcunic yokol uinicil te uinicil tun

44   oxlahun yn chacal batil ha uchic yn tuple/ a kinam hunac ah
siscunah hen cen ti ual hen yn tup a kinam cen a na cen a yum
hunac can ahau   Amen

VI

U coil tancas lae

hun can ahau u kinil hun can ahau y yakbilil u coil akab u coil
kin yx ti ti caan yx ti ti munyal

can edzlic yacantun can kin chilan u canil ch'ab can kin cu sut
ocan bacin pakal tech u coil tancase ten c lub a ch'u

45   cex ku/ cex bacabe macob cu pec be u coil bin ch'ab u coil bin akab
macob xan lay bin u nunil tancas be mac ech tah ch'ab u ch'ab ech
kin chac ahau colop u uich kin colop u uich akab ti topp ech tu kab kin
colop u uich mac ech tah ch'abi u ch'ab ech yx hun ye ta yx hun ye ton
la bacin dzai a kinam tech bacin chach chac [chachac] dzidzib kike

macx lappi hunac ah chibal hunac ah ch'uy hunac ah lappa max
46   a chich [ch'ich'] yx ko caan yx ko munyal/ macx cech xan tech bacin
cech mo tancase cech cuyum kike co tancase u cuyil kin u canil akabe
chocom [ch'ocom] kike

ten bacin tec ma ach tech tu can muc in pedz cech cat ualhen
oxlahunte yn yum la bacin a uenic hunuc can ahau   Amen

VII

U thanil kanpetkin tancas lae u pedzilob lae

47   hun can ahau hunuc can ahau can ahau bin ch'abe/ cante u hol u
dzulbal cante u hol acantun can tah kik can tah olom tu pach
acantun tu pach maxcal uchci u sihile cante u hol u dzulubal uchic u
sihil u kasil ch'abe

      max tah ch'abi u ch'ab kolop u uich kin tan yol can ti huni
[humni] u ch'ich'il chac tan pap yx kan tacay u ch'ich'il yx kan dzul
mo u na yal yx kantanen kin kantanen u yol [yal] bin oo tancas yal
48 bin ah ci tancas cat sihi tan yol/ can

      than ex to u kasil ch'abe ci bin yalabal ox tescun tancase ci bin
yalabal uoh ci bin u nuc than yal bacin uoh ti caan ix uoh ti munyal
yal bin ix kantanen kin ix kantanen u. yal bin yx koko can yx koko
munyal kanpetkin tancase chacal kanale chacal tupchace chacan
xanab chace dzidzil ah xuxe xux kike xux tancase

49   bax u hulbal [dzulbal]/ kante cech [kante ceeh] kantemo kan
dzutob kan pocob u kax u dzulubal uchci u sihile

      picch'int ex to pach can lakin tu hol yotoch chac pauahtun chac
chac toppen sac toppen tu hol yotoch chac pauahtun chac

      max toh [tah] ch'ab ti uli tu kas hon [hom] tu toc hon [hom] ci
bin u thanob oxlahun ti kuob ox texcun [tescun] tancase ci bin yalabal
uoh

50   ci bin u nuc than yal/ bacin uoh ti caan yx [uoh] ti munyal yx
kantanen kin yx kantanen u yal bacin yx kan dzul mo

      ti huni [humni] u ch'ich'il tancase chac tan pap sac tan pap yx
kan tacay u chi'ch'il kan dzul mo yal yx ko caan yx ko munyal yal
bin ah ci tancas yal bin ah oo tancas ca sihi

      tahlah tex u lubul bin pach caan [n]ohol max tah ch'ab . . . ac tu
kas hon [hom] tu toc hon [hom] ci bin u thanob oxlahun ti kuob
51 than ex to kan [p]pulen tu hol/ u dzulbal ox tescun tancase ci bin
yalabal tumen oxlahun ti kuob uoh ci bin u than yal bacin uoh ti can
yx uoh ti munyal yal ba yx kantanen kin yx kantanen u. yal yx ko can
ix ko munyal yal ah ci tancase yal bin oo tancas yal bin ix kan dzul mo

      cat sihi ti kanhi u tubi ti kanhi a dzulbal

      max tah ch'ab lae u ch'ab colop u uich kin tan yol caan u

52 picchintabal tu hol yotoch/ ek pauahtun pach can chikin max tah
ch'ab lae tu kas hon [hom] tu toc hon [hom]

ci bin u thanob oxlahun ti kuob kan ppulen ek ppulen tu hol u
dzulbal than ex tun ci bin u thanob oxtescun tancase ci bin yalabal uoh
ci bin u nuc than yal bacin uoh ti can ix uoh ti munyal yal bacin ah ci
tancase yal bin ah oc tancas yal bin ah oo tancas yal bin yx kan dzul mo

max u dzulubal kante cech [ceeh] kantemo kandzutob kan dzocob
u kax u dzulubal

53 max tah ch'ab la/ kin chac ahau kolop u uich kin tan yol can
picchinte u lubul bin tu chi kaknab ti huni [humni] u ch'ich'il chac
tan pap sac tan pap yx kan tacay u ch'ich'il ix kan dzul mo u na yal ix
ko caan ko munyal bay u dzulubal kante cech [ceeh] kandzutob
kandzocob u kax u dzulubal

than ex to ci bin yalabal tumenel oxlahun ti kuobi ox tescun tancas
ci bin yalabal tumen oxlahun ti kuob uoh ci bin u nuc than ti ul bacin

54 kanpetkin tancas/ chacal kanale chacal tupchace chacal xanab-
chace dzidzil ah xuxe xux kike xux tancase

max u na ca sihi yal bin ix ko caan ix ko munyal yal bin ix
kandzulmo u na cat sihi yal bin ah ci tancas oo tancas yal bin ah co
tancas kanpetkin tancas yal bin ix kantanen kin ix kantanen u

ti ualic [ualac] u sihil ti ualac u ch'abtabal oc bin ti xux tancasil u
chi kaknab kaxcie lubcie u kasal ch'abe

55 pichin bin pach can xaman/ tu hol yotoch sac pauahtun sac toplah
[topplah] tu dzulbal max tah ch'ab la tu kas hon [hom) tu toc hon
[hom] ci bin u than oxlahun ti kuob than ex to u kasil ch'abe ox tescun
tancase ci bin yal[a]bal tumenel oxlahun ti kuob uoh ci bin u nuc
than yal bacin uoh ti caan uoh ti munyal tii ul bacin

kanpetkin tancase chacal kanale chacal tupchace dzidzil ah xuxe
xux kike xux tancase ti huni [humni] u ch'ich'il chac tan pap u

56 ch'ich'il yx kan dzul mo/ u na yal ix kantanen kin ix kantanen u. yal
ah ci tancas yal co tancas yal ah oo tancas cu sihi u kasil ch'abe u kasil
akabe u picchintabal bin tan yol caan kan ppulen chac ppulen tu uich
kin tan yol caan max tah ch'ab lae tu kasah u uich kin

than ex to ci bin yalabal tumen oxlahun ti ku ox tescun tancase
ci bin yalabal uoh ci bin u nuc than yal bacin uoh ti caan yx uoh ti

57 munyal yal bin yx kantanen kin yx kantanen can yx/ kantanen u
kanpetkin tancase yal ix ko caan ix ko munyal ah ci tancas yal oo
tancas ca sihi

ti huni [humni] chac tan pap sac tan pap yx kan tacay ix kan dzul
mo u na ca sihi u kasil ch'abe u kasil akabe kante kantemo kan
dzutob kan dzocob u kax u dzulbal uchic u sihil

tii tu ch'ah u chibali tii tu ch'ah u kiname kanpetkin tancas

58 u pichintabal tan hom/ lah cab . . . tabal . . . tumenel . . . che yx . . .
tan yol caan u lubul pach can lakin tu hol yotoch chac pauahtun

Mac tah ch'ab la tu kas hon [hom] ci bin u thanob oxlahun ti kuob
than [ex to] ox tescun tancase ci bin yalabal uoh ci bin u nuc than

Yal bacin uoh ti caan yx uoh ti munyal dza ex yen u ba pichin bin

59 xux dzocob tii u na picchin bin dzacal mo/ pasismo la oc tu hol bal
picch'in bin u madzil uil la [o]c tu xib picchin bin yx mucuy la oc tu
yubal u pach picchin codzbil dzoc la oc tu . . . picchin bin u suhuy
pudz yx uuc metlah ahau la oc tu uach picchin bin u suhuy chachab
yx uuc metlah ahau la bin uch cu uenel oxlahun calab bin uchic a [u]
uenel u kasal ch'abe u kasal akabe

tii huni [humni] u ch'ich'il chac tan pap sac tan pap yx kan tacay

60 u ch'ich'il yx kan dzul mo u na yal/ bin yx kan tanen kin yx kan tan
en u. yal bin ah ci tancas yal bin ah co tancas yal bin oo tancas ca sihi
can kin sut tu chi kaknab el bin opol el bin tabche humucnac u pach
can kin cu tuhal cay uchic u sihil u kasil ch'ab oc bin tii xux tan sil u
chi kaknab lubcie u kasul ch'abe

kante cech [ceeh] kantemo kan dzutob kan dzocob u kax u
dzulbal

u kasic tan chacal chakan ti bin chok chocol sus tu cali u kuchul
bin ycnal sum chi sum pul [som ch'in som pul] tii tu ch'aah u thutz u

61 cali u kasic/ bin chacal boken haa uchci u patal u kasic bin chacal
kabal uchci u sihil uchci u patal

ta uilah yn tal ma ta uilah yn lukul

sam yn tup a kinam yokol uinicil te uinicil tun oxlahun yn chacal
batil haa uchic yn tupic a kinam oxlahun yn chacal moson yk uchic
yn tupic a kinam

sam yn ch'ab hunpic ti pap hunpic ti ch'el sam yn ch'ab huhunpic

Typical page of the Ritual of the Bacabs (see pages 76–77).

Intrusive material in a different hand; possibly a fragment of a malevolent incantation (see Appendix A).

tix tacay la [u] uayasba yn kab cen ti ualhen yn tup a kinam yokol uinicil te uinicil tun

hun ahau hunuc can ahau   Amen/

[*Pages 62–63, like pages 20–21, are in a different hand and evidently inserted from another book of incantations; see Appendix A.*]

VIII

64   U thanil coc u siam [sian] coc lae

hunuc can ahau can ahau bin ch'ab can ahau bin akab ti ualac u sihil can kin bin cu lothic u dzulbal can kin cu lothic maxcal can kin ix bin cu lothic yacantun ti ualac u sihil ti ualac u ch'abtabal tumen oxlahun ti ku tumen bolon ti ku

max u na yx uoh ti caan yx uoh ti munyal ix nap ti caan ix nap ti munyal

picchint bin tumen hun sipit caan ix hun sipit munyal u lubul/

65   bin lakin payil lakin ukumil

can kin cu lothic chacal temte [chem te?] can kin ix bin cu lothic chacal kobaa can kin cu lothic u uich chacal ix chel sacal ix chel kanal ix chel can kin nix bin cu lothic u uich chacal ytzamna

max tah ch'abi max tah akabi ti sihie u ciil sihil bin u ch'ab [b]acan bin ah cooc ba tun ca ti sihi sam bacan bin sihic

be a[h] tan coc be sin [sim] cal coc be nap tan coc be sam bacan

66   bin sihic be hobon che kak/ coc be ix loth coc be ix hol coc be ix bith ni coc be can coc be yx kan mucuy coc be kax che coc be nach'bac coc be yx pus coc be tuch'ub che coc be sot la coc be tus yk coc be hayab coc be hal bac [halabac?] coc be cuyum coc be mac ni coc be hunac ah chibale hunac ah kiname

u lubul bin ycnal sintun coc ycnal yx mac ni coc yx ma than coc lay bacan bin u na chee saban kak coc be bla u lubul bin ycnal hunpedzkin ti ix bin lubi dzi kike dzi nohole/

67   tix bin u ledzah u cabil u pach yx hunpedzkin ti ix bin tu ch'aah u chibali u kinami can kin bin chilani can kin bin copani u lubul bin yicnal sinic kik sinic nohole ti bin tu ch'aah u kinamobi heklay bin u pach naobe

u lubul bin yicnal chacal xulab u lubul bin yicnal chacal tok u

83

lubul bin chacal chuc u lubul bin yicnal chacal chem ti bin sutul
sutabi uet u lac bacan bin u kakil yn uoce uatal bacan bin yn cah yokol
68 chacal uinicil/ te sacal uinicil tun

oxlahun ueceb uchic yn uecic tu chi kaknabe mac tial mula yn tial
cu than chuchen coc cu nuc thani tu pach yacan tu pach u maxcalil
tu hol yacantuni pul ex tun bacin cu than u ch'ich'il cu nuc thani u
pulul bin yicnal yx macanxoc

lay bin u nayntah chacal puhuy u ch'ich'il yx huy tok [suhuy tok?]
bacin cu chibale ah thun ci yauat u ch'ich'ile

uatal ix yn cah hek macab u hol u nie hek u coil ch'abe hek u
69 coil/ akabe oxlahu[n] macab uchic yn macic u hol u nie u ch'abe u
coil akabe bax u ch'ich'il max u mutil chac tan coco can sac tan coco
can ek tan coco can kan tan coco can chacal coc ye sac tan coci ye ek
tan coci ye kan tan coci ye

mac tah ch'abi u ch'ab yn coc bal tun yal bin yx uoh ti can yal bin
yx culum can yal bin yx co pauah ek yal bin yx hun meklah yal bin
yx hun sipit munyal yal bin ix oc tun xix yx ocomtun/

[*Page 70 contains a part of an ordinary medical prescription in a
different hand. Page 71 is blank; page 72 is apparently a continuation
of the preceding or of another incantation for asthma.*]

72   . . . ti tzab yx ti ho [ko] ti munyal max tah ch'ab ti sihi be cex
cantul ti ku cex cantul ti bacabe xot ex u cal ppel ex tu holmal u xotol
bin u cal tumen cantul ti ku cantul ti bacab

ti bin oc ti kak bacili ti ix bin oc ti nococili u holmal ti ix bin oc ti
nocacil u holi tiix bin oc tu tan nocacil u tan tix bin oc ti nocaccil u
pachi tix bin oc tii mucacili tix bin oc ti yit nocacili yiti

pech'eb [pechech?] takin bin u ne ac takin oc tu tan sol takin/
73 bin oc tu pach uich u pichinil bin chan kas nen la bin oc tu uich u
pichinil bin sac bob tii la bin oc tu pet u uich pichinil bin sacal lukub
chacal lukub tii la bin oc tu canal co tu cabal co

pichinil bin cabil kantun ti ti bin u ch'aah u kinami tiix bin
pichintabi tu . . . hol chac hol ti bin tu ch'aah u holol u cali tix bin tu
ch'aah yom u chi tix bin tu ch'aah u bay chibali chucnahci

74   max u che max yaban lae/ chacal yx ox loth chacal bilim coc chacal

bacel ac chacal xihil ac [xich'ilac] la bin u che la bin yaban can kin
cu lothic chacal yx ox loth chacal bilim coc chacal bacel ac chacal coc
che chacal y[x] xich'ilac sihom takin u uich

u helpahal u hol u cal hech'eb bin yak pepem kan bin oc tu
pucsikal kas tun bin oc tu kah sum chebil kuch bin oc tu chochel dzipit
75 kab oc tu yit buc/ suyen oc tu pach sac pop bin oc tu tan u ledzci bin u
ca cobol u na tix pic dzacab tix ho dzacab

tix bin coh hu chii chibalnahcii tix bin oc ti suhuy pudzil u coii
chibalnahci ma uenci ma coylaci uinicilte uiniciltun tumenel tin chint
[ch'int] ex tu cal ual tu cal xol cex bolon ti kue

u kuchul bin xaman payil xaman ukumil can kin bin cu lothic
76 chacal boken ha can kin cu lothic sacal boken/ ha ekel boken ha kanal
boken ha can kin ix bin cu lothic chacal kabal can kin cu lothic sacal
kabal ekel kabal kanal kabal can kin ix bin cu lothic u uich sacal ix
chel can kin ix bin cu lothic u uich sacal ytzamna

max tun u ch'ich'il bax tun u mutil chac tan coco chan ek tun
77 coco/ chan kan tun coco chan chac tan coc ye sac tan coc ye ek tun
coc ye

u kuchul bin chikin payil chikin ukumil can kin bin cu lothic u
uich ekel yx chel can kin cu lothic ekel ytzam u lubul bin yicnal tan
sacal chakan can kin bin cu lothic u uich yx bolon puc can kin cu
lothic ah tabay can kin bin cu lothic u uich hun pic ti ku
78 ti bin xot u cal tumen hun pic/ hun pic ti ku ti bin oc ti nocacili u
kuchul bin ycnal ah can chakan tumen ah cantzuc che

ti bin oc tu canil ac can kin ix bin yan yicnal yx kan kinim tun yx
kan kinim te u kuchul bin yicnal ah som chi [ch'in] som pul ti tu
ch'aah u canil u chi ti tu ch'ah u u canil pul ti tu ch'ah u kinami/
79 can kin cu ledzic chac tukbil acan sac tukbil acan ek tukbil acan
kan tukbil acan ti tu ch'ah u sac put yki tix bin tu ch'ah u sot a cocili
ti u ch'ah u sac tub u sac hayabi u sac keluci ti tu ch'ah u sac cimili
chibal nah ci chuc nah ci

u kuchul bin nohol payil nohol ukumil can kin bin cu lothic kanal
boken ha can kin ix bin cu lothic u uich kanal yx chel kanal ytzamna
cu kuchul bin ycnal ah bolonte uitz/

80   ti xoti u cali ti oci tu kax mucabi ti oci tu maben hol chem u holi
tix bin oci yit chem yiti tix bin [oci] tu pach chem u pachi tix bin oci
tu tan chem u tani

can kin bin lic yukic u kab chacal kutz sacal kutz ekel kutz ti bin
ueni ti bin coplahi u kuchul bin yicnal hun ch'icib xul u kuchul bin
xoc ci be hil ti bin hux [kux] yoc ti bin han u kabi

81   u kuchul bin yic[nal]/ chac uaya[b] cat sac uaya[b] cat [cab]
ek uaya[b] cat[cab] u kuchul bin ycnal chacal yx chel sacal yx chel
ekel yx chel kanal yx chel tu kasah uinicil te uinicil tun

u lapal [lappal?] bin u lubul tu dzic u uich bi ci tancase bulan coc
ci bin yalabal u dzic pop dzoc hi bin buul suhuyhi bin buul canhi bin
u dzic pop tumenel

u kuchul bin yicnal yx ma uaye yx mac u hol cab la u mac u pachi
yaxal chac u sisal yn uoc u sisal yn kab ti machci uinicil te uinicil tun/

82   hunuc can ahau   Amen

IX

U pail can coc lae

chacau sintun bin po cabel bal tepan [teppan] tix koch hach chacau
tamuk u na nak yabal ti yothel kohan uinic he u thanil u pail lae
. . . ek tun chuc u uayasba . . . in paah tu pach ytzamcab . . . can
coc lae uet man yn suhuy kak ca tin paah can coc lae max u kax
yaban sacal mudz coc u kax yaban hun ahau can ahau/

X

83   U thanil yx hunpedzkin tancas lae

hunuc can ahau sihici hunte[n] hi u kinil hun ten hi yakbili hun
kin ca sihi hun kin cu pec tu nak u na

max u na yal yx hun ye ta yx hun ye ton yx hun lah dzib x hun
lah uoh

max u na yal x hun dzalab caan x hun dzalab muyal ix hun
tzelep kin x hun tzelep akab

max u kalo ci bin yalabal yax huh lo yax ytzam yax [a]h aam cab
yax bekeh

84   tux tu ch'ah yen u balo/ ti tu ch'ah yicnal u yum kin chac ahau

86

ytzamna tu ch'ah u cabil u pach hun kin codzan ti yol nicte ti yol
xuchit tux tu ch'ah u am yicnal x yaxal chuen ti tu ch'ah chacal yaxcab
tab tu ch'ah u uelal u uich ti tu ch'ah yicnal sac bat ti yol chuene ti tu
ch'ah chacal sabac sac ek sabac kanal sabac la oc tu uelal u uich sihom
85 takin oc tu uich suhuy pech'ech'/ la oc tu ne dzipit kab oc tu yit sum
chebil kuch oc tu chochel

max u kalo ci yalabal x hunpedzkin caan x hunpedzkin calam x
hunpedzkin kokob x hunpedzkin taxinchan x k . . . ti calam yx
paclah actun x muc sohol

max u kalo te dzoci u dzibtabal u pach lay chacal x hunpedzkin
lo dzibtabi u na kin tu pach hunpedzac u na kin dzibtab tu pach
hunpedz u na akab ti dzibtab tu pach
86 max u cuch u ch'abi chacal kanal sac ekel/ kanal kanpetkin chacal
ych uinic sac ekel kanal yche uinic chacal tupchac kanal tupchac

ti cha [ch'a] u cuchob ti ch'abi hunah [hunac] ah chibal u cuchob
chacal sinic sac ek kanal sinic chacal hoch' sac ek kanal hoch' la oc ti
hoch' can x hunpedzkinil lay u cuch a ah chac calam sac ek kan

bici ti dzoci u dzibtabal u pach ta uilah ua uchic u chibale ma tin
87 uilahi [ma] tin pactah ti uchic u chibale/ bin chibalnac cen tin pach

max u che max yaban uchic u sihile chacal hunpedzkin che x
hunpedzkin yaban tu kasah u dzulbal max u dzulbal chacal x hunpedzkin che hunpedzkin yaban tu kasah u dzulbal max u dzulbal
chacal x hunpedzkin che hunpedzkin yaban hun kin copan tu hol u
dzulbal hun kin cu sut ti yaban tan yol can tu kasah u pacabil u yum
hun kin pacan tu pacabil u yum ti tu kasah u uich kini ulicel tu uich u.
88 hun kin cu chibal u uich . . ./ caan tumen ca hadzni tu ne hadzni tu
holbal bici ci yalabal ma bici binel u cah ti ppebel u pucsikal

binel ix u cah ti xotol u cal tu kasah yax uinicil te yax uinicil tun
tu kasah ka bal hun ten hi hut cabal hun ten hix chuen tume[n] hun
ten acantun acante hu[n] tah kik tu pach acante acantun hun ten hi
chactun tun ha chac mosen ha
89 max yn uaesba [uayasba] cen ti ualhi chac tun ek pip/ sac chac tan
hun kuk bix yn uaesba uich'ac chacal chiuoh tok hek uich'ac ca tin
ppel hech cen ti uli yn chucub yax huh lo yax ytzam uatal yn cah yn
chucub yax huh lo

uatal yn cah yn paab u cuch bob lo puben chac tan tok pap yn
uaesba ca tin paah tu uich kin tin paah tu uich u. yokol yaxal chac yn
uaesba bax yn uaesba cen t . . . i x hatzab te x hatzab tun ti lukes
90 yokol/ yax uinicil te yax uinicil tun
   hunuc can ahau uchic u sihil uchic u ch'abtabal tu nen [tumen]
u yum tu nen [tumen] u na   Amen

XI

U thanil chibal oc lae
   uatal yn cah yn pab chacal sinic sac ek ka[n] Uatal yn cah yn
paab chacal tzaah sac ek ka[n] u tas u uay yax uinicil te yax uinicil
tun luksah yn cah ti chacal hoch' sac ek ka[n] la oc ti hoch' can yn
hunpedzkinil
91   luksah yn cah tii chacal ppoppox/ sac ek ka[n] yokol yax uinicil
te yax uinicil tun luksah yn cah ti chacal lal tu tas acantun tu tas
akab ti sihic
   sam tun ix bacin yn helbes u tas a uay bax tun bacin u hel u tas a
uay u tas ne yaxum u tas ne xop lahun u tasal be bolon tas oxlahun tas
u ne kubul u tas ne yaxum tin dzaah u tasic u uay uinicil te uinicil tun
   luksah yn cah tii h hunac ah chibal bax hunnac ah chibale chacal
92 yx/ u nic sac u cuch be bax yen u ba uchic u chibal chacal cheeb sac ek
ka[n] lay oc ti yach chibalnahci uatal yn cah yn paab u kinam ah
bolon paab en kakal ti cab budzal canal tin paah hunuc ah chibal
yokol yax uinicil te tin paah tu uich kin tu uich u
   chac hulub tii caan sac hulub ti caan chac hulub ti kakob sac
93 chac hulub ti calam/ sac la tii chibalni uatal yn cah chucub hunac ah
chibal uatal yn cah yn colpayte u kan uatal yn cah yn paab bla u kax
can x hunpedzkin caan kaxnahci chucnahci be chacal hunpedzkin
cante yn chacal ch'och [choch] yn sacal ch'ooch [chooch] max yn
uaesba [uayasba] ca ti ualhen chac tan ekpip chac tan hunkuk sac yn
uaesba cen tii uli cix hatzab te yx hatzab tun
   hetun x bacin chee ueteli cix hunac ti uenel yokol yax uinicil te/
94 ueteli cix hunac tii balam coan yokol uinicil te yax uinicil tun bax
hunac ah uenele tin luksah hunac ti ah chibal yokol yax uinicil tun
yax uinicil te sam yn dzaab u hel u tas u uay

coten [con ten] ix hay coten ix mudz coten yx nok coten yx lam
coten yx nat[h]

yax hun can ahau hun ahau uchic u sihil uchic ix u ch'abtabal
tumen yum tumen u na

u yax tas ne yaxum u yax tas ne kubul tin dzah u helint u tas
95 a uay yn paab lo hunac ah/ uenele yn luksic hunac ah chibale coten
hay coten ix mudz coten x nic coten x lam coten ix nat[h] coten x nok
hunuc can ahau can ahau   Amen

XII

U thanil yx hunpedzkin nohhol lae u pedzilob lae

Ocol tun bacin yn cah yn siscunt a uol ocebal tii sacal batan chacal
batan haa ti sacal sayaban chacal yoc haae ti sacal u uayesba chacal
uaya[s]ba tin paci a kinam/
96 he ba ti sacal batan chacal batan he ba ti sacal sayaba[n] tin tupci
a kinam he ba tii sacal sayaban tin chacal sayaban tal in cah yn loban
hunnac nah loben cen

tii ualhi ah chac mo xotena chac mo cotena sac mo xotena ten u
ch'ich'il na a mutil ten a chacal ek pip pam sacal ek pip pam coe coe
97 uatal tun bacin yn cah yn ualab chacal sinic chacal/ tzaahe chacal
ya sacal ya chacal popox [ppoppox] sacal popox

bax u uaesba [uayasba] u hel u tas uay he chacal yx hoch' chac
sacal hoch' hoch kik tun bocan bin tin paah tu uich kin tu uich u.

chac hulub ti can chac hulub ti kak kob chac hulub ti calam la tun
bacin tii chibal nah ci yokol uinicil te uinicil tun bin hunac ah chibale
98 chacal ix uinic/ u cuch be

balx yen u ba chacal cheb la oc ti yach chibal nah ci uatal bacin yn
cah yokol uinicil te uinicil tun yn siscunt u kinam uatal bacin yn cah
yn paab u kax can ix hunpedzkin can can te[n] kax nah ci can te[n]
chuc nah ci uatal yn cah yn chucul u moc can yx hunpedzkin can te[n]
chuc nah ci

u et u lac yn chacal choch la tin choch ci u kax caan yx hunpedzkin
99 u et u lac/ ah ch'ich'iil chac tan ek pip la tun bacin ti chuc nah ci u
kax can yx hunpedzkin can

yax hun ahau hunuc can ahau

he tun bacin he uet u lac bacin yn hunac ti balam caan yn pay
hunac ah uenel tun bacin sam tun bacin yn lukes ah chibale tin dzah
u hel u tas uay bax tun bacin u hel u tas uay u yax tas u ne yaxum u
yax tas ne kubul tin dzaah u helint u tas uay

100   in payic/ hunac ah ueneli yn luksic ah chibale coten yx nic coten
yx hay coten yx mudz coten yx nic coten yx lam coten yx noh
hunuc can ahau hun ahau hun can ahau
[Gloss] kak ti kohan

XIII

U thanil hobonte kake
cha cal . . . che pecbesabac tin ch'ab . . . tun . . . ix uucte lay ike se
. . . yokol . . . chac boken haa . . . ucul bin . . . ci bin hobonte kake . . .
101   tan yol can x uuc te lay yke/ u yum hobomte kake anal kake   Amen

XIV

U pedzil kakob chacuil tancasob blae
ten chub a chuc tech ydzin tancase macob kako[b] bacin xotom
bacin be chee chac mu[c]lah [ka]kob ocom kakob ho[bonte ka]kob
chacuil kakob hex u kumch . . . [tumen] u na tumen u citobe a
102   nayintaho[b] be che [x] h[un]/ ye ta x hun ye ton
can kin cu sut be hex u kuchul be yokol be uinicil te uinicil tun be
hek sam be yn pabe u kinam be hunac ah kinam be ti uen xa be ma
chee ma uenci ma coylaci ma be chee chac molonche kak
hex ox nicib sus be che oc tu tunilob chee cux u habalobe
hex u binel be ti holom kakil be chee cux u bacelobe hex u binelobe
tix ba[c] kakil be u bacelobe chee cux u kikel be hex u binel be tix
103   chac hulub/ ti kakil
be chee uac uudz hix ti caan chee uac uudz hix metnal xan . . . x
picchintabale chee pach can xaman be che hek tihi u kak hal actuni
tihi u kak hal hai uch cu sutobe xibnacobe tumen u na tumen u citobe
macobe chee u col al u cool ch'abe max tah ch'abobi u ch'abob citbil
be che
maco[b] be chee bobote kakob be che max a ch'ich'il u mutil
kakobe che hex u ch'abtabal be chee tumenel chee chac tan mo sac

104 tan mo ek tan mo/ che x u ch'abtabal be chee tumen chac tan dzidzib
sac tan dzidzib ek tan dzidzib be chee hex u chobal be chee tumen
chac ta[n] mo sac tan mo chac tan ppocinbe sac tan ppocinbe la u
ch'ich'il la u mutil kakob bacin xoton [xotom] bacin che max u che
max yaban kak be che u ch'abtabal be che tumen chacal colonte he ix u
ch'abtabal tumenel chacal nix che hex u kuchul be chee chacal chacah

105 be che/ hex u kuchul kakalobe che nacob che tumen u na tumen u
cito[b] be che

    max be che u sisal yn ka[b] be che ca ti ul en be yn pabe hunac ah
kinam be che uet u lac yn chacal sayab yn sacal sayab yn ekel sayab
tin siscunt ci u kinam be uet u lac be yn chacal dzonot yn sacal dzonot
yn ekel dzonot tin siscunt ci u kinam be uet u lac yn chacal kax ek be

106 ekel kax ek be yn siscun/ ci u kinam be che hex uet u lac be che yn
chacal batil yn sacal batil yn ekel batil tin siscun ci u kinam be
che   Amen

    yuklil chacah yetel cappel yc y cab dzedzec u kabil kutz dzedzec
bin yukub lae

XV

U pedzil x chac anal kak lae

Can ahau cab can ahau canal uchic u silhil uchic u ch'abtabal max
tah ch'abi max tah akabi u yum ti kin chac ahau kolop u uich kin

107 u chac kak bin kak tamaye kak ne chacpat [chapat]/ uuc ne
chacpat [chapat] yal bin yx chante kak yx chante oyoch yal bin yx ho
[ko] ti tzab yx ho [ko] ti munyal yal bin yx kantanen u. yal bin yx
hom ti tzab yx hom ti munyal yal bin yx culum chacah yal bin yx
meklah

    u sihci u pa ch'actabal bin tumen ah tabay ycnal uuc yol sip can
yah ual kak u mahantah yicnal ix ti cah puc yicnal ix moson cuc
ycnal ix u sihnal yicnal bolom [bolon] puc cu ... u ca al na ti som chi

108 [ch'in] ti som pul/ u tahlahtabal ti canil ual ti canal xolil

    u binel bin yicnal yx cocoyol cab yicnal ix ... yicnal ix ch'ich' cit
palum cit ch ... lum kik talebal ulenebal u kakil ulumbil tu yoxlahun
tas cab l ... nale yicnal yx hun ahau sisil ahau yicnal ix ... ci cech
kake cech ... e cex uchlome

mac tah ch'abi u ch'ab u yum kin chac ahau colop u uich kin u
109 ch'ab yn kak ti u lac kak/ tamaye kak ne chac pat [chapat] u yal bin
yx chante kak yal bin yx chante oyoch yal bin yx hom ti tzab yal bin
yx hom ti munyal yal bin yx kak tachel yal bin ix culum chacah yal
bin ix meklah oyte yal bin ix meklah u sip x

ximbal u cah sut u cah ulel u cah tali tan yol can yx ahau na yal
bin yx kuknab [kaknab] yal bin x tan dzonot yal bin ix hun cumlah
luk yal bin ix hun tip lah sus cat sihi u lah lah tabal ti canil ual/
110 ti canil xole

u binel bin yicnal ah nohole yicnal ah ych uitzil yicnal ix calap
yal bin ix chi ti cil uaclahun yal bin yx hun tzel ep uitz ix hun tuch uitz
u ch'a bin ah yax ceel uitz

la tah ch'abi akabi can kin nac u toc ci uitz ti el bin ah uuc calam
ti el bin ix ma ul ti el bin yx co ti pam ti el bin kuk ti el bin yaxum
uchic u toc uchic u kinam kakil xu tu [xuth u?] ni kak chac nicen
chac toppen/

111 cat sihi ximbal u cah sut u cah chacal hilib sacal hilib sut u cah
chacal nuchup sacal nuchup sut u cah ximbal u cah cat sihi u
tahlahtabal bin ti canal ual ti canil xol u lubul bin tan yol che tan
yol aban

max u na max meki yal bin ix kin sutnal cat sihi u tahlahtabal bin
ti canal ual ti canal xol u binel bin tan yicnal yx chac lah yeeb

112 u pulul bin tu pach u dzulbal/ ti el bin chacal ten [tem] tei ti el
bin chacal tun tun hai ti el bin chacal muzen hai ti tah ch'intabi ti pax
bin acantun uchic u toc uchic u kinam kaki kax u tunil kak chac
nicen kak chac toppen kak

ca sihi ximbal u cah sut u cah chacal hilib chacal nuchup u
tahlahtabal bin ti canil ual ti canil xol u lubul bin lakin kaknabil ti el
113 bin u chi susi ti el bin u chi kaknabi ti el bin yoc hai/ ti el bin sayabi
ti el bin phui ti el bin nab ti el bin halal uchic bin u haual buth ix . . .
al uchic u toc uchic u kinam kak kax u tunil kak cha[c] nicen chac
toppen

cat sihi ximbal u cah chacal hilib sacal hilib chacal nuchup max
tah ch'abi u ch'ab bin chac uayab xoc chac mumul am [chac mumul
ain] chacal hix lac yal bin   Amen/

XVI

114   Lay licil u ziscuntabal dzam chacuil ytt licil u siscuntabal kak lae
kak ti koh[an]o[b]

U zisal uoc u zisal yn kab ca tin sizcunah kak lae hoppel yn sacal
bat yn ekel bat kanal bat ca tin siscuntah kak oxlahun tas yn chacal
potz yn sacal potz ekel potz kanal potz tin kamci u kinam kak lae
ek picte [picite] yn uayasba ca tin kamah u kinam kak lae u et emic/

115   bacin yn sacal yxim ha yn kamci u kinam kak lae uet emic bacin yn
sacal nab uchic yn kam u kinam kak lae sam yn pak u sisal uoc u
sisal yn kab   Amen

XVII

Cantip[p]te lae u thannil lae

ten c lub a chuc tech max tah ch'ab u ch'ab bin u yum tah uuc yol
sip sam bacin sihic chacal cholop sacal cholop ekel cholop kanal cholop

116   yan ix bacin u uil yan ix/ u pak cat sihi sam bacin sihi u tab u chin
[chim] ah uuc yol sip u tab u chulul cat sihi tah uuc yol sip cat sihi

     max u na yal bin ix hun tiplah [tipplah] can yx hun tipptah
munyal tu tippah bin kin tu tippah bin u. tu tippah bin ek hunac ah
pec hunnac ah sut

     xot ex u cal cex cantul ti ku cex cantul ti bacabe cante yn chacal
ppeleb hek tin xotci u cal hek tin ppelci u holmal hek u col ch'ab u

117   cool akab/ ma uencii ma coylacii yokol uinicil te uinicil tun tumenel

     tim ch'im [tin ch'in] tex tahlah tex tu cal ual tu cal xol cex
cantul ti ku cex cantul ti bacabe dzam tun yn uayasba yn ualic ca tin
dzam chetah hech tu cacobol a na tu cacobol a yum

     liken a uile liken a pate cuyum kik kech kanch'aah kik kech bacin
kokob kik kech bacin calam kik kech bacin/

118   xot ex u cal ppel ex tu holmal cante yn chacal ppeleb hek cu xot cu
cal u cool ch'ab u cool akab ma uencii ma coylacii uinicil te uinicil
tun tumenel

     picch'im [picch'in] bin tumen hun sip can yx hun sipit munyal u
lubul bin pach can lakin ti ix tu tipah [tippah] yam ti ix tu tippah
susi ti tu tipah [tippah] tu hol chacal kabal ti tipp ix tu hol chacal
boken haa tu tippah chacal tente [chemte?] ma uenci ma coylaci

119   uinicil te uinicil tun/ tumenel

tim [tin] ch'im [ch'in] tex tahlah tex tu cal ual tu cal xol cex
cantul ti kui cex cantul ti bacabe

u lubal bin tu che tu yaban chacal pakam tu kam cu chi macx ba
uinicil te uinicil tun tu kam cu chi chac tan culix yx chac ek [chac ec?]
ix uixum chac tan ix uixum la baca u ch'ich'il la ba ca u mutil

u lubul bin yicnal sintun bul ahau tin ch'im [ch'in] tex tahlah tex
120 tu cal ual tu cal xol/ u lubul bin yicnal yx kam [kan] kinib te kan
kinib tun

tix tu ch'aah u kinami yetel u bay chibali chuc nah ci ti ix oc tu
kax mucabi hek u lubul bin yicnal yx kak yol mat u cool ch'ab u col
akab ma uene ma coylaci uincil te uinicil tun tumenel

tin ch'im [ch'in] tex tahlah tex tu cal ual tu cal xol xotex u cal cex
cantul ti ku cex cantul ti bacabe u lubul bin yicnal som ch'im [ch'in]
121 som pul/ yicnal can yah ual kak ke

tix tu ch'aah u kah u chi u sudz u chi tix tu kasah suhuy opi tix tu
kasah ix bolom [bolon] puci chibal nah ci chuc nah ci ti xoti u cal
tumen bolon ti ku oxlahun [ti ku] ti ma uene ci ma coylaci uinicil te
uinicil tun tumenel

u lubul yicnal sac buthul yk ti tu ch'ah u sac cimili u sac keluci u
sac hayabi u lubil bin yicnal tukbil acan tix tu ledzah yom acani ti tu
122 ch'aah u tuz yki cante yn chacal/ ppeleb tin can xotcuntah tin
maxcuntah u col ch'ab u cool akab ma uenci ma coylaci uinicil tun
uinicil te tumenel

tin ch'im [ch'in] tex tahlah tex tu cal ual tu cal xol cex cantul ti ku
cex cantul ti bacabe dzam tun yn uayasba ca tin dzam chektah ech tu
ca cobol a na tu ca cobol a yum cech cool ale cool mehene   Amen

XVIII

Ahaucan tu nak uinic lae
Can ahau hunuc can ahau

123   Sam ech tun bacin sihic u canil ch'ab u canil akabe/ same tun
bacin sihic chac u ba ahau sam ech tun bacin sihic sac u ba ahau same
tun bacin sihic ek u ba ahau same tun bacin sihic kan u ba ahau

cante u dzulub cante u yactunil hun yah ual cab hun yah ual anom
hek u xotol bin u cal tumen u na tumen u cool hek uidzil bin u

94

kikkel yocol bin tiix uixunil u kik kel oc bin x buhumil ix cuyum/
124 sucil yx cuyum chakanil yx ho ti tzab yal pentac yal ix munach yx
catil ahau yx ma dzil ahau yx pokol pic yx hun pudzub kik

hek u lubul bin yicnal kin patax uinic y ledzic bin yom to yom
acan u lubul bin yicnal bolon [h]obon u lubul bin yicnal sac dzom pul
acat u lubul bin yicnal yx bolon sut ni cal mak u chii ychcan [ich'can]
125 yocol bin tiix xulub mascabil/ u ni yocol bin ti zuhuy pudzil u co
yocol bin ti kupbil zahumil u yak yx luluth pechechech u ne u dzipit
kab [b]in ix huna ahau yantiic yocol bin yocol bin pixbil boc u
chochel sasac mukay bin u kikel

hek u puzikal le dzi kan he bin u kaahe yocol bin tu xihil ya ax
ca u kaxal bin tu hol uitz tu hol cacab u canhal bin chac acan bin uitz
kaxic u col ch'ab sutnical picch'im [picch'in] tex bin pach can lakin
pach can chikin
126 u kaxal bin tu chi kaknab/ u canhal bin ukum u canhal bin kaxic
u col al u col ch'ab u col akab u lubul bin pach can nohol yelel bin
dzidzic yelel bin musuy u canhal bin u chel bub u canhal bin u
chel macan

uuc can ahau hun ahau   Amen

XIX

kan ch'ah can tu nak uinic lae

Hunu[c] can ahau can ahau ac akab sam tun bacin yn kamab a
127 kinam chacal kan ch'ah sam tun bacin yn maxcun/ tech zacal kan
ch'ah sam tun bacin yn xotob a cal chacal cuyum sacal cuyum sam tun
bacin yn can maxcun ech yokol yax uinicil te yax uinicil tun sam tun
bacin yn copcun ech sam tun bacin yn chelcun ech

bal tun bacin u uayasba u hol a cal u yax cal hobon tab ti tun bacin
lic a zut tii zuhuy cat ti tun bacin ta ch'ah a kinam ta ledzci u chacau
128 haail ti zuhuy cat ti baca ta ledzah u yom cha[ca]u/ haa loe ti baca
ta ch'aah a kinam ti baca ta luk sacal sin tuni ti baca ta ch'ah u kinami

peluna ta uach sam tun bacin yn xotob ech yokol yax uinicil te
yokol yax uinicil tun bal tun bacin yn uayasba cen tii uli yn copcin ech
chacal kan ch'aah

95

bin a uilab yn tal ma a uilic yn lukul sam yn puch'ub a uich sacal
puch chacal pudz   Amen

XX

Can tu nak uinic lae/

129   Yax hun ahau uatal tun bacin yn cah yn pedzeb ech cech col ale
can kin tun bacin lic a zut can kin tun bacin lic a peclic a sut tumen
a na tumen a yum cech u col al u col akabe

sam tun yn can maxcun ech chacal uayan choche sih cech bacin
ti yol yke cech chacal ahau can ca tun bacan em ech yicnal sacal anom
sac uinic

130   max yn uayasba ca tin maxcunnah eche/ hunac ah thalcunah en
hunac ah chelcunah en hunac ah copcunah hen

hunuc can ahau kin a sihic u cool ch'ab u cool akab   Amen

XXI

Cantipte [cantippte] tu nak uinic lae hach utz lae

Sam tun bacin yn chuc ech cen a na cen a yum cech sacal can tipte
be che cech chacal can tipte be che max bin che cech ocic kin be che
131   ahic cabe che cech u coil/ al be che u coil ch'abe che

sam tun bacin yn chelcun ech cen a nae cen a yume sacal can tipte
can sut cenac ca tin chuch eche sacal can tipte tec[h] ch'uyen tech yn
picchin tech tan yol kaknab

tii tun bacin oc ech ti can ch'ocili ti tun bacin oc ech ti can cayili ti
tun bacin oc ech ti can hulubili ti tun bacin oc cech tii can sucili

max tun bacin a uayasba sacal kanch'aah cum ahau ti kin max tun
132   bacin tec[h]/ ch'uyen tech cech sacal can tipte

max tun bacin a mutil max tun bacin a ch'ich'il chee sacal ek pip
che sacal uakeh che sacal ah y che ti tun bacin tin kax hech ti yoc caa
ti nac cech tan yol can

sam tun bacin yn kuben tech ti ku ah tepal anbin chee anbin a ual a
mehen cu kuchul yn than pach can lakin anbin che a ppatah [patah]
hix uinicil ta culic tun a cul che/

133   cab kutz bin pedzbal u nak uinic lae ca nabsabac u kabil kutz tu
nak lae he yuklil can tipte lae bin dzabal sam tun bacin che yn ch'ab

sacal canchacche u che sam tun bacin sacal cantiplah tun bacin yukul
la tun bacin u ci sam tun bacin yn ch'ab yx kutz aban la tun bacin u ci
hun dzan [dzam] u ci la tun bacin uchic yn chelcunic cech cech sacal
can tipte lae   Amen/

XXII

134   Kanpedzkin tu pol uinic
kanal dzuto dzoc kintal y canppel yc yukulil
    hun Ahau can ahau ti ualac u sihil ti ualac u ch'abtabal u canil
ch'ab u cantul [canil] akab
    max tah ch'abi max tah akabi u ch'ab u yum ti kin chac ahau colop
u uich kin colop u uich akab tan yol can tan yol metnal tamuk bin u
sihil tamuk u ch'abtabal
    max u na max u col yal yx hun acay [hacay] kik yal ix hun acay

135   [hacay]/ olom tan yol can
    fe luna ti yach u canil ch'ab u canil akab hun yah ual uinic hun yah
ual anom ca ti ahi xot ex u cal ppel ex cex bolon ti ku oxlahun ti ku
yanac xi[1] uilal yanac xu[1] pak u col ch'ab u col akab
    sam u kasah uinicil te uinicil tun feluna ti yach kak bacin xotom
bacin che yal x hun tah kik x hun tah olom la bin u na la bin u col
ch'ab ca yum kin colop u uich kin colop u uich akab bacin kak yol ti/

136   bacin kak u bahan tok bacin
    cex bolon ti ku tahlah tex holmek tex u col ch'ab u col akab kak
bacin xotom paynum bacin u kinam paynum u chacuil fe luna ti yach
    sam u tocah dzulub sam u tocah ton ti ek [el] chacal ta sacal ta
tumen ti el chacal ton sacal ton chacal kanal tumeni sacal kanal tumeni
    yal ix hun pet ah kin x hun pet ah akab kin chac ahau canal

137   ti tu ch'ah u nah u ba ti tun bacin tu ledzah chac/ yut sac yut tu
ledzah chac pay sac pay ti tu ch'ah u hol u cali ti tu ch'ah u sac xei ti
tu ch'ah u sac cimili ti tu ch'ah u nath cali u dzuul [dzuil] cali fe luna
ti yach
    ti eli chacuil sac uil tumen hulbil soh hulbil akab tok hulbil holom
kak chac topplah kak tumen u canil ch'ab u canil akab can kin cu
kinam can kin cu chacuil fe luna ti yach xot ex u holmal ppel ex

138   ci bin yalabalob chacal kanal sacal kanal/ chacal kanpetkin sacal

kanpetkin chacal tupchac sacal tupchac u chopaytabal bin chac hol
sac hol la bin oc ta kinam ma kaki ma xotomi

max u na max u col yal x hun patah [petah] kin x hun petah akab
max u ch'ich'il u mutil sac pauahtun

uatal yn cah cen a na cen a yum yn poch'aac tech tu tu kazal metnal
139   sam yn cocin ech ta che ta uaban cech chacal kanale/ cech chacal
kanpetkine sacal kanpetkine cech chacal tupchace sacal tupchace cex
u che cex yaban chacal dzoc sacal dzooc a che a uaban ti ech ti ueni ti
ech ti coylaci yokol uinicil te uinicil tun

he tun bacin oxlahun ppul yn sis ha yn sisil ha yn sisil bat yn chacal
bat sacal bat yn sacal tulub yn sis nakat yn cel

140   cen a na cen a yum kin/ chac ahau canal oxlahunte yn sabal [cabal]
ha yn canil ha yn batil haa tin siscunci u kinam u col ch'ab u col
akab   Amen

XXIII

U thanil kanpetkin yah lae

tii lac u pec chacal bacab can thub lic ba [tu catil *crossed out*] tu
pulil can thub lic ba tu catil Mahan tux bacin in cah tech cech chac
tan pahap sac tan pahap laix ti chi laix ti payi mahan yn cah tech
141   cech chac tan ch'ahum/ mahan ix yn cah tech cech chac tan colonte
lay i chii layi payi candzit yn chacal haxab la y tin haxcii u nokol
uil u nokol uah tan ca:

ca ti hulihul tunx bacin u canil kin u canil akab ca ti uli chacal
bikib can taxlic tun bacin u kakil chacal toncuy [tuncuy] can techlic
[thechlic] tun bacin yn chacal xamach tun tin keelci chacal xux nokol
uuclahun bak tun bacin tin keelci nok chiic tun bacin/

142   ca ti uli can techlic [thechlic] tun bacin yn chacal xamach tun caa
tin kel hech yx mucul nok x tab cal nok x hunpedzkin nok u mehen
tun bacin chacal bacab

mahan yn cah tech cech chac tan uakeh mahan yx yn cah tech cech
chac tan pap lay ix tii chi lay ix ti payi he tun bacin chee pidzilpidz tex
to pokolpok tex to

143   can techlic tun bacin/ yn suhuy luch ca tin cotzah chacal ix
hunpedzkin sacal ix hunpedzkin kanpetkin yah   Amen

XXIV

he ca bin lubuc tancas yokol uinicce

ca ch'abac ye ci yan ych lum tamile ca tokok [tokoc] ti canppel ye bin u xay u chi tabantac tu bacel u pach lukul tu thethe lukul tu puczikal lukul tu ni yoc

he ca bin dzococ u tokole ca mansabac yokol hunppel [hun ppul] 144 chacbil ha yokol y hun pul zil/ tuntabil yalil paybe ti yoc uinic

he u thanil lae La tun bacin lubi hadz u hol tancase lubi yokol sac uinic tun: sacal yk yikal lubic dza ex tun a than yokol cacmansex cex cantul ti ku cex cantul ti bacabe

ekel yk u uayasba ca tali yokol ek uinic tun he tun bacina cante[n] yn ualic ca tin hadzah max u che max yaban sacal copo u yaban chacal copo yaban

145 lictun bacin yn ualic u sukin/ hun tenili bin hanebal hu[n]mac ti kin hun tenili bin ukul nahebal hu[n]mac ti akab xan lay u sukin lae   Amen

XXV

U thanil u siscunabal ha tii kak yan lae

Bolon che kak yn poch'actic u pol ytzamcab u uayasba u cumil yn kak cen ti ualhi yokol feluna ti yach

he tun bacin u tamnel ytzamcab u uayasba u koben he tun bacin u chacbacel ytzamcab u uayasba u siil yn kak cen tii ualhi yokol

146 u les [ledz]/ ak bacin ytzam cab u uayasba u ledz ak u kakil ox haben dzidz bacin u uayasba u chucil ca tin pochaktah [pochektah] chacal cocay sacal cocay u uayasba u ppiliz u kakil

ox nicib sus bacin u uayasba u tanil chac bubul can sac bubuy can u uayasba u budz dzit che

bax tun bacin che oxlahun ppul bacin che yn sisal bat tin tupci u kinam yokol uinicil te uinicil tun/

147 oxlahun ppul bacin yn sis ha tin siscunci u kinam yokol uinicil te uinicil tun he tun bacin che oxlahun ppul yn batil haa tin tupci tin siscunci

he tun bacin che u tamnel bacin ytzam cab u uases [uayasba] u cumil

99

he tun bacin che u pol bacin ytzam cab u uayas ba u koben
he tun bacin che u chacbacel ytzam cab u uayasba u chel u siil
148   he tun bacin che/ yak bacin ytzam cab u uayasba yelel u kakil
he tun bacin che hun ppis u ci ca tin siscunah
he tun bacin che chacal sus u uayasba u tanil
he tun bacin hun ppis u ci ca tin siscuntah chacal cocay sacal cocay
hunuc can ahau   Amen

XXVI

siscunah haxan lae
149   Oxlahun ppul tun yalil yn tan yol chac tulub/ sayab yalil
tin dzah oxlahun sutac tin sutci cen chacal ah culin cul sacal saca ah
culin cul oxlahun sutac tin sutci yicnal u chich tix bolom [bolon] puc
ca tin uensah yokol yax uinicil te yax uinicil tun likul ti can
cante u dzulbal chacal mucab sacal mucab oxlahun tzuc cac sacal
mucab naclic chac nacab tun sac nacab tun   Amen/

XXVII

150   U thanil kak cache [nach che] lae
pedzbal kak layli haxane
Hun can ahau tunx bacin oci tu uayasba a kak cech yax uinic ce
[che] u cum ix bolon puc la oci tu uayasba u kobenil a kak cech yax
uinicil che
u chacbacel yx hun ytzamna la oci t[u] uayasba u nach cheil a kak
cech yax uinicil che oxlahun munyal
151   tunx tun bacin oci tu uayasba u budzil a kah [kak]/ cech yax
uinicil che oxlahun can
tunx bacin la oci oci tu uayasba yelel a kak cech yax uinicil che
u tunichil tun bacin sayab oci t[u] uayasba u chucil a kak cech yax
uinicil che
ox nicib sus tunx bacin oci tu uayasba u tanil a kak cech yax
uinicil che
sam tun bacin uedzcun nech xuu sayab V. V. V. V. V. tin
152 uedzcunah chumuc a kak cech yax/ uinicil che
chacal kax ek sacal kax ek ekel [kax ek] kanal kax ek   tin
uedzcunah chumuc a kak cech yax uinicil che

sam tun bacin uluc cen che chacal yk sacal yk ekel yk kanal yk en
tun bacin cen ti ul en hunac ah sat en tun bacin cen ti ul en
    che chacal copo sacal copo ekel copo kanal copo chacal chacah sacal
153 chacah ekel/ kanal x kanan chacal puc ak sacal puc ak ekel kanal
puc ak la tun bacin kamlahic a kak cech yax uinicil che
    oxlahunppis tun bacin yn sisil bat tin kamci a kinam hek hunac ah
kinam feluna ta uach   Amen

XXVIII

U thanil chuhul u pedzil kak nach che yokol cabil
    kak chacah u xiuil nabsabil u sac heil yx cax ti ya yokol chuhlil lae
154   hunuc can ahau u kinil a sihic cech yax cabe/ chac petan kin a
yum te ti cane yx hanil ek a na te ti cane yx hochan ek a na te ti cane
yx pic tzab a na te ti cane yx hun tip [tipp] tzab a na te ti cane
    bal tun bacin yn uayasba ca ual hen yn tup a kinam yax hal chac
tun bacin yn uayasba cat ual hen yn tup a kinam
    bal oc ta pol holom kak oc ta pol bal oc ta uich kak oc ta uich bal
oc ta kab kak oc ta kab bal oc ta chochel kakal cab oc ta chochel bal oc/
155 ta uoc u chacbacel hun [y]tzamna oc ta uoc cech yax uinicil che
    paklah sus u kaba u binel bin yetun u na yx ppohal mum ti sihi u
binel bin yetun u na tix muk yah kutz ti sishi u kinam lae   Amen

XXIX

U thanil ti ticin kab tu cimpahal uinic laci ua bic cimpahalile
    hun ahau yx ticinte yx ticin tun
156   uet ulac [ulic] bacin yn chacal chacah uet ulic/ bacin yn sacal
chacah uet ulic bacin yn chacal bul tub yn sacal bul tub hunac ah ytz
en bacin hunac ah tzutz en
    la ba yn cuch ca ti ul en yn pa a kinam yn uec a kinam hunac ah
ytz en bacin hunac ah tzutz en bacin yx ticin te yx ticin tun
    uet ulic bacin yn chacal copo yn sacal copo uet ulic bacin yn
157 chacal bul tub/ yn sacal bul tub hunac ah ytz en bacin
    la ba yn cuch cat ul en yn pa a kinam yn uec a kinam hunac ah
ytz en bacin yx ticin te yx ticin tun   Amen

XXX

U thanil u siyan am am lae
 hunil am cabil am oxil am canil am yax am te yax am tun ox kin
ba yan ech tu chemil u cab ah uuc ti cab tii tun bacin a ch'ah u cabil
a pach/
158   can kin yan ech yalan u yamtunil u mukay a chich ti suhuy ix
chel chacal ix chel sacal ix chel u uayasba u pach yax am te yax am tun
 he tun bacin u suhuy pudz tun bacin suhuy ix chel sacal ix chel
chacal ix chel la bacin u uayasba a uach oxlahun uol u bon kuch suhuy
159 ix chel chacal ix chel/ sacal ix chel la tun bacin u uayasba a ka
 sam tun bacin yn colob sam tun bacin yn lukes sam tun bacin yn
chochob fe luna ta na uach cech yax am te yax am tun
 can heb tun bacin yn ekel nok la tun bacin tin dzudzci [zudzci] he
tun bacin canlahun ppul tun bacin yn battil ha oxlahun ppul yn
160 sissala la tun bacin tin siscunci u kinam yax/
 am am am   Amen

XXXI

U thanil sinan tu chibal lae
 chib chib chib bul moc a ne dzacal moc a tan tulix mo a pol
 pichint ech bin tu chi kaknab ti bin lub ech tu hol yuxi ti bin a
ch'ah u yuxil [huxil] kabi pichint ech bin yicnal saba yol tii chuen ti
161 bin lub ech ti sinan kabil ti a ch'ah a kaba ti/ sinanil cech fe luna ta
uach u suhuy pudz bin a chich a ch'ah oc ta uach u suhuy kak bin a
chich la bin oc t kinam ta uach ti lahan u nek sisbic ta uach
 pichint ech tan kula ti bin a ch'ah u yamulil a pachi pichint ech bin
tan yol che ti bin ta ch'ah u yax cheil a pachi a yax cheil naki cech/
162 fe luna ta uach chib chib
 bul moc a ne cech ix yal actun cech ix yal pox che cech fe luna ta
uach lub a cam a uach la bacam a sian tumen a na tumen a yum

XXXII

x nok ti co kakal nok lae
 x hetun bacin chee tech tun bacin cech

chacal bik [uik] sacal uik ekel uik kanal uik

163   sam tun bacin a ppel tu pucsikal chacal chulul chacal toncuy/ chac
tok uil chacal ek hub chacal yx kanpoc [kanpokolche?] chacal yx
malau

tech tun bacin ch'a u pucsikal uile bax chibal ni ci chacal pudz
bax u uayasba u kab a chi sacal hol chacal hol sacal hol

chac kakal nok cech nabal bac ti noke max tun a na macx a yum ca
sih eche x hun tah dzib x hun tah nok sam tun a dzib chacal lum

164   tab tah ch'ah/ [c]heb uchic a dzib chacal cheb tii ta ch'ah yetun
luum tii chuen la ta dzib tab ci u le chacal tudzi [tutzi] chacal chacah
habin chacal yax cab la ta dzibtabci u le chacal chacah chac tan
ch'ahun chac tan colonte la ti chuc ci tu pucsikal uil la tin chopay ti ci
chac tan uakeh

uatal yn cah yn ch'ab u kakil tin keelci tu pucsikal uil tu co
165   yax uinicil te/ yax uinicil tun chacal uik sacal uik ekel in uik kanal uik

bax cheil u che chacal chacah sacal chacah ekel chacah kanal chacah

bal bacin che u ch'ich'il chacal colonte sacal colonte ekel colonte
kanal colonte la bacin u ch'ich'il

la ba tii can tech lic yn chacal xamach tun yn sacal xamach tun ekel
166   kanal xamach tun ca tin kelah a uich cech chacal uik/ sacal uik ekel
uik kanal uik

picch'in tech bin ychil chacal tok sacal tok ekel kanal tok picch'in
tech bin ychil chacal hub sacal hub ekel [ka]nal hub

can tech lic yn chacal toncuy sacal toncuy yn ekel kanal toncuy yn
keelci a uich a chi

can tech lic yn chacal xamach yn ekel kanal xamach can tech [lic]/
167   yn chacal x kankilis che

la tah kakil tin kelci a uich ca tin kel heche co fe luna ta uach coe
co co co

XXXIII

lay xan nok ti co xan lae

hun can Ahau ten ch'ub a chuc sam bacin sihic chacben nok akab
noh [nok] x hunpedzkin nok kakal nok ahal nok sibis nok ten c lub
a chu

booh booh ti copo booh boh ti tzalam booh booh yaxnic booh boh/
168 tiix kulinche booh booh tix kan toppol can booh booh ti chacah
      hayci u binel bin yilabal bin tumen chacal ch'ahun sacal colonte la
bacin chii chee tan tzatza la bin yilabal bin tumen uah ah ek u ne
yilabal bin tumen ah tan xot u kuchul bin tan kukmal [kukmel?]
      yaxche u chicil bin ti cha ohoma [ohelma] ma bin kuchi ma bin nac
169 cii u chicil tun bin tii aklis/ bul la bin kuchci la bina naci la tun bakob
che u chopaytabal bin tumen uilob
      can kin bin cu sut same ti kax tu tzuc uil ti bin kaxi tu yol uil uakeh
uakeh bal uakeh citbal uakeh yum uakeh uakeh u munal uil u munal
uah ma ci chee cii u thanynte tin pucsikale
      bal a xot ex to ppel ex to can maxcun ex to
170 ma uenci ma coylaci u cool al u col ch'ab/ untzil [umtzil?] untzil
uakeh uakeh hae
      ci u binel bin u nacal ti caan yicnal u yum oxlahun [ti kuob?]
      edzlic bin suhuy coot ca bin u hol xux tah ti bin maci u lobhal tu
uich u pulul bin tu dzot yol hub yicnal yx hub tun Ahau
      can tech lic tun bacin yn chacal xamach tin kelci same bacin
171 yn keleb chacal uik/ sacal uik ekel uik kanal yn uik
      pay tun bacin yn cah yn chacal toncuy sacal toncuy la tun ba tah
kakal tin kelci chacal uik sacal yn uik
      bax bax yaban chacal chacah chacal kutz sacal kutz
      la u na same ul cencen a yum cech yx chac koh ten bin chic ech
ten bin chic u pach a xau hun Ahau ten c lub a ch'u tancase
      yax uec tii yax uec ti tun
172 hunuc can ahau sihci/ ch'abtabci tumen u na tumen u yum tii
kin colop u uich kin
      ten c lub a ch'uc tancase u dzoc tun hele lae

XXXIV

U thanil chac nich' max lae
      chacal olom kik tix chacal bao ua to ti chac tan uakeh chac pipican
sac pipican la bayili yalcab u kikel ti cab teni bacin u nupp tan ba
bacin u kakil cech ix ekel olon kik chac olon kike kanal olon kik/
173 sacal olom kik

cech ek pipi caan chac pipican sac pipi caan la bacin u uayasba ca
tin tupah u kakil

tin pay yah [payah] hunac ah ueneli coten yx hay coten yx mudz
bal tun bacin u hel u tas uay u yax tas u ne kubul tin dzah u helint
u tas u uay

in payic hunac ah ueneli yn luksic hunac ah chibale coten yx nic
coten yx hay coten yx mudz coten yx lam coten yx nat [nath] coten
yx nok

hunac can ahau/

XXXV

174   U pedzil ybin lae

he tun ta nup[p] tun top[p] tzilil

max tun bacin u co ol cit u co ol akabe yx hundzit balche tun
bacin u cool cit u col akabe

can chelic tun bacin yn chacal toncuy .4. la ten bacin tin tac cah
[tacah] yalan u homtanil ytzam cab can chelic tun bacin yn met u
met yit yn cat xani/

175   hunac pecni hunac chibalni ci picch'in tun bacin tu dzulbal ti
yacantun tumen u na tu chun bin kinim

can kin bin chel lan [chelan] tu chun kinib ti ba tu ch'ah u kinami
picch'in bin tu chun chacal chi ti ba tu ch'ah u kinami nan xani
picch'in tun bacin yicnal u yum chacal ku sinic .4. ti bin tu ch'ah
u chibali

bal tun bacin u uayasba u cabil chacal choc uah cab [chac uayab
176   cab]/ u uayasba u cabil yn ci

chac bolay tux bacin yn uayasba cat ual hen yn tac kab te u
homtanil ytzam cab yn oxlahun tzuc ech tun bacin

taba cech mucuil kutze tech tun bacin u cool cite u cool akabe sam
tun bacin chib hun yah ual uinicob hun yah ual anomobe satal sat bin
177   can satalsat yan bin bin luum/ tiob hun yah ual uinicob hun yah ual
anomobe oxlahun tzuc ech tun bacin

taba cech hunac ah kiname cech hunac ah chibale ca tin picch'intah
ychil u homtanil ytzam cabe oxlahun tzuc ech

taba cech chacal kanale sacal kanale oxlahun tzuc ech

taba cech [chacal] ah chuc tie sacal ah chuc tie cech ah chuc uke cech chacal tupchace sacal tupchace/

178   sam tun bacin a chib hun yah ual uinicob cech hunac ah kiname cech hunac ah chibale hek satalsat yan can satalsat yan lum tu uich hun yah ual uinicob

sam tun bacin hunnac hun pic tix uoh xani sam tun bacin hunnac tii pap xani tu hol ytzam cab a oxlahun cha'cat tun bacin sayab

179   yn cuntanma [cum than ma?] chacal culub tun/ bacin yn uayasba yn culic xan yan bin u mutil tumen u na tumen u yum chacal tacay bin u ch'ich'il u mutil

can tahlic tun bacin yn kak cat em en cenx kak tan mucuy sam tun bacin yn cumcint can yah ual kak yalan u homtanil ytzam cab xani oxlahun tzuc ech

taba tun bacin cech x muc uil kutz cech tin picch'intah ychil u homtanil ytzam cab

180   yn hek chacal yam sacal yam u/ uayasba yan yn culic yan yn ci chetun top tun tzilil   Amen

XXXVI

U thanil u siscunabal pib lae

sam tun ualac cen yokol chacal petay sam tun ualac cen yokol sacal petay sam tun ualac cen yokol ekel petay sam tun ualac cen yokol kanal petay

181   oxlahun ppul bacin yn dzonotil ha oxlahun ppis yn/ batil ha oc ti zintunil same tun ualac cen tu pach chac munyal yk [sa]me tun ualac cen tu uich sac munyal yk same tun ualac cen tu uich ek munyal yk same tun ualac cen tu uich kan munyal yk

sam tun bacin yn chochob chacal peet same tun yn chochob ekel pet same tun yn chochob kanal pet hunac ah choch en

182   sam tun bacin yn chochob/ kanal anicab sam tun bacin yn chochob ekel cibix sam tun bacin yn chochob chacal dzoy sacal dzoy sam tun bacin yn chochob chacal chunup hunac ah choch en bacin cen tii ualhi hunac a ppal en bacin cen tii ualhi

sam yn chochob sacal chuenchee sam yn chochob sacal kab lam yn

183   chochob chacal boken ha colpay tun bacin/ yn cah tix um xuchit
ppa a chi ytzam he tun tzilil   Amen

XXXVII

U sihil tok

can kin cu sut hek tun u na yal ech bacin yx u sik tok ten c lub
ch'unute cech ton cech chacal bacabe he ti kin ti akab cex cantul ti
bacab

he tun bacin cin can uudz tu nak can ten c lub a ch'un cex ku cex
bacab ch'ab tex yutzil mehene utzi uile ca ix u natab cuxanil on/

184   kam ex ch'ab yemel tun u ch'ab ti cab ch'imtok [chimtok] bici ma
iua alan uol mai tin natah a kuil ex xan

lay uile ten c lub a ch'un tex cex bacabe yn ch'ab bici cex ku cex
[bacabe] yn ch'ab mani manbal ta cibah tij ti mani xan

ma ua alan uol tex ti hun lukul bic tun be alan uol tex tu dzi uol
can kin cu sut tan yol ha bata u coil yxmehen bak a uich/

185   hun ahau hi u kinil hek u tal cii cii u can cucut hex yicnal u na
cex u canil ch'ab

sam yn kamab u kinam cex cantul ti ku cex cantul tii bacabe sam yn
pokolpokte sam yn pitzilpitz te cex cantul ti ku cex cantul ti bacab
cantul tu ba ca sihsabi bici

mac u che chacal x tok aban u dzulubtok cex cantul ti ku cex
cantul ti bacab cantulob tu ba kuob

186   hun ahau bin u kinil cex can[tul]/ ti ku cex cantul ti bacab sam
yn kamab u kinam canppel tu ba yn chacal ba[cab] cantul ti ku cex
cantul ti bacabe

sam tun ualac cen yn tec dzudzte yn kam u kinam he tun bacin
cen ti ualhi yn kamab u kinam chacal chimtok sam yn kamab u
kinam sacal dzulubtok sam yn kamab u kinam ekel dzulubtok-aban
cex hu [ku] cex bacabe/

187   sam yn kam u kinam chacal chuc tok sacal chuc tok sam yn kam
u kinam ekel chuc tok sam yn kam u kinam kanal chuc tok

sam ch'abac u kinam cex ku cex bacab bal u uayasba chacal pepen
sacal pepen ekel pepen kanal pepen u uayasba he tun bacin can tu ba
sam tun ualac cen hek u kam u chii ti chacal pakam sam u kam u

188 chi ti cha/ chacal chacah sam u kam u chi ti chacal opo [op] lay chac
tan sicil u uayasba cex ku cex bacab sacal tan sicil cex cex ekel tan
sicil cex kanal tan sicil cex cantul ti ku cex cantul ti bacab bici max
tah ch'abi ti sihci cex cantul tii bacabe

    sam yn kam u kinam hun ahau hi u kinil sihi cex ku cex bacab
197 hun ahau u sian/ tok hunuc can Ahau akabe

    sam tun bacin yn kamab [b]e chee sacal pepen chacal pepen bal
tun bacin yn uayasba tii chuc ech sac dzulub tok aban sacal tok aban
cech sacal pepen chacal pepen

    bal tun bacin u uayasba u kax u tokil sac lucum can bal tun bacin
u uayasba chac lucum can

    bal tun bacin yn halal yax kam [kanan?] lay tun bacin u uayasba
yn halal

198   bal tun bacin u chuchteil u natab [nathab]/ yn xbolon puc u
uayasba u chuchteil

bal tun bacin u uayasba u tab yn chulul sac lucum can u uayasba u tab
yn chulul cac yam [lam?] can bacin u chululil bal tun bacin u
uayasba yn sinci u chululil macal sin ni ni ni tzi ni ni ni tzin

    bal tun bacin yn uayasba sacal bab hay tii luum chacal bacab bal
tun bacin yn uayasba che sac dzulubtok chac dzulubtok lae u
189 uayasba/ tin pedzci

    sam bac[in] a uilah yn talel ma a uilic yn lukul sam tun bacin emec
yitz sacal kikche chacal kikche   Amen

XXXVIII

U thanil kal cab lae

    chacal ytzam kan ta te no oxlahun yal yn chacal chulul ti[n] mac
ci yn pach pach can lakin

    sacal ytzam kan ta te no oxlahun yal yn sacal chulul tin mac ci yn
pach pach can xaman

190   ekel ytzam kan ta te no oxlahun yal yn ekel chulul/ tin maci yn
pach pach can chikin

    kanal ytzam kan ta te no oxlahun yal yn kanal chulul tin maci yn
pach pach can nohol

chacal ytzam kan ta te no oxlahun yal yn chacal chaltun tin maci
yn pach pach can lakin

sacal ytzam kan ta te no oxlahun yal yn sacal chaltun tin maci yn
pach pach can xaman

191 ekel ytzam kan ta te no oxlahun yal yn ekel chaltun/ tin maci yn
pach pach can chikin

kanal ytzam kan ta te no oxlahun yal yn kanal chaltun tin maci yn
pach pach can nohol

chacal [y]tzam ka[n] ta te no oxlahun yal yn chacal kaknab tin
mac in pach pach can lakin

sacal ytzam kan ta te no oxlahun yal yn sacal kaknab [t]in
ma[ci yn] pach pach can xaman

192 ek kel itzam kan ta te no/ oxlahun yal yn ekel kaknab tin mac yn
pach pach can chikin

kanal ytzam kan ta te no oxlahun yal yn kanal kaknab tin maci yn
pach pach can nohol

chacal ytzam kan ta te no oxlahun yal yn chacal yk tin maci yn
pach pach can lakin

sacal ytzam kan ta te no oxlahun yal yn sacal yk tin mac in pach
pach can xaman

193 ekel ytzam kan ta te no/ oxlahun yal yn ekel yk tin mac ci yn pach
pach can chikin

kanal ytzam kan ta te no oxlahun yn kanal yk tin maci yn pach
pach can nohol

chacal ytzam kan ta te no chacal ytzam kan ta te no oxlahun yal yn
chacal kan chachac leon kanal leon ekel leon sacal leon ti[n] mac ci
yn pach tan yol can haycab ca u cab

oxlahun ticin en cen ti ualhi chacal chulul tin maci [yn pach]

194 tan/ tan yol metnal yokol uinicil te uinicil tun

max kali tii max tii kal a yum tin paci be a al

tunx ten bacin a than chacal Ahau sacal Ahau ekel Ahau kanal
Ahau

u xotol bin tun bacin che u ta cal tunx bacin sahom tu chie chac ya
pen[cech] kik tu chi   Amen

XXXIX

kal cab xan

mac yk kal yk canal cabal tii uayob xanab pasmo kaxnak mascab
ppoc u sian pay/

195   Layi coc ech layi ti kali ech yax kak budz oc ta uich ca coylah ech
ca a chuy [ch'uy] ech ta se yan

u lubul yn than ti yuyum acan yn yumtic ix oxlahunppel tuba bub
tun uitz yn hedzcunt yokol ueyulal yn hedzcun yokol ah uinclis sip yn
hedzcun yokol boboch ex oxlahun than tix hedzeb tun

ca yn homkaxh hech ti suhuy tzotz ti suhuy cibix ti suhuy dzoy
196   suhuy tabacan yx chac anicab yx kaxabyuc tin/ tin kaxci ech bla
bax ch'uylic cech u suhuy hohol kuch bacin yx hob hol

bax oc tu xich'il u pach u kasul ch'abe u suhuy bi x hob hol oc tu
xich'il u pach dzayen [tzayen] tal

bax oc tu mehen xich'il u pucsikal tac tu yoc tu kabob bala bax oc
tu pucsikale u ca cob hob hol u dzikin lubic ti chul uay pach chul uay
tan hedzlic chul uay tan culic/

[*Pages 197–98 were a continuation of page 188. Consequently page
196 is followed here by pages 199–200. The subject matter of page
199 seems uncertain, but page 200 is concerned with the breathing
passages.*]

199   chac ahau te canal chac ahau te cabal bla bax yn uayasba ca ualhen
tu bel hom bac tu bel hom tzekel bace tan sasil ti akab kak ken cabal
budz en canal ca ualhen tu tan u col ch'ab u col mehen

bla max a yum che bla tan a yum u cool mehen uah a muk che
hun kin cappel en cab hun akab ca kasic a yum che tu uuccul kin tu
200   uuccul akab ca nup tan cab nah on ti ye/ en bla pak ten u kasul ch'ab
u kasul akabe

max ti kali ech che hun mac canal hun mac cabal tin maci ech a
uikal tu macapil lum as tin sincabtah ta tan a paktic en

bla bax tzayi ta uikal u kasul ch'abe bla bax tzayi ta uoc chacal
luum luk tzayi ta muk che bla bax a a uayasba ca tin hedzcun hech
201   ca tin culcin hech/ ta cuntan chuen

chac ahau tok oc ta hobnel ua ualac te tin ch'uycint ci ech hun kin ca poklen cab t uucul akab t uucul kin ca nupp on nac ch'in in cah tech u kasul ch'abe

bla bax yn uayasba ca tin nupp hech chac tan leun [leum] sac tan leun ek tan leun kan chac leun yn uayasba ca nupp tan ca nupp pach yn hedzcunci ech

202   bla tux a tal ca tal ech tan yol yaxche tan yol lakin/ ti ta ch'ah a kinami ti ta ch'ah a uikali can nab ych luum tin maci a uikal. hun iche tin maci a uikal tin hom chachtic ech yn cocint ech ta se yan lum tab ueyulale

tux a tal ca tal ech tan yol yaxche tan yol xaman ti ta ch'ah a kinami ti ta ch'ah a uikali tin xulah a kinam tin xulci a uikal

yal ach [ech] ix uinic yal ech ix nae

203   tux ca tal ca tal ech tan yol/ yaxche tan yol nohol ti tah ch'ah a kinami ti ta ch'ah a uikali tin xulci a uikal bla hun kal tin xulci a uikal tin machci ech oyi ta ch'ab oyi ta yche uinic oyi ta tii uincliz oyi ta boboch oyi ta boboch metnal oyi ta boboch ti luum u lubul tan suyua yn thanab na kukulcan [can] tzuc dza yen u ba oyi ta boboch tii caan oyi ta boboch metnal oy ta boboch ti luum maili oyoc in uol ca oy a uol hun ye bobe hun ye uinclise/

204   blaxa [bala ix a] sian che u suhuy kikel x hob hol layi chuc ech hun ye bob hun ye uinclise lay oc ta kikel ca a lubi a muk

tux a tal ca tal ech tan yol metnal tan yol ha tux hok ech tu hol tan akab actun

kuchi [au] auat ti metnale kuchi au auat tu nak caan caa chuy [ch'uy] ech u kasul ch'abe u kasul toppole u kasul sihile

205   bax chuc ech yx hob hol su uin layi uacun ech/ edzedznac u uich u kasul ch'abe ca y i ua ocan yokol chee tuppi u xicin hun ch'uylahob tii canale tan yacan che tan yauat che

bala bax u uayasba yn nabte yn anate yn suhuy opp [op] u uayasba yn sahun yn nabte

ca tin tac chetah u pucsikal u hokol tun bacin yax ci tzem tzitz tu kikel haki yol che a muk cu lubul

Jesuz maria a uik cu lukul che a muk cu lubul che ti lakin maci a uikal xx xx

Jesuz maria a uik cu lukul che a muk cu lubu[l] xan maci a uikal
che xx xx/

206   Jesuz maria a uik cu lukul che a muk cu lubul che ti nohol maci
a uikal

u kasul ch'abe u kasul sihile can chelic tun bacin ma yn pecbes

macma[c] ti chuuen macmac ti munyal macmac ti luum macmac
macmac ti yikal macmac tii kin macmac ti akab macmac tin tan
macmac tin pach macmac ti hun suyi u macal che u dzoc   Amen

xxxxxx

te tun y pail [l]ae u pabal ykal tun be yx papa tun acan u dzoc/

XL

207   U thanil bac hun kin lae

Sam en ualac cen a yum cen a na x bolon dzacab yn uayasba cen ti
ualhen cen a na yn pakab yax uche yax uudze

Same ual ti chacal [ch'ay] bac same ual ti sacal chay [ch'ay] bac
same ual ti ekel chay bac same ual ti kanal chay chi [ch'ay bac] same
ual ti chac uah tan same ual ti ek uahtan same ual ti kan uahtan

same ua ix bacini ch'abi chacal kaxab ya che yax uudze

208   uatal tux bacin yn cah yn/ chopayte chacal huko chacal huke ekel
huke kakac che nol na kuke

sam tunx bacin i[n] kaxab chacal uudze sacal uudze ekel uudze
uuc seye   Almen

XLI

U thanil bac ox kin bac xan

Can Ahau kin can Ahau ch'ab

balx oc ti bacil che chacal xolob sacal xolob kanal xolob yax olom
bax oci ti xich'il chacal say sacal say kanal say yax ch'ich yax olom/

209   chacal ix chu uehe sacal ix chu uehe ekel ic chu uehe kanal ix chu
uehe hunac ah tzutze hunac mulute con tun pak u hol u bacel

chacal uah tane sacal uah tane ekel uah tane kanal uah tane

chacal ah ku eme sacal ah ku eme ekel ah ku eme kanal ah ku
eme hunac ah tzutze hunac ah p[a]ke hunac ah mulute con tun pak u
bacel

112

chacal uah tene [teme] sacal uah tene ekel uah tene kanal uah tene
210   chacal ah ku eme/ sacal uah tene chacal uah tene chacal ah xike
sacal ah xichi hunac ah tzutze hunac ah pake hunac ah mulute con
tun bacin ix tzutzub u bacel chacal uah tene

balx bacin u ch'ich'il balx bacin u mutil chac tan bac hol ba cen
chulub u ch'ich'il balx u che bax yaban dzacal bac bax u che bacel ac
u chel bacal che

211   bax u che bal in uayasba ca tin dze kaxtah/ ca tin noh kaxtah
chacal kaxixch'el sacal kaxixch'el chacal kaxixku sacal kaxixku

oxlahun ytz en yn chacal dzonot tin pedzkaxtici u kinam hunac
ah kinam hunac ah oxou hunac ah pec ten cel u ba chuc tex ku

mac tah ch'abi u ch'ab colop u uik [uich] kin colop u uich akab

ahen bace ahen olome ci tun be che tu kab Dios yumbil y Dios
mehenbil y Dios Espiritu san[to]   Amen/

XLII

212   U thanil ceh payab lae [*Untranslated.*]

Cu yahal can silim tun hun pokigi ucun sac tah kayun yk tah
kayun yk tah popol kayun sac tah yk. yk tah popol kay sac lahun
humun sanal yn than un sac tah yk top kay yk top kay tu sac lahun
kaun u xibil y u mep kabil y u yul cil u hole samal yn haual kayum
213   noh yk la ciman/ ti ceh o top sic ben u niteil [nicteil?] u cichpamil ax
may hin ci tah okol utzil ax may ta lahun tas metnal dzeh . . . ti ceh
a topsic ben u nicteil u ciychpamil ax may hin ci tah okol ax may tac
lahun . . . nal yalan man ti ceh u . . . ci bin u nicteil ax may . . . ta
hokol ax may tac lahun tas metnal yabac nenun . . . ti ceh a top sic
214   bin u nicteil ax may tac lahun tas metnal/ ti hun molahi hun haual
kayum   Amen

GLOSSARY OF PLANT NAMES

Ac ("turtle," "boar-peccary," "dwarf," also a patronymic). A tall grass with broad leaves used for thatching (Standley, *Flora of Yucatán*, which is well indexed; hereinafter cited as Standl.). In the Petén the *ac* is identified as *Imperata contracta* (HBK), Hitchc., and a grass of this name is also used for thatching (Lundell, *Vegetation of Petén*, 51). Prescribed for bowel complaints, chills, fever, biliousness, jaundice, headache, and a skin complaint (Roys, *Ethno-Botany*, 213). The *ac* is cited in an incantation for asthma (MS p. 78).

Acan ("a groan," also the name of a wine god). An herb with an angular stalk, cordiform leaves, and a milky sap (Standl.) Prescribed for toothache and snake-bite (Standl.; Roys, *Ethno-Botany*, 213). Cited in incantations for erotic-seizure and a snake in the abdomen (MS pp. 31, 124).

Akab-tok ("dark-flint"). Presumed to be a plant name; *akab* and *tok* are elements in known plant names. Cited in an incantation for *kanpedzkin* (a wasp?) at the head of a man (MS p. 137).

Aklis-bul ("vine-like bean"). Cited in an incantation for a worm in the tooth (MS p. 169).

Bacal-ac ("corncob-*ac*"). A tree bearing fragrant white flowers (Pío Pérez, *Coordinación alfabética*; hereinafter cited as P.P., 1898). Prescribed for toothache (Roys, *Ethno-Botany*, 215). Cited in an incantation for asthma (MS p. 74). *Bacal* is also a Maya patronymic.

Bacal-che ("corncob-tree"). *Bourreria pulchra*, Millsp., a shrub or tree. Prescribed for skin diseases, fevers, and loss of speech (Standl.; Roys, *Ethno-Botany*, 215). Cited in an incantation for erotic-seizure, of which fever is a symptom (MS p. 31). *Che* is a common patronymic.

Balam-kuch-ci ("jaguar-vulture-agave"). Name not found elsewhere, but the ending *-ci* suggests an agave. Cited in an incantation for tarantula-seizure and tarantula-eruption (MS p. 36). *Balam* and *Ci* are also patronymics.

Balche. Lonchocarpus yucatanensis, Pittier (Standl.). An intoxicating drink was made from fermented honey and the bark of this tree. The crushed leaves were a remedy for smallpox, a post-Conquest disease, and an infusion was drunk for loss of speech (Roys, *Ethno-Botany*, 216). It is cited in an incantation for the placenta (MS p. 174). *Balche* is also a patronymic.

Bat-can ("axe-shoot"). The name is not found elsewhere, but a plant named *bat-aban* ("axe-bush") is prescribed for chills and fever (Standl., Roys, *Ethno-Botany* 216). The *bat-can* is cited in an incantation for various seizures (MS p. 12). *Can* is also the word for "snake," as well as being a patronymic.

Bub-tun-uitz ("canopy-stone-hill"?). Only doubtfully a plant name. It is cited in an incantation for obstruction of the breathing passages (MS p. 195).

Bubul-can ("canopy-shoot"?). There is a cenote named Bubul (Roys, *The Titles of Ebtun*, pl. 1). *Bub* could mean "frog-spawn," and *bul* could mean "submerged." *Bubul-ha* is a beetle-like water insect. The syllable *can* is a frequent element in plant names. The *bubul-can* is cited in an incantation for cooling water on a fire (MS p. 146).

Bubuy-can could well be a form of *buy-can* ("eye-film-shoot"). The *buy-ak* ("*buy*-vine") is a woody vine, the sap of which is a cure for eye complaints (Roys, *Ethno-Botany*, 219). The *bubuy-can* is cited in an incantation for cooling water on the fire (MS p. 146).

Can-tiplah (*can-tipplah*, "snake- or worm-pulsation"). Its wine (*ci*) is prescribed in an incantation for that complaint in the abdomen (MS p. 133). This may well be referable to the unidentified *"cantibte-ak"* (Standl.), which I would correct to *can-tippte-ak*.

Cibix. Amerimnon cibix, Pittier (Standl.). A scandent shrub, its inner bark is used for cordage. It is cited in an incantation for cooling a pit-oven and in one for an obstruction of the breathing passages (MS pp. 182, 195).

Coc-che ("asthma-tree"). Various parts are prescribed for asthma, phthisis, the testicles, and an abscess of the throat (Roys, *Ethno-Botany*, 225). It is cited in an incantation for asthma (MS p. 74).

Copo. Ficus cotinifolia, HBK. This is the *álamo*, a sacred tree. The sap and leaves are a remedy for wounds and abscesses (Roys, *Ethno-Botany*, 226). It is cited in incantations for seizures, fire biting on wood, and a running sore (MS pp. 144, 152, 156). *Copo* is also a patronymic.

Cumux-can ("*cumux*-shoot"). Not cited elsewhere; here it is mentioned in an incantation for seizures (MS p. 12). We know *Cumux* only as the patronymic of a ruling family on Cozumel Island (Roys, *Political Geography of the Yucatán Maya*, 156), and such patronymics are often referable to plant names.

Chacah. Bursera simaruba (L.), Sarg., gumbolimbo. Applied externally or internally, it is used for many complaints (Roys, *Ethno-Botany*, 227–28). It is cited in incantations for eruptions, fevers, and seizures (MS pp. 104, 106), for fire biting on wood (p. 153), for a running sore (p. 156), for a worm in the tooth, (pp. 164–65, 168, 171), for chipping a flint point (p. 188).

Chac-anicab ("great" or "red" *anicab*). *Cydista aequinoctialis* (L.), Miers (Standl.). A woody vine used in construction. Cited in an incantation for obstruction of the breathing passages (MS p. 195).

Chac-tok ("red flint"). Probably Standley's *chac-toc* (*Hamelia Patens*, Jacq.). The *chac-tok* is prescribed for inflammation of the throat (Roys, *Ethno-Botany*, 232), and cited in an incantation for a worm in the tooth (MS p. 163).

Chac-topplah-kak ("red-budding-fire" or "-eruption"). Many plants are named for the disease they cure. Cited in an incantation for a complaint called *kanpedzkin* (a wasp?) at the head of a man (MS p. 137).

Chac-ya ("red sapote"). Cited by Standley and P.P., 1898. Prescribed for dysentery and fevers (Roys, *Ethno-Botany*, 232). It is also cited in an incantation for obstruction of the breathing passages (MS p. 194).

Chankala. Canna edulis, Ker. (*lengua de dragón*). Considered a remedy for nervous pains and spider bites (Standl.). Cited in an incantation for certain seizures (MS p. 11).

Chi ("mouth," "shore," "edge"). *Byrsonima crassifolia* (L.) DC. (Standl.), widely known as the *nance*. Prescribed for dysentery, blood-vomit, and yellow fever (Roys, *Ethno-Botany*, 235). Cited in incantations for tarantula-seizure and tarantula-eruption and also for asthma (MS pp. 36, 78). *Chi* is also a familiar Maya patronymic.

Chichibe. *Sida acuta*, Burm., also *Melochia pyramidata*, L., a common weed. The stems were used to make cord (Standl.). Prescribed for phthisis, asthma, stomach ailments, headache, skin diseases, and other complaints (Roys, *Ethno-Botany*, 236). Cited in an incantation for erotic-seizure (MS pp. 31–32).

Chim-tok ("flint-capsule"). *Krugdendron ferreum* (Vahl.), Urban. The axe-master, a thick tree noted for the hardness of its wood (Standl.). Prescribed for pleurisy, asthma, dysentery, ulcers, and toothache (Roys, *Ethno-Botany*, 237). Cited in an incantation for chipping a flint point (MS pp. 184, 186).

Chiuoh-xiu ("tarantula-plant"). Cited in an incantation for tarantula-eruption and tarantula-seizure (MS pp. 33, 35). Possibly referable to the *chiuoh-kaak*, also unidentified, listed by Standley: "A small plant of the form of a black spider; leaves thick; has no flowers or fruit. Root a remedy for gangrene (Cuevas)."

Chuc-tok ("charcoal-flint"), presumably a plant name. Cited in an incantation for chipping a flint point (MS p. 187). It is associated with other plant names containing the syllable *tok* ("flint").

Chulul. *Apoplanesia paniculata*, Presl. (Standl.). A tall tree; its hard wood was used to make bows, wooden swords, daggers, and shields. Cited in an incantation for "a worm in the tooth" (MS p. 162).

Chunup. *Clusia flavia*, Jacq. A large tree, various parts of which are used to make pails or to cure wounds, headache, or syphilis (Standl.). It is cited in an incantation for cooling a pit-oven (MS p. 182).

Dzii-kan. I would reconstruct this word as *dzin-can* ("cassava-shoot").

117

Maya medical texts call the *dzin-can* a synonym of the *dzay-can* (*Sesuvium portulacastrum*, L., or *verdolaga de la playa*) (Roys, *Ethno-Botany*, 314). The *dzin-can* is prescribed for wounds, ulcers, skin complaints, and vomiting blood. The "*dzii-ḳan*" is cited in an incantation for certain seizures (MS p. 12).

Dzoc ("end," "to finish"). I do not find this elsewhere but we are reminded of the *ḳan-dzocob*, a palm. The red *dzoc* and the white *dzoc* are stated to be trees or bushes in an incantation for *ḳanpedzḳin* (a wasp?) at the head of a man (MS p. 139).

Dzoy ("weak," "overcome"). Cited in incantations for cooling a pit-oven and for an obstruction of the breathing passages (MS pp. 182, 195). Apparently a shrub or vine.

Dzulub-toḳ ("festooned flint"). *Bauhinia divaricata*, L. The inner bark is used for cordage (Standl.) Prescribed for pleurisy, fever, swollen head or neck, and dysentery (Roys, *Ethno-Botany*, 315). The *dzulub-toḳ* is cited in an incantation for chipping a flint point (MS pp. 185–86, 189).

Dzuto, or *dzubto*. Cited by Pío Pérez, 1898. Its leaves are poulticed on bites of reptiles (Roys, *Ethno-Botany*, 315). Cited in an incantation for *ḳanpedzḳin* (a wasp?) at the head of a man (MS p. 134).

Eḳ-acal ("black *acal*"). *Acal* is listed as an unidentified plant name (Standl.). Here the context suggests a tree or shrub. Cited in an incantation for various seizures, convulsions, and fever (MS p. 27).

Eḳ-hub ("black conch"). Not mentioned elsewhere. Here something hard is called for, apparently a tree. Possibly the *eḳ-huleb* is intended, but the latter is not identified (Standl., P.P., 1898). The *eḳ-hub* is cited in an incantation for a worm in the tooth (MS p. 163).

Habin. Piccidia communis (Blake) Harms. A large tree with a strong, heavy wood. The bark is used for stupefying fish (Standl.). Decoctions of the leaves are prescribed for asthma, fever, and ringworm (Roys, *Ethno-Botany*, 242). Cited in incantations for *ḳanpedzḳin*-poisoning and a worm in the tooth (MS pp. 141, 164).

Halal ("reed," "arrow"). The name has been ascribed both to *Phragmites communis*, Trin., a reed, and to *Scirpus validus*, Vahl., a bulrush. Standley believes that arrows were made of the former. The *halal* is prescribed for phthisis, fainting, dysentery, retention of the urine, and hiccoughs (Roys, *Ethno-Botany*, 243). It is cited in incantations for tarantula-eruption, and for tarantula-seizure as well as for ulcers (MS pp. 41, 113).

Halal-kan ("reed-cord"). I can find no other mention either of *halal-kan* or of *halal-can*. The *halal-kan* is cited in an incantation for various seizures (MS p. 12).

Hol. Hibiscus clypeatus, L., or possibly *H. tiliaceus*. It is a tree, the bark of which is used for cordage (Motul Dict.). The *hol* is cited in incantations for *kanpedzkin* (a wasp?) at the head of a man, and for a worm in the tooth (MS pp. 138, 163).

Holom-kak, or *x-holom-kak*, "*holom*-insect-eruption" or "-fire." A medicinal plant (P.P., 1898). Cited in incantations for *kanpedzkin* at the head of a man and for making a fire burn (MS p. 137, 154).

Hulub ("something with which something is pierced or something on which something is strung, like beads or fish"). *Bravaisia tubiflora*, Hemsl. A bush growing near the sea; its stalks are used to string fish. It is used to cure an abscess of the breast (Standl., Roys, *Ethno-Botany*, 246). Cited in incantations for *hunpedzkin*-vein and snake- or worm-pulsation of the abdomen (MS pp. 97, 131).

Hunpedzkin. The name of an apparently mythical reptile. A tree or bush of this name, however, is cited in an incantation for a seizure of the same name (MS p. 87). A medicinal plant of this name is employed to relieve headache and neuralgia, which might be *Tillandsia sp.* (Standl.). It is prescribed for gas in the bowels, headache, and fainting spells (Roys, *Ethno-Botany*, 246).

Ic. Capsicum annuum, L. Used for skin eruptions or blistering (Standl.) Maya manuscripts prescribe it for phthisis, delayed parturition, blood in the stools or urine, vomiting blood, and other ailments (Roys, *Ethno-Botany*, 247). Cited in an incantation for *kanpedzkin* (a wasp?) at the head of a man (MS p. 134).

Ich'-can ("claw-shoot"?). Various Maya manuscripts and Pío Pérez (1898) state that it is a synonym for the *pahalcan* or very similar to it (*Solanum nigrum*, L.). The latter is employed to reduce inflammation (Standl.). The *ich'-can* is cited in an incantation for a rattlesnake in the abdomen (MS p. 124).

Ixim-ha ("maize-water"). Variously reported as the name of *Lemna minor*, L., or duck-weed, and *Wolffia brasiliensis*, Wedd.; both are small aquatic plants (Standl.). Cited in an incantation for an eruption accompanied by fever, but apparently only as a symbol of cooling, as with water (MS p. 114).

Kak-chacah ("fire- *chacah*"). It is stated to be a plant (*xiu*) and is cited in an incantation for a burn and for making a fire burn (MS p. 153).

Kan-dzocob ("yellow-" or "cord-finisher"). The *dzocob* is a *"palma de cocos ó de cocoyoles"* (Vienna Dict., f. 155r.). In an incantation for wasp-seizure the *kan-dzocob* is cited as one of the binders of an arbor (MS pp. 52, 53, 57, 60).

Kan-dzutob ("yellow-" or "cord-*dzutob*"). Possibly referable to the unidentified *dzuto* (P.P., 1898, p. 112). The latter is prescribed for the bite of a snake or *hunpedzkin*-reptile (Roys, *Ethno-Botany*, 25). In an incantation the *kan-dzutob* is called the binder of an arbor (MS pp. 52, 53, 57, 60). I suspect that *dzutob* is a bad pun on *zut*, "to make a turn around something."

Kan-kilis-che ("cord-" or "yellow-*kilis*-tree"). *Acacia Farnesiana* (L.), Willd. A spiny shrub or small tree; its wood is hard and heavy (Standl.). Certain parts are prescribed for jaundice, bile, dysentery, toothache, and abdominal pains caused by sorcery (Roys, *Ethno-Botany*, 251). Like other trees with a hard wood, it is cited in an incantation for a worm in the tooth (MS p. 167).

Kan-mukay-che ("yellow-cochineal-tree"). This name is not found elsewhere. The *mukay-che*, *mucuy-che* ("dove-tree") and the *kan-mucuy-che* are cited by Standley and by Pío Pérez (1898), but none of these are identified. The *kan-mukay-che* is cited in an incantation for erotic-seizure (MS p. 31). This association of *coccus cacti* with eroticism among the Maya is of interest.

Kan-pocob ("yellow-" or "cord-*pocob*"). Apparently a play on the word *ppoc*, which can mean to bend something in a circle, like a crown or wreath. The *kan-pocob* is said to a binder of an arbor in an incantation (MS p. 49).

Kan-pocol-che (or *kan-pokol-che*). *Durante repens*, L., a spiny shrub. The wood is said to be medium hard, and the leaves were used in making ink (Vienna Dict., f. 18r.). Here the *kan-pocol-che* is cited in an incantation for a worm in the tooth (MS p. 163).

Kante. In the Petén this has been described as a tree with yellow flowers. In Yucatán the roots are used to make a yellow dye (Standl.). It is prescribed for coughs, asthma, and certain spasms (Roys, *Ethno-Botany*, 252). In the incantations it is cited in connection with a certain wasp-seizure and is said to be one of the binders of an arbor (MS p. 57).

Kante-cech. Probably the *kante-ceeh* is intended.. The latter is cited by Standley, but it is unidentified. The *kante-cech* is cited as a binder in an incantation for wasp-seizure (MS pp. 48, 52, 53, 60).

Kante-mo ("macaw-*kante*"). *Acacia angustissima* (Mill.), Kuntze, reported as a remedy for an enlarged spleen (Standl.). It is also prescribed for a certain kind of spasm (Roys, *Ethno-Botany*, 208–10). Here it is cited as the binder for an arbor in an incantation for wasp-seizure (MS pp. 52, 53, 57, 60).

Kan-toppol-can ("yellow-budding-shoot"). I do not find this name elsewhere; but here it is associated with a number of known trees. It is cited in an incantation for a worm in the tooth (MS p. 168).

Kaxab-yuc ("brocket-binder," better known as the name of snake of the constrictor type). "A plant or small vine, which is good fodder for horses" (Motul Dict.). It produces a handsome blue flower, has a round leaf, and climbs on trees. It is prescribed for dysentery (Roys, *Ethno-Botany*, 253–54). It is cited in an incantation for obstruction of the breathing passages (MS p. 195).

Kinim. A tree, probably *Spondias* (Standl.). It is cited in an incantation for the placenta (MS p. 175).

Koch, or *ix koch*. This is now the name of the castor bean, an African plant; but apparently a native plant of that name is the one now called *kaxil-ix-koch* ("wild-*ix-koch*") (Roys, *Ethno-Botany*, 255–56). Here it is cited in an incantation for asthma (MS p. 82).

Kokob-tok ("*kokob*-snake-flint"). I do not find this name elsewhere, but it is associated with various known flora in an incantation for certain seizures (MS p. 12).

Kulim-che (" *kulim*-tree"). *Kulim* is the name of a certain eruption and also of a small garrapata. The *kulim-che* is *Astronomium graveolens*, Jacq., an important timber tree. Parts of it are prescribed for abscesses and pustules (Roys, *Ethno-Botany*, 258). It is cited in an incantation for a worm in the tooth (MS p. 167).

Kutz. Nicotiana tabacum, L. (Standl.) It is prescribed for asthma, bites and stings, bowel complaints, chills and fever, seizures, sore eyes, skin diseases, and urinary complaints (Roys, *Ethno-Botany*, 259). Here it is cited in incantations for eruptions, fever, a snake in the abdomen, a worm in the tooth, and for the placenta (MS pp. 80, 106, 133, 171, 176).

Lal, or *la. Urera baccifera* (L.), Gaud.; *U. carcasana* (Jacq.), Griseb. A shrub or small tree (Standl.). It is prescribed for aching bones, chills and fever, and dysentery (Roys, *Ethno-Botany*, 261). Cited in an incantation for a sore leg (MS p. 91), where it is mentioned as an irritant.

Loth-coc ("cramp-asthma"). Cited by Standley; probably the same as the *lot-coc* listed by Pío Pérez (1898). It is prescribed for asthma (Roys, *Ethno-Botany*, 262). Cited in an incantation for asthma (MS p. 74).

Luch. Crescentia Cujete, L., calabash (Standl.). It is prescribed for coughs, asthma, retarded parturition, diarrhea, and skin diseases (Roys, *Ethno-Botany*, 262). It is cited in an incantation for a certain wasp poisoning (MS p. 143).

Lukub-tok ("flint-remover"). Possibly not a plant name. It is cited in an incantation for various seizures (MS p. 28).

Macapil-lum ("earth-stopper"). Possibly not a plant name. It is cited in an incantation for obstruction of the breathing passages (MS p. 200).

Ix Malau. Considered to be a plant name because it appears in a group of names of trees. It is cited in an incantation for a worm in the tooth (MS p. 163).

Max-cal ("monkey-throat"). A herb said to resemble the maguey (Standl.). Since the *maxcal* is associated with the *acantun* and with a mention of splotches of blood, it is suggested that its spines were employed to make blood sacrifices. The *max-cal* is cited in incantations for a certain seizure and for asthma (MS pp. 5, 8, 47, 64, 68).

Nab, or *naab* ("palm of the hand"). *Nymphaea ampla* (Salisb.), DC., water lily. It is cited in incantations for ulcers and a certain eruption (MS pp. 113, 115).

Nicte ("flower-tree"?). A generic name for the *Plumerias* (more correctly, *Plumieras*). It was a symbol of erotic practices, and is prescribed for dysentery and burns (Roys, *Ethno-Botany*, 269–70). The *nicte* is cited in an incantation for erotic-seizure (MS p. 30).

Nicte-max ("monkey-Plumeria"). Cited in an incantation for several mental disorders (MS p. 6).

Nix-che, or *nii-che* ("inclined-tree"). *Coccoloba uvifera* (L.), Jacq., sea-grape. Prescribed for diarrhea, dysentery, and venereal diseases (Standl.; Motul Dict.) Cited in an incantation for eruptions, fever, and certain seizures (MS p. 104).

On. Persea americana, Mill., aguacate. Prescribed for diarrhea, bladder complaints, and certain skin eruptions (Standl.; Roys, *Ethno-Botany*, 271). Cited in an incantation for erotic-seizure (MS p. 30). This is apparently due to the meaning of its Mexican name: *"Auacatl, fruta conocida, o el compañon"* (Molina, *Vocabulario de la lengua Mexicana*, II, 9).

Op. Annona sp. (Standl.). Here it is perhaps *A. reticulata*, the custard apple. The leaf is burned over the perforation of a snake-bite, and it is prescribed for diarrhea, cramps, and certain eruptions (Roys, *Ethno-Botany*, 272). The *op* is cited in incantations for obstruction of the breathing passages and for snake or worm-pulsation of the abdomen (MS pp. 121, 205).

Oppol. Unidentified, and cited elsewhere only by Pío Pérez (1898, p. 108). The well-known *oppol-che* ("*oppol*-tree") is *Adeno-calymmna Seleri*, Loes. (Standl), which is a woody vine. The *oppol* is cited in incantations for tarantula-seizure and wasp-seizure (MS pp. 42, 60).

Ox-loth ("severe cramp"?). In an incantation the context seems to call for a plant name (MS p. 74). It is cited in an incantation for asthma.

Pakam. Nopalea cochinillifera (L.) Salm-Dyck. This is the food plant of the cochineal insect (Standl.). It is cited in an incantation for chipping a flint point (MS p. 187).

Ppoppox ("something rough or itchy"). *Tragia nepetaefolia,* Cav. (Standl.). Prescribed for pimples, cough, aching bones, convulsions, and abdominal pains caused by sorcery (Roys, *Ethno-Botany,* 278). Cited as an irritant in an incantation for a sore leg (MS pp. 90, 97).

Puc-ak ("mouse-vine"?). *Notoptera Gaumeri,* Greenm. or *N. leptocephala,* Blake. Described as a large shrub (Standl.). A Yucatecan writer describes it as a vine that winds around the *kan-chunup-*tree. It is a remedy for abscesses (Roys, *Ethno-Botany,* 279) and is cited in an incantation concerning a fire (MS p. 153).

Puh (also the word for pus). *Typha angustifolia,* L., cattail (Standl.). The rush is employed for mats (Pérez Dict.)

Pul, or *puul Psidium sp.,* apparently a wild form of guava. "*Guayaba montesina: puul*" (San Francisco Dict., Span.-Maya).

Sabac-nicte ("soot-colored-*nicte*"). *Plumeria rubra,* L. (cf. *nicte*). Used to make a laxative conserve; prescribed for dysentery, venereal diseases, and to expel intestinal parasites (Standl.). Cited in an incantation for erotic-seizure (MS p. 31).

Sac-nicte ("white *nicte*"). *Plumeria alba,* L. Prescribed for throat complaints, aching bones, convulsions, and as a charm for flatulence. The *chac-*("red")*nicte* and the *sac-*("white")*nicte* were considered to be the father and mother of the head of the Lacandón pantheon (Roys, *Ethno-Botany,* 306; Tozzer, *A Comparative Study of the Mayas and the Lacandóns,* 93). The *sac-nicte* is cited in an incantation for erotic-seizure (MS p. 31).

Sahom, or *sahum. Zexmenia hispida,* var. *ramosissima,* Greenm., (Standl.). Considered good fodder today. Prescribed for asthma, aching bones, convulsions, liver complaint, and chills (Roys, *Ethno-Botany,* 308). Cited in an incantation for obstruction of the breathing passages and a snake, or possibly a worm, in the abdomen (MS pp. 125, 194, 205).

Sicil. Squash seed. Cited in an incantation for chipping a flint point (MS p. 188).

Sihom. Probably *Sapindus,* or soapberry (Standl.). A small fruit used for soap (Motul Dict.). Its leaves were spread in the temple court for certain ceremonies (*Landa's "Relación,"* 105). The seeds are employed as beads for necklaces and rosaries, and here the word sometimes seems to represent a gold bead. It is cited in incantations for asthma and a certain seizure (MS pp. 74, 84).

Sisbic. Vanilla fragrans (Salisb.), Ames. Supposed to be an excitant and aphrodisiac (Standl.). Cited in an incantation to charm a scorpion, in which the tail is likened to a vanilla pod (MS p. 161).

Soh, or *sooh. Gossypium religiosum,* L. (Standl.). The word can also mean "dry." It is cited in an incantation for what is called *ḳanpedzḳin,* possibly a certain wasp, at the head of a man (MS p. 137).

Suc, or *zuuc.* A general name for grass. It is cited for what is called snake- or worm-pulsation in the abdomen (MS p. 131).

Tab-can ("cord-shoot"). *Cissus sp.,* perhaps *C. sicyoides,* L., *uvas del monte* (Standl.), a woody vine. It is prescribed for snake-bites and skin complaints (Roys, *Ethno-Botany,* 261). It is cited in an incantation for obstruction of the breathing passages (MS p. 38, 195).

Tab-che ("cord-" or "rope-tree"), possibly referring to its prop-roots. The name is applied to *Conocarpus erecta,* L., and *Rhizophora mangle,* L., both mangroves. It is cited in an incantation for tarantula-seizure and tarantula-eruption (MS p. 60).

Tancas-che ("seizure-tree"). *Zanthoxylum Fagara* (L.) Sarg. A medicinal tree of the coast, said to cure any disease, even buboes. On the northeast coast it is called *uole* ("frog-leaf"?) (Motul Dict.). It is prescribed for skin complaints and fevers and convulsions (Roys, *Ethno-Botany,* 283). In British Honduras it is "a charm worn by nearly all the children," which "consists of a small cross of *tancas-che*-bark," and is a remedy for flatulence (Gann, "The Maya Indians . . . of Northern British Honduras," 19). It is cited in an incantation for jaguar-macaw-seizure (MS p. 6).

125

Tiuoh-xoc. I suspect that it is a form of *Chiuoh-xoc,* as it is associated with the tarantula (*chiuoh*). It is cited in an incantation on p. 39 of the manuscript. Possibly *chiuoh-xiu* is intended, although I know of no such name.

Tix-um-xuchit. Only doubtfully a plant name. *Xuchit* is a form of *xochitl,* which means "flower" in Nahuatl. *Tix-um-xuchit* is cited in an incantation for cooling a pit-oven (MS p. 183).

Too. "A herb with broad leaves." It is used for wrapping (Pérez Dict.; Motul Dict., Span.-Maya). The *too* is cited in an incantation for a rattlesnake in the abdomen (MS p. 124).

Tok-aban ("flint-bush"). Variously identified as *Trixis radialis* (L.), Kuntze, and *Eupatorium odoratum,* L. Both are herbs. Prescribed for gonorrhea and intestinal affections (Standl.; Roys, *Ethno-Botany,* 286). It is cited in an incantation for chipping a flint point (MS pp. 185).

Ton-cuy, apparently the same as *tun-cuy* ("stone-heel"?). The latter is reported as the name of *Pithecolobium sp.,* but it is also defined as the heart-wood of the *habin*-tree which is very strong (Standl., Motul Dict.). The *ton-cuy* is cited in an incantation for a worm in the tooth and for the placenta (MS pp. 162, 166, 171, 174).

Tukbil-acan ("hiccough-groan"), may be an improvised plant name. *Tuk* is the well-known wine-palm, and there is an unidentified herb called *acan,* which was also the name of a wine god. *Tukbil-acan* is cited in an incantation for asthma (MS p. 79).

Tudzi, probably intended for *tadzi,* identified only as a timber tree. The *tudzi* is cited with the *habin* and *chacah* in an incantation for a worm in the tooth (MS p. 164).

Tzalam. Lysiloma bahamense, Benth. A tall tree with a hard, tough wood (Standl.). It is prescribed for phthisis and asthma (Roys, *Ethno-Botany,* 290). A preparation from the bark was employed for whitewashing or plastering (Vienna Dict., f.18r.). The tree is cited in an incantation for a worm in the tooth (MS p. 167).

Xan, or *xaan. Inodes japa* (Wright), Standl., *palma de guano,* widely used for thatching. It is considered a remedy for affections of the air passages and the sexual system (Standl.). Maya manuscripts prescribe it for snake-bites, stings by insects, dysentery, sores, and ulcers. An imitation fetus made of its interior was a charm to accelerate parturition (Roys, *Ethno-Botany*, 293). It is cited in an incantation for tarantula-eruption and tarantula-seizure (MS p. 41).

Xihil-ac, probably intended for *xich'il-ac* ("tendon-grass"?), but not mentioned elsewhere. We find reported a *"xichil-ax," Galactia striata* (Jacq.), Urban, and a *xichil-ak* [*xich'il-ak*], *Kallstroemia maxima* (L.), Torr. & Gray. The *xihil-ac* is cited with the *bacal-ac* in an incantation for asthma (MS p. 74).

Xuchit. An archaic form of the Nahuatl *xochitl* ("flower"), which, like the *nicte* (Maya), was associated with carnal sin (cf. Roys, *Chilam Balam of Chumayel*, 83n.). The *xuchit* is cited in an incantation for *hunpedzkin*-seizure (MS p. 84).

Xux-dzocob ("wasp-*dzocob*-palm"). Cf. *kan-dzocob*. Both names may be referable to the nuciferous *dzocob*-palm, and both are cited in an incantation for wasp-seizure (MS p. 58).

Yax-cab ("green" or "fresh earth" or "honey"). Either the name of a plant or of a type of earth. *Yax-kax* is a certain soil, between red and black. There are at least three cenotes in Yucatán named Yax-cab-a ("water at the *yax-cab*"), and many cenotes in Yucatán are named for trees or other flora. The *yax-cab* is cited in incantations for a certain seizure, also for fire biting on wood and for a worm in the tooth (MS pp. 84, 153, 164).

Yax-ci ("fresh" or "green agave"). *Agave sisalana*, Perrine (Standl.). It is used for making hammocks. Cited in an incantation for obstruction of the breathing passages (MS p. 205).

Yax-che ("first," "fresh" or "green tree"). *Ceiba pentandra* (L), Gaertn. A large shade tree, very important in Maya mythology (Thompson, *Rise and Fall of Maya Civilization*, 225; Roys, *Chilam Balam of Chumayel*, 299). It is cited in incantations for a worm in the tooth and obstruction of the breathing passages (MS pp. 168, 201–203). Elsewhere we read of certain signs or symbols (*dzalab*) on the *yax-che*-tree.

Yax-kam. This name is not found elsewhere, and I suspect that *yax-ḳanan* is meant (cf. P.P., 1898). *Kanan* is *Hamelia patens,* Jacq., a shrub or small tree. The *"yax-toc"* (*yax-toḳ,* "fresh-flint") is reported as a synonym for the *yax-ḳanan* (Standl.). The *"yax-ḳam"* is cited in an incantation for chipping a flint point (MS p. 197).

Yax-nic ("green" or "blue flower"). *Vitex Gaumeri,* Greenm. A large tree, fifteen meters high; its wood is unusually tough and used for carts, boats, and agricultural implements (Standl.). It is prescribed for asthma, malaria, ulcers, and abscesses (Roys, *Ethno-Botany,* 300). Along with other trees having a similar wood, the *yax-nic* is cited in an incantation for "a worm in the tooth" (MS p. 167).

Yax-um ("green fowl"?). See also Glossary of Fauna Names. It is a term applied to Kukulcán and the quetzal cult. *Yaxum,* however, is also the name of a tree growing between Ixil and the north coast (communication from J. Martínez Hernández). It is listed by Pío Pérez (1898). The *yax-um* is cited in an incantation for tarantula-eruption and tarantula-seizure as a feature of the coastal area and apparently associated with the mangrove (MS p. 42).

Yuyum-acan ("oriole-*acan*"). I do not find this name elsewhere, but I suspect that it is the same as the *yuyum-can* ("oriole-shoot"), which was considered to be a remedy for loss of speech (Roys, *Ethno-Botany,* 301). The *yuyum-acan* is cited in an incantation for obstruction of the breathing passages (MS p. 195). Cf. *acan,* above.

GLOSSARY OF FAUNA NAMES

T HE MASCULINE AND FEMININE ARTICLES, *ah* and *ix*, even though they are often used, are not invariably employed with a number of the names in this glossary.

Ahau-can, ("king-snake"). Probably *Crotalus basilicus* or *C. terrificus*. In modern Maya it is often called *tzab-can* ("rattlesnake"). (Cf. Roys, *Ethno-Botany*, 327.) Cited in an incantation for a rattlesnake in the abdomen (MS p. 122). Many people still believe that a witch can plant a rattlesnake in a person's bowels. Cf. Appendix C.

Ain. Crocodile. Reported to have been worshiped (Lizana, *Historia de Yucatán*, f. 23*v*.). Possibly this is a reference to the mythical monster named Chac-mumul-ain ("great-muddy-crocodile") mentioned in the Maya prophecies and cited in an incantation for ulcers (MS p. 113). See Glossary of Proper Names.

Am. Described as a certain deadly spider with a red tail (Motul Dict.; *RY*, I, 301). *Am* was also the name of a divining stone used by medicine men (Roys, *Ethno-Botany*, 326). Cited in incantations (MS pp. 84, 157–58, 160).

Ah am-cab ("spider-bee"). The name is cited, along with those of three different lizards, in an incantation for *hunpedzkin*-reptile-seizure (MS p. 83). We are reminded of the name, *am-can* ("snake-spider"), defined as that of a spider that fights with snakes (Motul Dict.).

Ah bab, or *bab* ("paddler"). A certain large frog (Motul Dict.) It is associated with one of the Bacabs in an incantation for chipping a flint point (MS p. 198). Boys still impersonate frogs in the rain ceremonies (Redfield and Villa, *Chan Kom*, 142).

Balam. Jaguar, *Felis hernandesii goldmani*, Mearns. The word appears only in an element of the names of certain so-called seizures (*tancas*). Here the jaguar is apparently a symbol of the violent behavior of the patient (MS pp. 4, 10). *Balam* was a term formerly applied to town priests and officials and, today, to certain protective spirits (Roys, *Ethno-Botany*, 328; Redfield and Villa, *Chan Kom*, 113–14).

Balam-caan ("jaguar-sky"). It is apparently a pun on *balam-can*, ("jaguar-snake"), also called *balam-chan*. In this context, however an actual fauna is not implied. (Cf. Roys, *Ethno-Botany*, 338). The *balam-caan* is cited in an incantation for *hunpedzkin*-vein or -humor (MS p. 99).

Bekech. A certain offensive small lizard (Motul Dict.; S. Pacheco Cruz, *Léxico de la fauna Yucateca*, 116). Cited in an incantation for a seizure (MS p. 83).

Bob. An unidentified animal (Pérez Dict.). *Bobilche* ("forest-*bob*") was a general name for the jaguar (*RY*, I, 169). Cited in an incantation for obstruction of the breathing passages (cf. MS pp. 203–204).

Bob-och ("*bob*-opossum"). A mythical animal (Pérez Dict.). In the Book of Chilam Balam of Chumayel it is mentioned as a destroyer of crops (Roys, *Chilam Balam of Chumayel*, 155, 166). Cited in an incantation for obstruction of the breathing passages, where it seems to be associated with terror (MS pp. 195, 203).

Bobote. Apparently the name of a certain wasp, for there is a reference to its nest and it is associated with the *kanpetkin*-wasp (Roys, *Ethno-Botany*, 139). It is also the name of a certain eruption (MS p. 103).

Buhum. Apparently the same as the *ah-buhum-chakan* ("buhum of the savanna"). These are defined as "large snakes, which make much noise when they move about, and are very poisonous" (Motul Dict.). Cited in an incantation for a rattlesnake in the abdomen (MS p. 123).

Cab ("bee"). Here an element in the name Chac-uayab-cab ("great-demon-bee"). See Glossary of Proper Names.

Calam. Described as a snake a meter or more in length, colored black and yellow, with reddish and dark rings. Its bite is dangerous

(Pacheco Cruz, *Diccionario de la fauna yucateca*, 43–44; Pérez Dict.). It is cited in incantations for a sore leg, seizure, ulcers, snake-pulsation (MS pp. 86, 92, 110, 118). It is also part of the proper name Ah Uuc-calam. Cf. Glossary of Proper Names.

Ix cax. The name of the European hen. Its egg is prescribed for a burn (MS p. 153).

Ah ceh. *Ceh* means "deer," but *ah ceh* is defined as "hunter" (Motul Dict.). It is an element in the name of a complaint named *ah-ceh-tancas* (hunter-seizure).

Cocay ("firefly"). Cited in an incantation for cooling water on the fire, apparently as a symbol of the sparks of the fire (MS pp. 146, 148). The sky god Itzamna was associated in some way with the firefly, for one of his names was Yax-cocay-mut ("first-" or "green-firefly-bird") (*Landa's "Relación,"* 145).

Coco-can. Apparently a variant of *coco-chan*. It is cited in an incantation for asthma (*coc*), perhaps as a pun (MS p. 69).

Coco-chan ("trogon-serpent"?). A small species of trogon (Maler, "Explorations of the Upper Usumacintla," 151). Cited in an incantation for asthma (MS pp. 76–77). We are reminded of the Chontal name for Kukulcán, which was Cuculchan (Scholes and Roys, *The Maya Chontal Indians of Acalan-Tixchel*, 395).

Colonte. *Ceophloeus scapularis*, Vigors. (*Bull. Mus. Comp. Zool.*, Harvard [1916], Vol. L, p. 130). DeLattre's woodpecker. The bill is used to bleed the gum to relieve toothache (Roys, *Ethno-Botany*, 185). It is cited in an incantation for eruptions, fever, and a seizure (MS p. 104), and in one for a worm in the tooth (MS pp. 164–65, 168).

Cuc. *Sciurus yucatanensis*, Allen, Yucatán squirrel (Gaumer, *Monografía de los mamíferos de Yucatán*, 100). Cited in an incantation for ulcers (MS p. 107).

Culix. The name of what is ritually called a "bird" in an incantation for snake-pulsation of the abdomen (MS p. 119). Since we find it associated with the *chac-ec*-wasp, it may well be the name of an insect.

Cuyil. Apparently a form of *cuy* ("clothes moth"). The context suggests the grub. It is cited in an incantation for erotic-seizure (MS p. 46).

Cuyum. Considered to be a snake because of its association with the rattlesnake and *ƙan-ch'ah*-snake. It is cited in incantations for snake-pulsation and for various snakes in the abdomen (MS pp. 46, 117, 124, 127).

Chab-can ("anteater-snake"). Found only as a part of the name of a disorder called *chab-can-tancas* ("anteater-snake-seizure"). Cited in an incantation for jaguar-macaw-seizure (MS p. 7). *Chab*, which can also mean "scurf," is an element in several plant names.

Chac-bolay. *Felis hernandesii goldmani*, Mearns., jaguar. Spreading its skin in the market place was a symbol of war (Roys, *Ethno-Botany*, 331). *Chac-bolay* was also the name of an evil spirit. It is cited in an incantation for the placenta (MS p. 176).

Chac-dzidzib ("red-variegated"). *Cardinalis cardinalis yucatanicus*, Ridgway, Yucatán cardinal. Its feathers were a remedy for blood-vomit, dysentery, and spotted-macaw-spasm (Roys, *Ethno-Botany*, 62, 64, 208). We also find the term *chac-dzidzib-ƙik* ("red-variegated-blood") in an incantation for the lewd madness of seizure (MS p. 44).

Chac-ec. Substituted for *chac-eƙ* ("great-star"), which is defined as "morning star" (Motul Dict.). The *chac-ec* is a stingless reddish wasp, which nests in trees and makes an edible comb (Pacheco Cruz, *Diccionario de la fauna yucateca*, 97). It is, however, "*chac-eƙ*" that is cited in an incantation for snake-pulsation of the abdomen (MS p. 119). The context calls for either a bird or an insect.

Ch'ahum. *Melanerpes dubius*, Cabot, Uxmal woodpecker (*Bull. Mus. Comp. Zool.*, Harvard [1916], Vol. L, p. 130). "A crested magpie or woodpecker with a red head" (Motul Dict.). Cited in incantations for *ƙanpetƙin*-wasp-poisoning and a worm in the tooth (MS pp. 140, 164, 168).

Chapat ("centipede"). Here it appears only as part of the name of Kak-ne-chapat ("fire-tailed-centipede") in an incantation for ulcers (MS pp. 106, 109). See Glossary of Proper Names.

Ch'el. Cyanocitta yucatanica, Dubois (*Proc. Zool. Soc. Lond.*, 1883, p. 446), a jay. It was also the patronymic of the ruling family of Ah Kin Ch'el. Cited in an incantation for *ƙanpetƙin*-wasp-seizure (MS p. 61).

Chiichii. A bird of omen (Vienna Dict., f. 24r.). Cited in an incantation for jaguar-macaw-seizure (MS p. 10).

Chiuoh ("tarantula"). Said to be the same as *couoh*, which was also the patronymic of the ruling family at Champotón. The *chiuoh* is cited in incantations for tarantula-seizure, tarantula-eruption, and tarantula-blood (MS pp. 33–40, 42).

Ah ch'uy ("he who holds something suspended"). Defined as any bird of prey (Motul Dict.). Today it is the name of the kite (Pacheco Cruz, *Diccionario de la fauna de yucateca*, 129). Cited in an incantation for seizure characterized by erotic behavior (MS p. 45).

Eƙ-pip. A bird of prey said to be the same as the *coz*, *Micrastur melanoleucus*, Viellot (*Bull. Mus. Comp. Zool.*, Harvard [1906], Vol. L, p. 121). Cited in incantations for seizure, sore leg, *hunpedzƙin*-vein or -humor, and snake-pulsation of the abdomen (MS 88, 93, 96, 99, 132).

Eƙ-u-ne ("black-his-tail"). A very large snake, mottled gray and blackish. It is said to be dangerous, but the one I saw killed did not appear to inspire much fear (Pacheco Cruz, *Diccionario de la fauna de yucateca*, 13). Cited in an incantation for a worm in the tooth (MS p. 168).

Hoch' ("to drill"). A long-bodied, ash-colored ant living in old tree trunks (Pacheco Cruz, *Diccionario de la fauna de yucateca*, 139). The nest is a remedy for a skin complaint (Roys, *Ethno-Botany*, 175). Cited in incantations for seizure, sore leg, *hunpedzƙin*-vein or -humor (MS pp. 86, 90, 97).

Hoch'-can ("boring snake"). The contexts imply a poisonous serpent. Cited in incantations for *hunpedzƙin*-seizure and a sore leg (MS pp. 86, 90).

Holom. An insect, with a severe sting, resembling a wasp but larger. It builds a nest of clay or earth, and it is called an *abejorro* (Pacheco

Cruz, *Diccionario de la fauna de yucateca* 146). A poultice made of its nest is applied for nightmare (Roys, *Ethno-Botany*, 85). Cited in incantations for eruptions, fever, seizure, and one concerning a fire (MS pp. 102, 154).

Hub. Conch, here apparently meaning the shell. Cited in an incantation for a worm in the tooth (MS p. 170).

Huh. A general term for iguana. Its gall is a remedy for granulation of the eyelids, and its ashes will render painless the extraction of a tooth (Roys, *Ethno-Botany*, 167, 186). Cited in an incantation for *hunpedzkin*-seizure (MS pp. 83, 89).

Hunpedzkin. "Among the many poisonous insects, reptiles and serpents there is especially one, which the Indians call *ix hunpedzkin*. It is of the size and form of a small lizard, with white and black spots and a shining body. It breeds in the forests and in old houses among the stones and is so poisonous that, when it touches a person, even on the garment, without biting or stinging, it kills completely and in so short a time that [the victim] does not last an hour. Nor is there time for any remedy. Its name in the language of the natives sounds like 'brief time,' because it kills quickly" (*RY*, I, 65–66). A modern writer describes it as a small lizard three or four inches long with blackish and reddish stripes on its belly. It is believed that it can, by biting only the shadow of a person's head, cause a headache that can be fatal if not properly treated (Pacheco Cruz, *Diccionario de la fauna yucateca*, 289–90). The seventeenth-century San Francisco Dictionary, however, describes it as a snake, and such a belief is confirmed by Eugenio May, a well-known archaeological worker (letter, E. W. Andrews). It is cited in incantations for seizures, sore leg, and *hunpdezkin*-vein or -humor (MS pp. 83, 85, 90, 93, 98).

Ah ii. "A certain hawk" (Motul Dict.). Resembles the *ah ch'uy*, but is smaller; it has a short, curved beak and is yellowish; it is designated *Odontriorchis palliatus mexicanus* (Pacheco Cruz, *Diccionario de la fauna yucateca*, 146). Cited in an incantation for snake-pulsation of the abdomen (MS p. 132).

Ich-uinic, or *iche-uinic.* The context indicates some species of wasp. Cited in an incantation for *hunpedzkin*-seizure (MS p. 86).

Itzam. "Land or water lizards, like iguanas" (Vienna Dict., f. 134*v.*). Izamal (Maya, Itzmal) and a number of mythological names are derived from *itzam.* Cited in incantations for *hunpedzkin*-seizure and for the placenta (MS pp. 83, 89, 183).

Kanal. Described by E. May as a large red wasp, living a few to a small nest (letter, E. W. Andrews). Cited in an incantation for *kanpetkin*-wasp-seizure (MS pp. 48, 54, 55).

Kanch'ah ("yellow or orange drop"). A large nonpoisonous snake (Vienna Dict., f. 54*r.*). Cited in incantations for seizures and a snake in the abdomen (MS pp. 28, 117, 126, 131).

Kan-dzul-mo ("yellow-foreign-macaw"). Not found elsewhere, but apparently a synonym of the *kan-dzul-oop.* The latter is a short-tailed macaw abounding in Tabasco (Beltrán de Santa Rosa, *Arte de el idioma maya,* 229; Seler, *Gesammelte Abhandlungen, IV,* 552). The *kan-dzul-mo* is cited in an incantation for *kanpetkin*-wasp-seizure (MS pp. 47, 50–54, 59).

Kanpedzkin. E. May considers this a more correct form for the *kanpetkin*-wasp (letter, E. W. Andrews). (MS pp. 134, 137.)

Kanpetkin ("yellow-round-sun" or "yellow-round-*kin*-insect"). A large yellow wasp with a painful sting. It produces a round, flat comb (Pacheco Cruz, *Diccionario de la fauna yucateca,* 156). Cited in incantations for *kanpetkin*-seizure and other seizures (MS pp. 46, 48, 55, 57, 86); also for *kanpetkin*-poisoning (MS pp. 138–40, 143).

Ix kantanen-kin ("yellow-colored-*kin*-insect"). Probably the same as the *ix kantanen* described by Jacinto Cunil, who states that it is a caterpillar covered by "*como plumas de gallina,*" not spines. It is round and about two inches long (letter, J. E. S. Thompson). Cited in an incantation for *kanpetkin*-seizure (MS pp. 47, 48, 50, 51, 54, 56, 60).

Ix kantanen-u ("yellow-colored-moon"). Since *kin* can also mean "sun," this might be a poetic fiction to contrast with *Ix kantanen-*

ƙin. Nevertheless, such a contrast does actually exist in the plant names, like *pet-ƙin* ("round sun") and *pet-u* ("round moon") (Roys, *Ethno-Botany*, 275; Motul Dict., Span.-Maya). The latter item is *"yerva trepidora para dolor de muelas."* The *ƙantanen-u* is cited in incantations for *ƙanpetƙin*-seizure and ulcers (MS pp. 47, 48, 50, 51, 54, 56, 60, 107).

Kin. Described as a variety of locust, light green, with a flat body and long rear legs. It often flies at night and brings good luck to the person or house on which it lights (Pacheco Cruz, *Diccionario de la fauna yucateca*, 163–64, pl. 1, fig. 10). Several towns are named for compounds of *ƙin*, such as Calkini, Numkini, Kini; and *Kin* is also a somewhat rare Maya patronymic. The *ƙin* insect is cited in an incantation for seizure (MS p. 85).

Ix ƙo. *Ko* means "the belly of an animal," "the crop of a bird," or it can be a plant name, *Sonchus oleraceus*, L.(?). We read of *ix ƙo* in the Rattles constellation. Sometimes the context seems to call for a bird, as when it is associated with the kite. It is also associated with the sky and clouds. Cited in incantations for seizures, ulcers, and a snake in the abdomen (MS pp. 10, 45, 50, 53, 54, 107).

Kokob. "There are other kinds of snakes called *ƙoƙob*, three or four yards long and as thick as a lance. They are very poisonous. Anyone who is bitten exudes blood from the whole body and from the eyes" (*RY*, I, 66). The descriptions by colonial and modern writers generally describe it as "venomous in the hemotoxic manner, i.e. a pit-viper" (letter, E. W. Andrews). One modern writer, however, describes the *ƙoƙob* as a poisonous but inoffensive tree snake (Pacheco Cruz, *Diccionario de la fauna yucateca*, 163). It is cited in incantations for seizure and snake-pulsation of the abdomen (MS pp. 85, 117).

Kubul. Oriole. Cited in incantations for a sore leg, *hunpedzƙin*-vein or -humor, and inflamed gums (MS pp. 91, 99, 173).

Kuƙ ("shoot, sprout"). In the Books of Chilam Balam *ƙuƙ* sometimes means "quetzal." Cited in an incantation for ulcers (MS p. 110).

Kul-sinic, or *ku-sinic*. "A certain black ant" (Vienna Dict., f. 125*v*.). Cited in an incantation for the placenta (MS p. 175).

Leum. "A certain species of spider" (Motul Dict.). It is today considered to be the same as the *am* (Pacheco Cruz, *Diccionario de la fauna yucateca*, 11). It is cited in an incantation for obstruction of the breathing passages (MS pp. 193, 201).

Lucum-can, or *lucum*. Angleworm. It is roasted, ground to powder, and mixed with *atole* or chocolate for a drink to cure an itching rash on the mouth or head (Roys, *Ethno-Botany*, 178). It is cited as a symbol of a bow-string in an incantation for chipping a flint point (MS pp. 197–98).

Mo. A general name for a large macaw (Seler, *Gesammelte Abhandlung, IV*, 552). In this manuscript it usually appears in compounds. The expression *mo-tancas* ("macaw-seizure") indicates a feature of various complaints, including convulsions and aberrations (MS pp. 6, 10, 24, 25, 46). The macaw is cited in incantations for *hunpedzkin*-vein or -seizure, eruptions, and to charm a scorpion (MS pp. 96, 103, 160).

On a high pyramid at Izamal was a shrine and an idol named Kin-ich-kak-mo ("sun-eye-fire-macaw"), and here at midday a macaw flew down and consumed the sacrifices with fire. Whenever there was a pestilence or great mortality, many people came bringing offerings (Lizana, *Historia de Yucatán*, f. 4*v*). Also a macaw bearing a flaming torch is portrayed on page 40b of the Dresden Codex, apparently as a symbol of drought (Thompson, *Maya Hieroglyphic Writing: An Introduction*, 270).

In the Kaua manuscript is a picture of a macaw astride a snake, entitled *Am-can-mo-ik-tancas* ("spider-snake-macaw-wind-seizure"). Here apparently the macaw is likened to the *am-can*, a certain poisonous spider that fights vipers (Motul Dict.).

In spite of the Kaua passage, today these "macaw-seizure" spirits are not considered winds. They are still believed to be death-dealing birds that kill children. Flying over houses, they vomit a substance which drops into a sleeper's mouth and causes death. The soul of an unbaptized child becomes a *mo-tancas* (Redfield and Villa, *Chan Kom*, 169). Nevertheless, it must be admitted that some of the modern evil winds (*ik̇*) are ascribed to the noun macaw or to *tancas* ("seizure"). We are told of the *tatac-mo-ik̇*, named for an unidentified large greenish nocturnal bird of the high forest (Pacheco Cruz, *Diccionario de la fauna yucateca*, 232). There is also a *tancas-ik̇*, which I would translate as "seizure-wind" (Redfield and Redfield, "Disease and Its Treatment in Dzitas, Yucatán," 62).

Mucuy. Columbigallina rufipennis, Bonaparte, ground dove. *Tórtola* (Motul Dict.). Cited in an incantation for the placenta (MS p. 179).

Ix mumuc-sohol ("covered by dry leaves or twigs"). Associated with known snakes in an incantation for seizure (MS p. 85). This would seem to apply to the coral-snake, but no doubt equally well to others.

Nok̇. A worm or maggot. Cited in an incantation for a worm in the tooth (MS pp. 162, 163, 167).

Oo. Stated to be a "bird" and so implied in the contexts here, although sometimes, perhaps, a mythical bird. Insects, however, are often ritually designated "birds" in this manuscript. Cited in an incantation for traveler-seizure (MS pp. 17–19, 22, 24). It is also the name of a seizure (*oo-tancas*) (MS pp. 47, 50–52, 54, 56, 57, 60).

Op, or *ix op*. A large macaw with red plumage, bluish wings, a long tail, a yellowish or reddish beak, and a yellowish circle around the eye (Pacheco Cruz, *Diccionario de la fauna yucateca*, 301). Cited in an incantation for gout (MS p. 91).

Ix paclah-actun. This name is associated with those of snakes, and it could well mean "cave-lurker." Cited in an incantation for seizure (MS p. 85).

Pap, or *paap* ("that which stings like chile"). Yucatán brown jay, *Psilorhinus mexicanus vociferus*, Cabot (*Bull. Mus. Comp. Zool.* Harvard [1916], Vol. L, p. 318). The colors red and white are probably only ritual terms; but it is harder to tell what is meant by "8,000 *pap*-jays." We are reminded of an idol in the form of a woman at Tahdziu, which was named Hun-pic-dziu ("8,000 cow-birds"). (Roys, *Political Geography of the Yucatán Maya*, 76). The *pap*-jay is cited in incantations for complaints associated with the *kanpetkin*-wasp and for expelling the placenta (MS 47, 50, 53, 55, 57, 61).

Pay. Conepatus tropicalis, Merriam (Goldman), *zorrito*. The context, however, seems to call for something like the bezoar stone, rather than a skunk. Possibly *ppay* ("a powder or something crushed into small particles") is intended. In any case, *pay* is cited in an incantation for "*kanpedzkin*" (*kanpetkin*-wasp?) at a man's head (MS p. 137).

Pepem, or *pepen* ("butterfly"). Cited in an incantation for chipping a flint point (MS pp. 187, 197). We also read of the *pepem-kan* ("butterfly-shell-bead"), which seems to be a figurative term for some part of the throat, possibly the uvula. Cited in an incantation for asthma (MS p. 74).

Pipican. The context calls for some fauna that is considered to be an irritant. Possibly the *pic-can* is meant. Identified by Pacheco Cruz (*Diccionario de la fauna yucateca*, 217) as *Magazoma elephas*. This is a flying insect, six to ten centimeters long, injurious to cattle. "Certain large bugs which, they say, fiercely sting serpents" (Motul Dict.). The *pipican* is cited in an incantation for inflamed gums (MS pp. 172–73).

Ppot-sinic ("downy-ant"?). A black, stingless ant often seen on the kitchen table (Pacheco Cruz, *Diccionario de la fauna yucateca*, 230). Cited in an incantation for eruptions, fever, and seizures (MS p. 104).

Puhuy. Pájaro pluma, Parauque. Variously designated *Nyctidromus albicollis yucatanensis*, Nelson (*Bull. Mus. Comp. Zool.*, Harvard [1916], Vol. L, p. 127). and *Geococcyx mexicanus* (Pacheco Cruz, *Diccionario de la fauna yucateca*, 212). It is a nocturnal bird of omen (Vienna Dict., f. 158*v*.). Cited in an incantation for asthma (MS p. 68).

Sibis. "Wood-louse or the dust made by it" (Pérez Dict.). *Ah sibis*, however, is defined as a large green fly or gadfly, which infects wounds and produces worms (Vienna Dict., f. 148r.). The *sibis* is cited in an incantation for a worm in the tooth (MS p. 167).

Sinan ("stretched out"). Scorpion. *Hadrurus azteca* (Pacheco Cruz, *Diccionario de la fauna yucateca*, 338, pl. 1, fig. 15). There is an incantation to charm a scorpion (MS pp. 160–61).

Sinic. Apparently a general term for a certain type of ant. Cited in an incantation for *hunpedzkin*-seizure (MS p. 86).

Sipip. Not found elsewhere. In view of the occasional doubling a a syllable, this might indicate the Sip. The Sip was a hunter's god with the form of a small deer (Redfield and Villa, *Chan Kom*, 117). *Pip* ("the fat of a fowl"), however, is part of the name of the ek-pip-hawk. In an incantation for various seizures the *sipip* is associated with the *ko*-bird of the sky and clouds, which suggests something like the *ek-pip* (MS p. 10).

Ix tacay. Myozetes similis superciliosis, Bonaparte. Mexican large-billed tyrant, Couch's kingbird (*Bull. Mus. Comp. Zool.*, Harvard [1916], Vol. L, p. 133). In an incantation for a certain wasp-seizure we read of "8,000 *tacay*-birds" (MS pp. 47, 61). In another, we find it cited for the placenta (MS p. 179).

Ti. Probably an insect, from its context. It is associated with the *uk*-louse and the *tup-chac*-wasp in an incantation for the placenta (MS p. 177).

Tok-pap ("flint-jay"). Cited in an incantation for *hunpedzkin*-seizure (MS p. 89).

Tulix. Dragonfly (Pacheco Cruz, *Diccionario de la fauna yucateca*, 241). Cited in an incantation to charm a scorpion (MS p. 160).

Tup-chac, or *tup-chaac* ("stop the rain"?). A large ash-colored wasp, which nests in trees. Its sting is severe (Pacheco Cruz, *Diccionario de la fauna yucateca*, 249). Cited in incantations for various seizures, *kanpedzkin*(-wasp?) at a man's head, and the placenta (MS pp. 48, 54, 55, 86, 138–39, 177).

Uakeh. Uak can mean the sound of something bursting. The *uakeh* is associated with the hawk, jay, and woodpecker. It is cited in incantations for snake-pulsation in the abdomen, *kanpetkin*-wasp-seizure, and inflamed gums (MS pp. 132, 142, 164, 169–70, 172).

Uixum. Although it is called a "bird," the context suggests a flying insect. Cited in an incantation for snake-pulsation in the abdomen (MS p. 119).

Uk. "The louse found on man and animals" (Motul Dict.). *Pediculus capitis*, and *P. vestimenti* (Pacheco Cruz, *Diccionario de la fauna yucateca*, 271). Cited in an incantation for the placenta (MS p. 177).

Ul. "Certain small mottled snails, which live among bushes and in rocky places" (Motul Dict.) Cited in an incantation for a worm in the tooth (MS p. 171).

Uoh, or *ix uoh* ("glyph," "to write," "sound of falling water"). Apparently a super-tarantula. See Glossary of Proper Names. Cited in an incantation for *kanpetkin*-wasp-seizure (MS pp. 48, 51–53, 56, 58).

Xacat-be ("road-jumper"?). An ash-colored or brown insect resembling a locust (Pacheco Cruz, *Diccionario de la fauna yucateca*, 275). Cited in an incantation for "tarantula-seizure" and "tarantula-eruption," where it is repeatedly called a "bird" (MS pp. 33–35, 37, 40, 42).

Xanab-chac ("rain-god-sandal"?). A certain wasp (Eugenio May, letter, E. W. Andrews). Cited in an incantation for wasp-seizure (MS pp. 48, 54).

Xoc, or *xooc*. Shark. (San Francisco Dict., Maya-Span.). Part of the name Chac-uayab-xoc. See Glossary of Proper Names. (MS p. 113.)

Xulab. A stinging ant (Motul Dict.). Found in moist places. These ants move in batallions, invade houses, and destroy bees. Designated *Atta barbata* (Pacheco Cruz, *Diccionario de la fauna yucateca*, 308). An eclipse of the moon was ascribed to the sting of these ants (Sánchez de Aguilar, *Informe contra idolorum cultores del obispado de Yucatán*, 122), but this was due to confusing them with the name of the morning star, Venus, which is still named Xulab in eastern Yucatán (Thompson, "Ethnology of the Mayas of . . . British Honduras," 63). The *xulab* is cited in an incantation for asthma (MS p. 67).

Xux. A general term for wasp. Its nest is cited in an incantation for a worm in the tooth (MS p. 170).

Yaxum ("green bird"). Apparently a name for the quetzal (Roys, *Chilam Balam of Chumayel,* 63). Cited in incantations for a sore leg, *hunpedzkin*-vein or -humor, and ulcers (MS pp. 91, 94, 99, 110).

GLOSSARY OF PROPER NAMES

T HE MASCULINE AND FEMININE PREFIXES "Ah" and "Ix" are not considered in the alphabetical arrangement of these names.

Ac-uinic-ik ("dwarf-wind" or "turtle-man-wind"). A relief figure corresponding to the latter appears on the Iglesia at Chichén Itzá. The name is cited in an incantation for erotic-seizure (MS p. 32). *Ac-ek* ("turtle-star") was the name of a constellation composed partly of the stars of our Gemini (Motul Dict.).

Ix Ahau-na ("palace-lady"). She is said to come into the heart of the sky and is associated with a "cenote lady." Cited in an incantation for certain ulcers (MS p. 109).

Anom. Defined as "the first man, Adam" (Motul Dict.). In compounds, however, it sometimes seems to imply humanity in general. See Hun-yah-ual-anom.

Bacab. One of the four deities stationed at the four world-quarters. They were sky bearers and apparently had other functions as well (Roys, *The Indian Background of Colonial Yucatán*, 74–75; Thompson, "Sky Bearers," 211, 215, 235–36; *Maya Hieroglyphic Writing*, 10, 85–86, 116, 124; *Landa's "Relación*," 135). They often appear in this manuscript. Cited in incantations for seizures (MS pp. 9, 10, 22, 26, 45), obstruction of the breathing passages (p. 72), snake-pulsation of the abdomen (pp. 116–17, 120, 122), wasp-poisoning (p. 140), birth of the flint (pp. 183–88). The word *bacab* is defined in the Motul Dictionary as *representante* ("actor") and *zingles*. J. E. S. Thompson (letter) notes that the latter could well be intended for *zingales*, apparently the equivalent of *zincali*, meaning either "gipsy" or "strolling player." The San Francisco Dictionary (Span.-Maya) gives *bacabyah* as the Maya word for *representante*.

Ix Bolon-can ("lady nine-sky" or "lady nine-snake"). Cited in an incantation for traveler-seizure (MS pp. 17, 18).

Ix Bolon-che ("lady nine-" or "many-trees"). Cited in an incantation for tarantula-eruption (MS pp. 33, 41). *Bolon-che*, however, has been reported as a plant name, *Phaseolus sp.*

Bolon-choch ("nine-" or "many-releases"). Cited in an incantation for traveler-seizure (MS p. 19). Here the context seems to indicate a proper name.

Bolon-ch'och'ol ("nine-" or "many-times-salted"). Cited in an incantation for tarantula-eruption and tarantula-seizure (MS p. 41).

Bolon-hobon ("many colors"). Cited in an incantation for a rattlesnake in the abdomen (MS p. 124). Ah Bolon-hobon is defined as "accomplished painter" (Motul Dict.).

Ix Bolon-puc, Ix Bolon-pucil ("lady nine-" or "many-hills"). Associated with the names of known deities. Cited in incantations for a pathology of the breathing passages, for ulcers, to cool a drill, and to chip a flint point (MS pp. 77, 107, 149, 198).

Ix Bolon-sut-ni-cal ("lady many-neck-turns"). Possibly a plant name. Cited in an incantation for a rattlesnake in the abdomen (MS p. 124).

Bolon-ti-ḳu ("nine-gods"). The well-known deities of the nine underworlds, or lords of the night (Thompson, *Maya Hieroglyphic Writing*, 12, 54, 210). Cited in incantations for asthma (MS pp. 64, 75), snake-pulsation (p. 121), *ḳanpedzḳin* at the head of a man (pp. 135–36).

Ah Bolonte-uitz ("lord nine-mountains"). We are reminded of a site named Bolonppel-uitz, or Bolonte-uitz, and of Salinas de los Neuve Cerros on the Chixoy River (Roys, *Chilam Balam of Chumayel*, 64, 121, 139). Ah Bolonte-uitz is cited in an incantation for a pathology of the breathing passages (MS p. 79).

Bolon-yocte ("he of nine" or "many strides"). Cf. Roys, "The Prophecies for the Maya Tuns," 166; Thompson, *Maya Hieroglyphic Writing*, 56, 291). Cited in an incantation for traveler-seizure (MS p. 23).

Ah Can-chaḳan ("lord high-savanna" or "lord-savanna-snake").

X-canchakan appears on maps as a rural site between the railroad and the ruins of Mayapán. Ah Can-chakan is cited in an incantation for a pathology of the breathing passages (MS p. 78).

Ah Can-tzuc-che ("lord four-clumps-of-trees" or "lord high-clump-of-trees"). Cited in an incantation for a pathology of the breathing passages (MS p. 78).

Can-yah-ual-kak ("vigorous-enemy-of-fire" or "-of-eruptions"). Cited in incantations for jaguar-macaw-seizure, ulcers, and the placenta (MS pp. 9, 12, 107, 179). Associated with Ix Ma-uay ("lady detrimental-one"), "who keeps closed the opening in the earth," and with Ah Tabay, a god of the hunters.

Ix Catil-ahau ("lady mistress of the water-jars"?). Cited in an incantation for a rattlesnake in the abdomen (MS p. 124).

Ix Cocoyol-cab ("lady abstinence"). Cited in an incantation for certain ulcers (MS p. 108).

Colop-u-uich-akab ("snatcher-of-the-eye-of-the-night"). Apparently a reference to a lunar eclipse. Cited in incantations for an erotic-seizure and *kanpedzkin* (a wasp?) at the head of a man (MS pp. 45, 134). Here, just as a solar eclipse is associated with the sky, Colop-u-uich-akab is associated with Metnal.

Colop-u-uich-kin ("snatcher-of-the-eye-of-the-sun" or "-day"). "The principal idol [god], which the Indians of this land had, and from whom they said all things proceeded, and who was incorporeal, hence they made no image of him" (Vienna Dict., f. 129r.). Cited in incantations for various seizures, *kanpedzkin* at the head of a man, and a worm in the tooth (MS pp. 34, 35, 45, 52, 108, 134, 172). Apparently a solar-eclipse god. See also Kolop-u-uich-kin.

Ix Co-pauah-ek. The prefix is feminine. *Co* could mean "tooth" or "beak," but in this manuscript it usually signifies "mad," "fierce," or "lewd." *Pauah* is an untranslated element in the name of the important Pauahtuns. *Ek* can mean *"star," "black,"* or *"tumor."* It is also the name of the logwood tree. Ix Co-pauah-ek is cited in an incantation for asthma (MS p. 69).

Ix Co-tancas-ek ("lady mad-seizure-star" or "tumor"). Cited in an incantation for a certain seizure (MS p. 8).

Ix Co-ti-pan. If it were Ix Co-ti-pa*m*, it could mean "indecent-young-woman." Cited in an incantation for a seizure and associated with an arbor (*dzulbal*) (MS p. 24).

Ix Cucul-patz-kin ("lady sun-stroke"). Cited in an incantation for tarantula-eruption and tarantula-seizure (MS p. 41).

Ix Culum-can ("*culum*-snake," "*culum*-shoot," or "*culum*-of-the-sky"). I can find no meaning for *culum*. The name is associated with several terms that might indicate celestial phenomena. Ix Culum-can is cited in an incantation for asthma (MS p. 69).

Ix Culum-chacah. *Chacah* is the common gumbolimbo tree. Here, too, there is an association with celestial phenomena. Cited in an incantation for certain ulcers (MS pp. 107, 109). One of the terms for ulcer or tumor is *ek*, which can also mean "star."

Cum Ahau ("seated lord"). This could well be the same as "Cumhau," identified as "Lucifer, the prince of the devils" (Motul Dict.). Here the name is associated with the *kanch'ah*-snake and, less closely, with a "place of great putrefaction." Cited in an incantation for snake-pulsation in the bowels (MS p. 131). The underworld was characterized by its stench.

Chac Ahau ("great lord"). A title of Kolop-u-uich-kin. Cited in an incantation for *kanpetkin*-wasp-seizure (MS p. 53).

Chacal Ahau ("red lord"). Cited in an incantation for obstruction of the breathing passages (MS p. 194).

Chacal Bacab ("red Bacab"). Cited in an incantation for *kanpetkin*-wasp-poisoning (MS p. 140). See Bacab.

Chacal Itzamna ("red Itzamna"). Cited in an incantation for asthma (MS p. 65). See Itzamna.

Chacal Ix Chel ("red Ix Chel"). Cited in incantations for jaguar-macaw-seizure, asthma, and a pathology of the breathing passages (MS pp. 4, 65, 81, 158). See Ix Chel (under "I").

Chac-bolay ("great-" or "red-beast-of-prey"). One of the words for "jaguar," but also the name of a certain evil spirit (*demonio*) (San Francisco Dict., Maya-Span.). Cited in an incantation for the placenta (MS p. 176).

Ix Chac-lah-yeeb ("lady rain-face-dew"). Associated with a savanna. Cited in an incantation for ulcers (MS p. 111).

Chac-mumul-ain ("red-" or "great-muddy-crocodile"). Associated with Chac-uayab-xoc here and in one of the prophecies (Roys, "The Prophecies for the Maya Tuns," 166). Cited in an incantation for ulcers (MS p. 113).

Chac Pauahtun ("red Pauahtun"). Cited in an incantation for tarantula-eruption (MS pp. 34). See Pauahtun.

Chac-Pauahtun Chac ("red Pauahtun Chac"). This name suggests a close relationship, almost an identity, of the four Pauahtuns with the four Chacs, or rain gods. Chac Pauahtun Chac is cited in an incantation for macaw-seizure and in one for *ḳanpetḳin*-wasp-seizure (MS pp. 29, 49). In the latter we find a mention of the house of one of the rain gods, which is said to lie beyond the east horizon.

Chac-petan-ḳin ("great-" or "red-rounded-sun"). Associated with a star name and the snake-rattles-constellation. Cited in an incantation for a fire (MS p. 154).

Chac-uayab-cab ("great-" or "red-ominous-bee"). This obviously mythical name has survived as that of the *chac-uayacab*, a dark red ant which nests underground and inflicts a painful sting (Pacheco Cruz, *Diccionario de la fauna yucateca*, 101; Roys, *Chilam Balam of Chumayel*, 152). Cited in an incantation for a pathology of the breathing passages (MS p. 81), and for the placenta (p. 175).

Chac-uayab-xoc ("great-" or "red-ominous-shark"). Associated with Chac-mumul-ain (Roys, "The Prophecies for the Maya Tuns," 166). Cited in an incantation for ulcers (MS p. 113).

Ix Chante-ḳaḳ ("lady notable-eruption" or "-fire"). Associated with Tzab, the snake-rattles-constellation, and possibly with other celestial phenomena. Cited in an incantation for ulcers (MS p. 107).

Ix Chante-oyoch ("lady notable-pauper"?). MS pp. 107, 109.

Chel. See Ix Chel under "I."

Ix Ch'ich'-cit ("lady bird-father"). Cited in an incantation for ulcers (MS p. 108).

Ix Chiticil Uaclahun. Chiticil might possibly refer to the ravelled edge of a fabric; and Uaclahun is the numeral 16. Cited in an incantation for ulcers (MS p. 110).

Chuen. One of the Maya day names and associated with a monkey-god (Thompson, *Maya Hieroglyphic Writing,* 80). *Ah Chuen,* however, is defined as "artisan," and in the Chumayel manuscript *chuen* seems to mean "industry." Yaxal-Chuen ("green-rain-Chuen") is the "aspect" of a Katun 12 Ahau (Roys, *Chilam Balam of Chumayel,* 158). Gates ("Commentary upon the . . . Pérez Codex," 30) reproduces a glyph from the Paris Codex combining the elements *yax* and Chuen. We find a glyph of this description in the Dresden Codex (p. 34c; Zimmerman, *Die Hieroglyphen der Maya-Handschriften,* Glyph 75:1331; Thompson, *A Catalog of Maya Hieroglyphs,* 47, 123, Glyph 74:521). Chuen is cited in incantations to charm a scorpion and for a worm in the tooth (MS pp. 160, 164).

Ekel Ahau ("black lord"). Cited in an incantation for obstruction of the breathing passages (MS p. 194).

Ekel Ix Chel ("black Ix Chel"). Only in the Bacabs manuscript have I found a black aspect of this goddess. Cited in an incantation for a pathology of the breathing passages (MS pp. 77, 81). See Ix Chel (under "I").

Ekel Itzamna ("black lizard-house"). Cited in an incantation for asthma (MS p. 77). See Itzamna.

Ek Pauahtun ("black Pauahtun"). Cited in an incantation for wasp-seizure (MS p. 52). See Pauahtun.

Tix Hochan-ek ("lady scraped-star"). Apparently associated with the snake-rattles-constellation and Yax-hal Chac, a rain god. Cited in an incantation for a fire (MS p. 154).

Tix Ho-dzacab ("lady five-generations"). There may be a figurative meaning for this name, just as *bolon-dzacab* ("nine-generations") means "eternal." Tix Ho-dzacab is cited in an incantation for a pathology of the breathing passages (MS p. 75). Cf. Tix Pic-dzacab.

Ix Hol-can-be ("lady opening-at-the-four-roads" or "-crossroads").

Cited in an incantation for traveler-seizure (MS p. 19). Cf. Roys, *Chilam Balam of Chumayel*, 103 and note; also Yum Hol-can-lub below.

Ix Hom-ti-tzab ("she-who-sinks-into-the-rattles-constellation"). Cited in an incantation for certain ulcers (MS pp. 107, 109).

Ix Hom-ti-muyal ("she-who-sinks-into-the-cloud"). MS p. 109.

Hub-tun Ahau ("lord stone-conch"). Cited in an incantation for a "worm in the tooth" (MS p. 170). Cf. Thompson, *Maya Hieroglyphic Writing*, 12, 133–34.

Ix Hun-acay-ḳiḳ (Ix Hun-hacay-kik) ("lady unique-slippery-blood"). Said to be in the heart of the sky. Cited in an incantation for a *ḳanpedzḳin* (-wasp) at the head of a man (MS p. 134).

Ix Hun-acay-olom ("lady unique-slippery-clotted-blood"). (MS p. 134).

Hun Ahau ("unique lord"). Thompson shows a close connection between the planet Venus and the god Hun Ahau, also with the day 9 Lamat, which falls eight days after the day 1 Ahau. "Hun Ahau is the day of Venus and undoubtedly serves also as a name of the Venus god at the time of heliacal rising, when he emerges from the underworld." In late colonial almanacs we read in connection with the day 1 Ahau: "There comes forth a great putrescence from the underworld by day and night. Sudden death." (Thompson, *Maya Hieroglyphic Writing*, 299–301). The glyph for the day Lamat is the sign for the planet Venus, and the Venus cycle ended on a day Lamat. (Thompson, *ibid.*, 77; see also Roys, "The Prophecies for the Maya Tuns," 174, 177).

Ix Hun Ahau ("lady One Ahau"). Here obviously the wife and consort of Hun Ahau, the lord of Metnal. She would correspond to the Mexican Micteca-cihuatl, the consort of Mictlan-tecutli. Cited in an incantation for traveler-seizure, where she is associated with "the opening in the earth"; also in others for seizures, ulcers, and a rattlesnake in the abdomen (MS pp. 25, 30, 108, 125). Cf. Appendix A.

Ix Hun-dzalab-caan ("lady unique-seal- [in the] sky"). We read of "three" or "many seals on the trunk of the ceiba," a sacred tree (Tizimin MS, p. 19). Cited in an incantation for *hunpedzkin*-seizure (MS p. 83).

Ix Hun-dzalab-muyal ("lady unique-seal- [in the] cloud"). MS p. 83.

Ix Hun-dzit-balche ("lady unique-slender-*balche*-tree"). MS p. 174.

Ix Hun-itzamna ("lady unique-lizard-house"). Cited in an incantation for a fire (MS p. 150).

Ix Hun-lah-dzib ("lady all written," or "painted"). Cited in an incantation for *hunpedzkin*-seizure (MS p. 83).

Ix Hun-lah-uoh ("lady unique-all-glyph"). (MS p. 83).

Ix Hun-meklah ("lady all-embracer"). Apparently associated with celestial phenomena. Cited in an incantation for asthma (MS p. 69).

Ix Hun-petah-kin ("lady unique-circular-sun"). Apparently a play on the syllables of the word *hunpetkin* (a certain wasp). Cited in an incantation for *kanpedzkin* at a man's head (MS p. 136).

Ix Hun-petah-akab ("lady unique-circular-darkness"). Possibly an improvised term for a rhetorical contrast to the preceding name. (MS p. 136).

Hun-pic-ti-ku ("8,000-gods"). Apparently a figurative expression meaning all the countless deities. We are reminded of a god at Izamal named Hunpic-toc (Hunpic-tok) ("8,000-flints"), and of a deity at Tahdziu called Hunpic-dziu ("8,000-cowbirds) (Thompson, *Maya Hieroglyphic Writing*, 87; Roys, *Political Geography of the Yucatan Maya*, 76). Hun-pic-ti-ku is cited in an incantation for a pathology of the breathing passages (MS pp. 77–78).

Hun-pic-ti-uoh ("8,000-*uoh*"). The *uoh* is not identified, but this expression is associated with the *pap*-jay, and I can recall *hun-pic* only as being associated with gods or bird names. Hun-pic-ti-uoh is cited in an incantation for the placenta (MS p. 178).

Ix Hun-pudzub-kik ("lady unique-needle-remover-of-blood"). Cited in incantations for seizure and a rattlesnake in the abdomen (MS pp. 7, 124).

Ix Hun-pudzub-olom ("lady unique - needle - remover - of - clotted - blood"). Cited for a seizure (MS p. 7).

Ix Hun-sipit-can ("lady unique-releaser-" or "discharger-in-the-sky"). Cited in incantations for asthma and snake-pulsation in the abdomen (MS pp. 64, 69, 118).

Ix Hun-sipit-muyal ("lady unique-releaser-in-the-cloud"). Cited, MS pp. 64, 69, 118.

Ix Hun-tah-acay-olom ("lady unique-splotch-of-clotted-blood"). Cf. Ix Hun-acay-kik. Cited in an incantation for a seizure (MS p. 8). Here *tah* has been translated only from its contexts, such as blood and coloring matter. *Tah* is defined as "splinter," but I do not know that a splinter was used in connection with a blood sacrifice.

Ix Hun-tah-dzib ("lady unique-splotch-of-paint"?). Cited in an incantation for a worm in the tooth (MS p. 163).

Ix Hun-tah-ḳiḳ ("lady unique-splotch-of-blood"?). Cited in an incantation for *hunpedzḳin* at a man's head (MS p. 135).

Ix Hun-tah-nok. *Nok* means a worm or grub, as distinguished from an earthworm (MS p. 163).

Ix Hun-tah-olom ("lady unique-splotch-of-clotted-blood"). MS p. 135.

Ix Hun-tip-tzab (Ix Hun-tipp-tzab) ("lady unique-pulsating-rattles-constellation"). Cited in an incantation for fire (MS p. 154). Associated with other celestial phenomena.

Ix Hun-tipplah-can ("lady unique-pulsating-sky"). Cited in an incantation for snake-pulsation-of-the abdomen (MS p. 116).

Ix Hun-tipplah-muyal ("lady unique-pulsating-cloud"). MS p. 116.

Ix Hun-tzelep-aḳab ("lady unique-inclination-of-the-night"). Meaning two hours after midnight (MS p. 83).

Ix Hun-tzelep-ḳin ("lady unique-inclination-of-the-sun" or "-day"). Meaning two o'clock in the afternoon. Cited in an incantation for *hunpedzḳin*-seizure (MS p. 83).

Hun-yah-ual-anom ("unique-enemy-of-Anom"). Anom was the name of "the first man, Adam" (Motul Dict.). Cited in an incantation for a rattlesnake in the abdomen (MS p. 123).

Hun-yah-ual-anomob ("unique-enemy-of-the-Anoms"). Apparently meaning the enemy of the human race. Cited in an incantation for the placenta (MS pp. 176, 177).

Hun-yah-ual-cab ("unique enemy of the world"). Cited in an incantation for a rattlesnake in the abdomen (MS p. 123).

Hun-yah-ual-uinicob ("unique-enemy-of-men"). (MS pp. 176, 178).

Ix Hun-ye-ta ("lady unique-point-of-the-flint-lancet"). Cited in incantations for *hunpedzkin*-seizure and for eruptions and fevers (MS pp. 83, 101). The mother of a personified disease.

Ix Hun-ye-ton ("lady unique-point-of-the-genitals"). MS pp. 83, 102. It seems inconsistent to find such an expression as a feminine name, but the context refers to it as the name of the mother of a personified disease. This and the preceding expression seem to be associated with Hun Ahau, the ruler of the katun of that name; and that katun was indeed a bad one (Roys, "The Maya Katun Prophecies," 40, 51).

Itzam-cab ("earth-lizard"). I suggest that this was the earth monster and take this to be the same name as Itzam-cab-ain ("earth-lizard-crocodile"), although Beltran (*Arte de el idioma maya*, 230) defines it as a "whale." The Chumayel manuscript, however, writes it Itzam-kab-ain ("lizard-[with]-crocodile-legs"), and states that it was fecundated by Ah Uuc-chek-nal ("lord seven-fertilizer-of-the-maize") (Roys, *Chilam Balam of Chumayel*, 101). Itzam-cab is cited in incantations for asthma (MS p. 82), cooling water on the fire (pp. 145, 147), and the placenta (pp. 174, 176–79).

Itzam-kan. *Itzam* means "lizard" and *kan* ("yellow" or "cord") is also a word for lizard in other languages of the Maya stock. Here Itzam-kan would appear to be a bad pun on Itzam-caan ("sky-lizard"). See the Dresden Codex, pp. 4 and 74. Other equally bad puns are not unusual in our manuscript. Itzam-kan is cited in an incantation for an obstruction of the breathing passages (MS pp. 189–93). Another play on the name, Itzam-caan, is to be found in an account of a deified ruler of Izamal. When asked who he was, he replied, "*Itz en caan, Itz en muyal*" ("I am the dew, or essence, of the sky and the clouds") (Lizana, *Historia de Yucatán*, cap. 2, f. 3r.). Surely this is a play on the words, Itzam-caan ("sky-lizard") and Itzam-muyal ("cloud-lizard") much like what we find here.

Itzam-na ("lizard-house"). See Chacal Itzamna, Ekel Itzamna, Kanal

Itzamna. No Sacal ("white") Itzamna is mentioned. Thompson (*Maya Hieroglyphic Writing*, 11) explains the Itzamnas as four celestial monsters often represented as alligators or lizards. These celestial monsters are deities of the rain and of the crops and food.

Ix Chel. *Chel* is the word for "rainbow," but I do not know whether or not there was any association in Maya mythology. She was a goddess of medicine, childbirth, weaving, and probably erotic love. Strangely enough, in this manuscript she is on one occasion called "virgin Ix Chel." As a patroness of medicine, her shrine on Cozumel Island was one of the three most important centers of pilgrimage for both the Mayas and the Tabasco Chontals, although many people went there to obtain forgiveness for sin (Roys, Scholes, and Adams, "Report and Census of the Indians of Cozumel, 1570"; Scholes and Roys, *The Maya Chontal Indians of Acalan-Tixchel*, 57, 395; Roys, *The Indian Background of Colonial Yucatán*, 25, 77–78, 94–95, 109; Roys, *Political Geography of the Yucatán Maya*, 54). The worship of Ix Chel and the related cults in Mexico have been covered in the past by Thompson ("Sky Bearers," "The Moon Goddess in Central America," and *Maya Hieroglyphic Writing*, 47–48, 83), and he has more recently identified her glyph and pictures and noted her activities as portrayed in two of the hieroglyphic codices (Thompson, "Symbols, Glyphs, and Divinatory Almanacs," 349–64). See also Chacal Ix Chel, Ekel Ix Chel, Kanal Ix Chel, and Sacal Ix Chel.

Jesus Mary. This appears twice, apparently only as an exclamation and not related to the context, in an incantation for an obstruction of the breathing passages (MS pp. 206–207).

Kak-ne-chapat ("fire-tailed-centipede"). One description of the *chapat* is that it is only a certain worm or caterpillar found in wet places (Pacheco Cruz, *Léxico de la fauna yucateca*, 52). It is, however, also defined as a centipede (Pérez Dict.). Beltrán (*Arte de el idioma maya*, 227) explains "*ah-uac-chapat*" (apparently a misprint for *ah-uuc-chapat*) as a "serpent with seven heads." Seler (*Gesammelte Abhandlung*, IV, 742–43, 747) illustrates the centipede in Mexican art but states that he has not found it in the Maya codices. Kak-ne-chapat is cited in an incantation for ulcers (MS pp. 106, 109). Ulcers, although they have a special name, could be considered to be an eruption (Maya, *kak*), and *kak* is a homonym meaning "fire" also.

Kak-tamay. Since it is cited in an incantation for ulcers (MS pp. 106, 109), this appears to be a reference to the term *kak-tamay-ek*, which could mean literally "fire-ill-omened-star" or "ulcer"). Both terms, however, are defined as meaning "carbuncle" and "a fabulous monster." (See Beltrán, *Arte de el idioma maya*, 228; Pérez Dict.). *Tamay* is also the name of a large tree, which is a remedy for ulcers (Roys, *Ethno-Botany*, 283). We are reminded of the word carbuncle, which can mean either a boil or a semiprecious stone.

Ix Kak-yol-mat ("lady fire-heart-*mat*"). Cited in an incantation for snake-pulsation of the abdomen (MS p. 120).

Kanal Ahau ("yellow lord"). Cited in an incantation for an obstruction of the breathing passages (MS p. 194).

Kanal Ix Chel ("yellow Ix Chel"). Only in this manuscript have I found a yellow aspect of this goddess. Sacal ("white") Ix Chel and Chacal ("red") Ix Chel are more familiar figures, both in colonial Maya literature and in the codices. Kanal Ix Chel is cited in incantations for a pathology of the breathing passages (MS pp. 65, 79, 81). Associated with Itzamna, a rain god.

Kanal Itzam-na ("yellow Itzamna"). Associated with Kanal Ix Chel. Cited in an incantation for a pathology of the breathing passages (MS p. 79). See Itzam-na.

Ix Kan-kinib-te ("lady yellow-wooden-heater"). *Kin* can mean "to heat"; *-ib* implies the instrument of an action; and *-te* is a common suffix indicating that an object is of wood. Cited in an incantation for snake-pulsation of the abdomen (MS p. 120).

Ix Kan-kinib-tun ("lady yellow-stone-heater"). MS p. 120.

Ix Kan-kinim-te ("lady yellow-*ciruela*-wood"). Cited in an incantation for a pathology of the breathing passages (MS p. 78). It is associated with the *chi*-plum, or *nance*.

Ix Kan-kinim-tun ("lady yellow-*ciruela*-pit" or "-stone"). MS p. 78.

Ix Kantanen-u. See Glossary of Fauna Names. Here the context seems to call for a proper name. Cited in an incantation for ulcers (MS p. 107).

Kauil. The name of a god representing some aspect of food or crops. *Kauil-yah* means "to beg for alms." Kauil is a title of Itzamna, and we frequently find it in colonial Maya literature. (Cf. Thompson, *Maya Hieroglyphic Writing*, 82, 169, 286; Roys, *Chilam Balam of Chumayel*, 152, 165, 168; "The Prophecies for the Maya Tuns," 170; "The Maya Katun Prophecies," 38, 48). Cited in an incantation for traveler-seizure (MS p. 25). Cf. Uaxac-yol-kauil.

Kin Colop-u-uich-kin ("sun snatcher-of-the-eye-of-the-sun"). Cited in incantations for *kanpedzkin* at a man's head and a worm in the tooth (MS pp. 135, 172). Cf. Colop-i-uich-kin.

Kin Chac Ahau ("sun great lord"). A title of Colop-u-uich-kin. Cited in incantations for traveler-seizure, frenzied seizure, and *kanpedzkin* at a man's head (MS pp. 17, 18, 45, 134).

Kin Chac Ahau Canal ("sun great lord on high"). Cited in an incantation for a *kanpedzkin*-wasp at a man's head (MS pp. 136, 139).

Kin Chac Ahau Itzamna ("sun great lord lizard-house"). Cited in an incantation for *hunpedzkin*-seizure (MS p. 84) Cf. Itzam-na.

Kinich-kak-mo ("sun-eye-fire-macaw"). Cited in an incantation for macaw-seizure (MS p. 27). Cf. *Mo* in Glossary of Fauna Names.

Kin-patax-uinic. Cited in an incantation for a rattlesnake in a man's abdomen (MS p. 124).

Ix Kin-sutnal. Cited in an incantation for ulcers (MS p. 111).

Kolop-u-uich-kin ("wounder-of-the-eye-of-the-sun"). Cited in incantations for tarantula-seizure and ulcers (MS pp. 42, 106). Practically a synonym for Colop-u-uich-kin, used for rhetorical effect.

Ix Ko-ti-tzab ("lady *ko* [-bird?]-in-the-rattles-constellation"). Possibly the name of a star. Cited in incantations for ulcers, and a rattlesnake in the abdomen (MS pp. 107, 124). Cf. *ix ko* in Glossary of Fauna Names.

Ku-ah-tepal ("God-the-ruler"). Possibly a reference to the Christian God. Cited in an incantation for snake-pulsation in the abdomen (MS p. 132).

Ix Kuk-nab ("lady water-lily-bud" or "sprout"). For the water-lily in

Maya symbolism, see Thompson, *Maya Hieroglyphic Writing*, 89, 115, 134, 136. Cited in an incantation for traveler-seizure (MS p. 22).

Ix Macan-xoc. *Xoc* means "shark" or "count." The context seems to call either for a proper name or a fauna name. Macan-xoc is known elsewhere only as a well-known site at the ruins of Cobá. Cited in an incantation for asthma (MS p. 68).

Ix Ma-uay ("lady detrimental-one"). Characterized as "she who keeps closed the opening in the earth." Cited in incantations for jaguar-macaw-seizure and a pathology of the breathing passages (MS pp. 9, 10, 81).

Ix Ma-ul. *Ma* is the Maya negative; and *ul* could mean "to arrive," "a certain small snail," "*atole*," and "*gullet*." Cited in an incantation for ulcers (MS p. 110).

Ix Meklah ("lady embracer"). Cited in an incantation for ulcers (MS p. 107).

Ix Meklah-oyte. A forced translation would be "she who embraces the dismayed one." Cited in an incantation for ulcers (MS p. 109).

Ix Meklah-u-sip. Cited, MS p. 109. Sip was a hunters' god.

Metnal (also written *Mitnal*). The name of the underworld and the abode of the dead, with certain favored exceptions. It is evidently referable to the Mexican Mictlan. (*Landa's "Relación,"* 132; Thompson, *Maya Hieroglyphic Writing*, see index). Cited in incantations for jaguar-macaw-seizure and an obstruction of the breathing passages (MS pp. 9, 10, 194, 203, 204).

Ix Moson-cuc ("lady whirlwind," or "lady whirling-squirrel"). Cited in an incantation for ulcers (MS p. 107).

Ix Mukyah-kutz ("she who-strengthens-the-tobacco"). Cited in an incantation for a burn and for a fire (MS p. 155).

Ah Nohol ("lord of the south"). *Nohol* could also mean "right hand," "great," and "vein." Cited in an incantation for ulcers (MS p. 110).

Ix Ocom-tun ("lady stone-pillar"). Cited in an incantation for asthma (MS p. 69).

Ix Octun-xix. *Octun* is the sinker for a fish net; *xix* usually means "sediment," but *sac-xix* is the word for alabaster. Cited in an incantation for asthma (MS p. 69).

Ah Olon-tzin. Since a written "m" sometimes becomes an "n" before a dental, possibly *olom* ("clotted blood") is meant. Cited in an incantation for traveler-seizure (MS p. 24). Cf. U-lam-tzin.

Oxlahun-calab ("13x160,000"). Cited in an incantation for *kanpetkin*-wasp-seizure (MS p. 59).

Oxlahun-ti-kuob ("thirteen-gods"). The deities of the thirteen heavens and those representing the thirteen coefficients of the day names (Thompson, *Maya Hieroglyphic Writing*, 10, 12). Cited in incantations for tarantula-eruption and *kanpetkin*-wasp-seizure (MS pp. 34, 39, 49, 51, 52, 53, 56, 58). In most cases it is the words or commands of these deities that are cited. Note that the plural form, *-kuob*, is employed. Elsewhere it is usually written Oxlahun-ti-ku.

Oxlahun-tun-muyal ("supreme-jeweled-cloud"). This translation is made from a figurative meaning of *oxlahun*, and not its usual one, which is "thirteen." It is apparently a reference to the sparks in a cloud of smoke from a fire. Cited in an incantation for a fire (MS p. 150).

Pauahtun. The four Pauahtuns, usually named with their respective colors, Chac ("red"), Sac ("white"), *Ek* ("black"), and Kan ("yellow") are each assigned to one of the four world-quarters. They are associated with the Chacs, or rain gods, and the Bacabs, or sky bearers; also occasionally with the "four changing winds" (Thompson, *Maya Hieroglyphic Writing*, 161; Roys, *Chilam Balam of Chumayel*, 67, 110). The last association is sometimes called *can-hel* ("four-change"). This aspect of the Pauahtuns, I surmise, was what led Beltrán (*Arte de el idioma Maya*, 228) to define *can-hel* as meaning "*dragón*." So I infer that the Pahuahtuns were pictured as lizard monsters.

Ix Pic-tzab ("lady 8,000-" [or "countless-] rattles.") Associated with other celestial phenomena and obviously referable to the snake-rattles-constellation called Tzab. Cited in an incantation for a fire (MS p. 154).

Tix Pic-dzacab. ("lady 8,ooo-" [or "countless-]generations"). Apparently a paraphrase of the familiar expression, *bolon-dzacab* ("nine" or "many generations"), meaning "eternal." Cited in an incantation for a pathology of the breathing passages (MS p. 75).

Saba-yol. The context indicates a star name. Cited in an incantation to charm a scorpion (MS p. 160). Zinan-ek ("scorpion-star") is the name of a constellation (Motul Dict.).

Sacal Ahau ("white lord"). Cf. Chacal, Ekel, and Kanal Ahau above. Cited in an incantation for an obstruction of the breathing passages (MS p. 194).

Sacal Itzamna ("white Itzamna"). Associated with Sacal Ix Chel. Cited in an incantation for a pathology of the breathing passages (MS p. 76). See Itzamna.

Sacal Ix Chel ("white Ix Chel"). Cited in incantations for a pathology of the breathing passages and to charm a spider (MS pp. 81, 158). See Ix Chel, under "I."

Sac-mumul-ain ("white-muddy-crocodile"). In the Tizimin manuscript, we read of Chac-("red")mumul-ain (Roys, "The Prophecies for the Maya Tuns," 166). *Mumul* is also defined as a dark ring around the sun or moon, a sign of rain (Motul Dict.). Sac-mumul-ain is cited in an incantation for traveler-seizure (MS p. 22).

Sac Pauahtun ("white Pauahtun"). Cited in an incantation for *ƙan-pedzƙin*-(wasp?) at a man's head (MS pp. 38, 138). Here Sac Pauahtun is said to be a "bird of tidings" (*mut*), but I suspect that this is an error of the scribe. See Pauahtun.

Sac-uayab-xoc ("white-ominous-shark"). Associated with Sac-mumul-ain. Cited, MS p. 22, in an incantation for traveler-seizure. Cf. Chac-uayab-xoc, Roys, "The Prophecies for the Maya Tuns," 166. Here its association with travel might perhaps refer to the dangers of canoe transport.

Sin-tun-bul Ahau ("flat-stone-game lord"). Cited in an incantation for snake-pulsation in the abdomen (MS p. 119).

Sip ("sin" or "error"). A hunters' god, described as a small deer (Thompson, *Maya Hieroglyphic Writing*, 76, 108, 135). Cited in an incantation for an obstruction of the breathing passages (MS p. 195). See Ah Uuc-yol-sip.

Som-ch'in, Som-pul ("sudden hurling, sudden casting," at the place of). Cited in an incantation for tarantula-eruption, *ƙanpetƙin*-wasp-seizure, and a pathology of the breathing passages (MS pp. 43, 60, 78).

Som-pul-acat ("suddenly-cast-seed-capsule"). Cited in an incantation for a rattlesnake in the abdomen (MS p. 124).

Suhuy-ƙaƙ ("virgin-fire"). The spirit of the new fire and goddess of healing and young girls. She was the deified daughter of a ruler and founded a religious order of virgins (Cogolludo, *Historia de Yucatán*, bk. 4, ch. 8). Cited in an incantation to charm a scorpion (MS p. 161).

Ah Tabay ("lord deceiver"). A hunters' god, not to be confused with Ix Tabay, a modern malign female forest-spirit (*Landa's "Relacion,"* 155). Cited in an incantation for a pathology of the breathing passages and for ulcers (MS pp. 77, 107).

Ix Tah-ƙab ("mistress of the broth or juice," very doubtful). Associated with Ix Co-ti-pan. Cited in an incantation for traveler-seizure (MS p. 24).

Ti-cah-puc ("at-the-dwelling-on-the-hill" or "of the mouse"?). Associated with Ix Moson-cuc in an incantation for ulcers (MS p. 107). Apparently an assonance was sought for the rhetorical effect.

Ix Ti-ho-tzab ("lady at-the-five-rattles" or "fifth-rattle"). Said to be at the fifth layer of the sky and evidently associated with the snake-rattles-constellation (Tzab). Cited in an incantation for traveler-seizure (MS p. 22). This association with a traveler suggests that the constellation may have served as a guide at night.

Tzab ("the snake-rattles-constellation," defined by Motul Dict. as the *Cabrillas*, or Pleiades). Cited for asthma and ulcers (MS pp. 72, 107). Cf. Pic-tzab, Ix Hun-tip-tzab, Ix Ko-ti-tzab.

Uaxac-yol-ƙauil ("eight-heart-of-food"). Cf. Kauil. This may be one of the appellations of the maize god (Thompson, *Maya Hieroglyphic Writing*, 269, 286). In an incantation for traveler-seizure

(MS p. 25) this name is associated with the opening in the earth and with Ix Hun Ahau, the mistress of Metnal, the underworld. Ix Ma-uay ("lady detrimental-one"), who is elsewhere cited in a very similar context, is not mentioned here. Could they be the same?

U-lam-tzin. *Lam* can mean "to sink," or "to submerge." Cited in an incantation for macaw-seizure (MS p. 24). Cf. Ah Olon-tzin.

Ix Uoh, or *Uoh*. A proper name associated with *chiuoh* ("tarantula"). Uoh is also associated with the sky and clouds and with Sac Pauahtun. Sometimes Uoh is invoked. Cited in an incantation for tarantula-seizure (MS pp. 34, 35, 38, 42).

Ix U-sihnal ("lady moon-birth"). Associated with various celestial phenomena. Cited in an incantation for ulcers (MS p. 107).

Ah Uuc-calam ("lord seven-*calam*-snake"). The word *calam* is defined as "excessive." Ah Uuc-calam is cited in an incantation for ulcers (MS p. 110). Cf. *calam*, Glossary of Fauna Names.

Uuc-metlah-Ahau ("seven-timid," or "refused lord"?). In this manuscript the Maya *th* is often written *t*. Associated with a needle and a sieve. Uuc-metlah-ahau (Uuc-methlah Ahau) is cited in an incantation for *ḳanpetḳin*-wasp-seizure (MS p. 59).

Uuc-ne-chapat ("seven-tail-centipede"). Associated with Kak-ne-chapat ("fire-tailed-centipede") in an incantation for ulcers (MS p. 107).

Ah Uuc-ti-cab ("lord seven-earth"). Cited in an incantation to charm a spider (MS p. 157). This is possibly an earth monster (Thompson, *Maya Hieroglyphic Writing*, 276).

Ah Uuc-yol-sip ("lord seven-heart-of-Sip"). Sip was a god of the hunters, and here the name is associated with Ah Tabay, another god of the chase. Cited in an incantation for ulcers (MS p. 107). Cf. Roys, *Chilam Balam of Chumayel*, 157.

Yaxal Chac, or *Yax-haal Chac* ("green-water rain god"). Rain is colored green in the Maya codices. Yaxal Chac is the celestial patron of several katun periods in the Books of Chilam Balam (Roys, *Chilam Balam of Chumayel*, 77, 132–34, 151; "The Maya Katun Prophecies," 30, 37; Thompson, *Maya Hieroglyphic Writ-*

ing, 61, 261). Ix Ma-uay (*q.v.*) is said to be the guardian of Yaxal Chac, possibly implying that she is at the point underground where the rain water stops and where Metnal, the underworld, begins. Yaxal Chac is cited in incantations for asthma, *hunpedzkin*-seizure, and fire biting on wood (MS pp. 81, 89, 154).

Ix Yal-hopoch ("lady offspring of the *hopoch*"). I can find no meaning for *hopoch*, but the context suggests a fauna name. Cited in an incantation for tarantula-eruption (MS pp. 33, 41).

Yum Ho-can-lub (Yum Hol-can-lub) ("father four-resting-places"). The *lub* is the place, or the erect flat stone, where the traveler rests his pack at the crossroads. Cf. Ix Hol-can-be. Yum Ho-can-lub is cited in an incantation for traveler seizure (MS p. 19). Cf Ix Hol-can-be, which has the feminine prefix.

APPENDIX A
Intrusive Material in a Different Hand

[*Intrusive material in a different hand. The purpose of the incantation on pp. 20–21 is not disclosed.*]

20   The great (or old) men of the sky.

Jesus Mary! What would be your rattle (*sot*)? Oh! This is the gold rattle of Ix Hun Ahau.

What would be the symbol of your tail, Oh! It would be the gold spindle of Ix Hun Ahau.

What, then, would be the adornment (*atavio*)? The gold rings of Ix Hun Ahau.

What, then, would enter into your hide? The red mat of Ix Hun Ahau.

What then, would enter into the ribs (*ch'ibil*, [*ch'ilibil*?]) of your back? The gold rosary of Ix Hun Ahau.

What, then, would be your ribs (*ch'alatil*)? Oh! The gold comb of Ix Hun Ahau.

What, then, would enter into your bowels? It would be the virgin [unused] prepared cotton of Ix Hun Ahau.

What, then, would enter into the tendons of your back? It would be the spun yarn of Ix Hun Ahau.

21   What, then, would enter into his [your?] stick (*cheel*)?/ It would be the gold weaver's bar of Ix Hun Ahau.

What, then, would be your head? The gold spindle-cup of Ix Hun Ahau.

What then would be your ear-wax? The virgin white crown (*sac pet*) of Ix Hun Ahau.

What, then, would enter to your eye? It would be the gold *sihom*-seed bead of [Ix] Hun Ahau.

What, then, would enter your nostril? The . . . *chab* of gold of Ix Hun Ahau.

What, then, would enter to your tooth? It would be the virgin needle of Ix Hun Ahau.

What, then, would be the opening in your neck? Oh, the genitals of Ix Hun Ahau.

What, then, would be the symbol of your tongue? Oh, the virgin cord of Ix Hun Ahau.

What, then would be your breath? Oh, the . . . of the breath of Ix Hun Ahau.

[*Apparently an incantation for some form of "seizure"* (tancas).]

62   To make good . . . a seizure, when it falls on a man.

Ox-chochola of wood, *ox-chochola* of stone. Much (or thrice) embraced in the cloud, vigorously (or four times?) embraced in the wind, supremely (*oxlahun*) . . . am I, when I stand erect to break the wind-lust. Three times gushes the trickling water to you, Bacab in the heart of the sky; three times it gushes for you, ye Bacabs in the heart of the earth. Ye fathers, ye gods! Chac Pauahtun is your symbol.

Then ye shall distrust the wind of Ix Tan-yobal-nicte ("lady in the heart of the *nicte*-flower"), Ix Tan-yol-caan ("lady in the heart of the sky"), Ix Tan-yol-metnal ("lady in the heart of Metnal").

Things sink on high, things sink on earth, when I stand erect to pull down the wind of Ix Tan-yobal-nicte. I cast you (pl.) into the heart of Metnal. Supremely (*oxlahun*) I take the fiery whirlwind. Vigorously I represent you. Embraced in the wind of Ix Uuc-yobal-nicte ("lady seven-heart-of-the-*nicte*-flower") [I] cast you into the heart of Metnal./

63   Supremely (*oxlahun*) I took the red *pahdza*-herb, when I soured (*pahah*) the . . . . Twelve hearts of the *nicte*-flower in the heart of the earth.

Supremely I take the place of Chac-ualom-kin, to suck up the wind (or breath) of the *nicte*-flower and the wind (or breath) of Ix Canlahun-tzuc-nicte ("lady fourteen-cluster-*nicte*-flower"). Then I stopped the throat of Chac-ualom-kin. Then I went to close the mouth of Ix Yan-coil ("lewd lady"). The genitals of Ix Hun Ahau are the symbol of the mouth of Ix Yan-coil.

Supreme (*oxlahun*) is the broom with which I sweep the wind
of lust from her heart and from her hand with my broom-axe (or
broom-hail).

Supreme (*oxlahun*) is the filling (or stopper) in the mouth of
Ix Yan-coil. Then I stopped it with the handle of the fan, with the
end of the *xicul* ("jacket"?).

Supreme deputy am I for the hairy Bacab, my symbol, when I
went to sour his wind (or breath).   Amen.

MANUSCRIPT TEXT

[Intrusive material in a different hand. Subject unknown.]

20 U noh uinicil can lae

[je]sus maria Bax bin a sot be [c]he u sot takin bin x hun a[h]au

bax bin u uayasba a ne be [c]he u pechech takin bin x hun ahau

bax tun bin otavit [atavio] u sortijas takin x hun ahau

Bax bin oc ta keulel u chachac pop bin [x] hun ahau

Bax tun bin oc tu ch'ibil [ch'ilibil] a pach u Rosario takin bin x
hun ahau

Bax [t]un bacan bin a ch'alatil be [u] xalche takin x hun ahau

Bax tun bin oc ta chochel u suhui bi bin x hun ahau

Bax tun [b]acan bin oc tu xich'il a pach [u] hohol kuch bin x
hun ahau

21 Bax tun baca bin oc tu cheel/ u xumche takin bin x hun ahau

Bax tun baca bin a pol u thohol takin x hun ahau

Bax tun bin u ta xicin u suhuy sac pet bin x h[un] ahau

Bax tun bin oc ta uich U sihom takin bin [ix] hun ahau

Bax tun bin oc tu hol a ni u . . . chab takin bin x hun ahau

Bax tun bin oc ta coo U suhuy pudz bin x hun ahau

Bax tun bacan u hol a cal be che u ca cobol x hun ahau

Bax tun bin u uayesba a uak be u suhuy tab x hun ahau

Bax tun bacan bin a uik be che u y . . . u yik bin x hun ahau

[Apparently an incantation for some form of "seizure"]

62 Licil u yutzcin . . . [apparent erasure] tancas tu lubul yokol uinice
ox chochola te ox chochola tun ox meklah ti munyal can meklah

164

ti yk oxlahun . . . cen cat ualhen yn pa ykal coil ox ten chuluba tech bacabe tan yol can ox ten chuluba tex bacab ex tan yol cab yumex kuex chac pauahtun a uayasba

ca bin a paholt ex yikal x tan yobal nicte x tan yol can x tan yol metnali

hom canal hom cabal uchic yn uatal yn hom chach yikal x tan yobal nicte yn picch'in tex tun [tan] yal [yol] can x tan yol metnal oxlahun ch'a en ti kakal moson can chac yn mahan tech u hol mek t yikal x uuc yobal nicte a [in] picch'in tex tan yol metnal/

63 ten oxlahun ch'ah en ti chacal pa padza uchic yn paha ti . . . l lahca yobal nicte tan yol cab

oxlahun mahan en ti chac ualom kin hapic yikal nicte y yikal x canlahun tzuc nicte ti tin macah tu hol u cal chac ualom kin ti tun bin en yn nupp u . . . x yx yan coyl u cacobol ti chac ti x hun ahau u uayasba u chiil

oxlahun mis uchic yn mistic yikal coil tu pucsikal y tu kab y yn misib bat

oxlahun macap tu chii x yan coil ti . . . tin macah t yoc ual t yoc xicul

oxlahun mahan en ti tzotzotz bacan yn uayasba in . . . uchic yn paholtic yika ye sam   Amen.

APPENDIX B
Malevolent Magic

MALEVOLENT MAGIC TOOK SEVERAL forms in Yucatán. The first, so far as we can learn, consisted largely of incantations, accompanied no doubt by appropriate ceremonial acts and gestures, intended to inflict disease or death upon the victim. Our chief source of information consists of items in the colonial Maya dictionaries, especially the Motul Dictionary.

These items tell of the nature of the misfortunes inflicted by sorcerers, but they vouchsafe little of the actual methods employed. For the latter Redfield and Villa give us an excellent account of such sorcery in modern times.[1]

One important method is to "send the enchantment into" the victim by control over the personified "evil winds" (*malos aires*). I find no earlier mention of these than in an undated manuscript in Harvard Peabody Museum entitled "*Libro del Judío*," which might date from the late eighteenth century, and in the Book of Chilam Balam of Kaua, probably compiled in the early nineteenth century.[2] Consequently I believe that the conception came late to Yucatán. I doubt the antiquity of the modern device of burying, cutting, or piercing a beeswax image of the intended victim. Another method is to inflict illness by sending one or a number of evil insects believed to have come from Metnal, the underworld.[3]

The second form of evil magic, which is widely spread in southern Middle America, is generally known as nagualism. Brinton has published a volume on this subject,[4] but he has given few examples of it in Yucatán. It could well be considered to be lycanthropy, although there are no wolves in the area.

Redfield and Villa describe this magic as it is known to the modern

1 *Chan Kom, a Maya Village*, 177–78, 227–28, 372.
2 A. M. Tozzer, *A Maya Grammar*, 190, 195.
3 Redfield and Villa, *Chan Kom, a Maya Village*, 178.
4 Daniel G. Brinton, 1894.

Maya.[5] Like the werewolf, the sorcerer or witch has a familiar animal called a *uay* and can take its shape, when he desires, to accomplish an evil purpose.

In the historical allusions found in a prophecy for a Katun 5 Ahau (A.D. 1342–62) we find the Itzá rulers in Yucatán and their supporters transforming themselves into lynxes and prowling about, allegedly to the disgust of their subjects.[6] These people were later driven out of Yucatán and settled in what is now northern Guatemala.

Nagualism still had an official standing of a sort among the Itzás on Lake Petén when they were conquered about the end of the seventeenth century.

We are told of a female slave of the high priest Kin Canek: "She was a great sorceress [*maga*] and witch, whom he had instructed in his diabolical cult, treating her, as it were, like a priestess." When a party of Spaniards encountered her and asked where she was coming from, "the false priestess" replied: "It was from seeing the *Xagual* [that is, her suitor], who always came out to visit [her] at the shore of the Lake in the form of a puma or jaguar and presented [her] with rabbits, pheasants, and other fowl and game." She refused to conduct them to him, for, if they killed him, she herself would die.[7]

Nagualism, however, appears to have been limited to the priesthood. Father Avendaño, who visited the Itzás shortly before they were conquered, reported: "I saw an Indian, the oldest one that I had seen up to that time in the nation of the Cehaches, nor up to the present time in that of the Itzaes, since they have the custom of beheading them when they pass fifty years, so that they shall not learn to be wizards and to kill; except the priests of their idols, for whom they have great respect. And this man must have been one without doubt."[8]

A third form of reprehensible magic was also practiced. The

[5] *Chan Kom, a Maya Village*, 178–80.

[6] Roys, "The Maya Katun Prophecies of the Books of Chilam Balam," 9, 14, 37–38.

[7] Juan de Villagutierre y Soto-Mayor, *Historia de la conquista de la provincia del Itza*, 528–29.

[8] P. A. Means, "History of the Spanish Conquest of Yucatán and of the Itzas," 131–32.

Plumeria blossom (*nicte*), which is cited in an incantation for "erotic seizure" (MS p. 30), was subjected to a certain ceremony performed by a witch. This turned it into a powerful love charm, which the recipient of the blossom could not resist. According to an old Maya legend, Hunac Ceel of Mayapán used this charm to induce Chac Xib Chac of Chichén Itzá to abduct the bride of the ruler of Izamal during the wedding festivities, at which Chac Xib Chac was a guest. Realizing later that he was not powerful enough to resist the injured bridegroom, the offender abandoned Chichén Itzá and led his followers to the region of Lake Petén in northern Guatemala. Here Cortés found their descendants still living in the sixteenth century.[9]

It would seem obvious that a reputable shaman must have some knowledge of malevolent magic in order to protect or cure his own patients. In any case, such a man is sometimes suspected of secretly practicing sorcery. During the late 1930's one of my informants was Benito Cauich of Pisté near Chichén Itzá, where he was a highly respected *yerbatero*. A Mexican woman, who was a spiritualist medium, moved into the town and was reported to be attempting to undermine his reputation. Finally, when one of his patients, a young girl, suddenly died, some members of her family were persuaded that Benito had caused her death by means of sorcery. Warned that these men were planning to kill him, he fled in the night to Uayma; and a year later he had not yet dared to return home.

In the following list of terms related to malevolent magic and lycanthropy all the items are quoted from the Motul Dictionary except as otherwise stated.

Terms relating to malevolent magic

Ah cunal can, ceh, balam: enchanter or wizard, who can charm snakes, [deer], jaguars, etc.
Ah cunal than: enchanter or wizard, who knows spells.
Ah cunil cizin: wizard or sorcerer, who has traffic with the devil.
Ah cunyah: wizard, witch, etc.

[9] P. Sánchez de Aguilar, *Informe contra idolorum cultores del obispado de Yucatán*, 124; Roys, *The Book of Chilam Balam of Chumayel*, Appendix C.

Ah dzac-yah: doctor in general and surgeon. Ordinarily it is taken in a bad sense as a wizard, who speaks with evil and idolatrous words.

Ah ez: enchanter (Pío Pérez dict.).

Ah koh keuel ("he with the hide mask"): sorcerer or wizard dressed in jaguar skins, who terrorizes people to rob them.

Ah mac ik ("wind-stopper"): conjurors of the winds, and one who, with words of the devil, cures children whose bellies have been bewitched. [I suggest that this refers to gas in the bowels.]

Ah paycun: wizard, who, with words and enchantment, attracts a person, jaguar, or deer.

Ah pul abich kik: wizard, who causes blood in the urine.

Ah pul abich puh: wizard who causes pus in the urine.

Ah pul auat, ah pul auat-mo ("he who causes a cry," "he who causes a macaw-scream"); wizard, who makes children scream.

Ah pul cimil: wizard who causes sickness in others.

Ah pul ch'ub chi: wizard who makes children refuse the breast.

Ah pul holok ta: wizard who causes repeated involuntary stools.

Ah pul kantzac: wizard who causes the spell called *pul kantzac*. [The *kantzac* is a species of wild bee, *Trigona jaty*, Sm. (Redfield and Villa, *Chan Kom*, 379).]

Ah pul kazab: wizard who causes strangury.

Ah pul nach'bac: wizard who causes consumption.

Ah pul ti yit uinic ("he who casts a spell on a man's rectum"): wizard who casts worms.

Ah pul uenel: wizard who causes sleep.

Ah pul xan-kik: wizard who causes bloody flux in women.

Ah pul yah: wizard in general, who causes illness in another.

Ah uaay: wizard (*brujo*).

Ah uaay balam: one who takes the form of a jaguar (Vienna Dict., f. 30v.).

Ah uay xibalba: wizard or conjuror, who speaks with the devil.

Ah uay ch'amac: a wizard who takes the form of a *ch'amac* ("gray fox").

Ah uay miztun: a wizard who takes the form of a cat. [*Miztun* is a new word, and there were no cats in pre-Spanish times.]

Balhol: wizard or witch, or conjuror and enchantment.

Calam ḵoh-che: wizards who are said to transform themselves into jaguars and kill people. [*Koh-che* means "wooden mask" and the *calam* is a well-known snake. See Glossary of Fauna Names.] (Vienna Dict., f. 130r.).

Cunal than: spells and witchcraft; also to enchant or charm people with words.

Cunul: to be enchanted or bewitched.

Çian: spell of enchantment. *A uohel ua u çian can, ch'uplal, ettz.?* Do you know how to charm or bewitch snakes, women, etc.?

Choch-cuntah, choch-cunyah: disenchant or exorcise what has been bewitched.

Ch'a-uay-tah: to take the form of another, as they say wizards (*brujos*) do, those called *uaytan*. *U ch'a uaytan ch'amac*, the wizard took the form of a *ch'amac* ("fox").

Dzutan: wizard (Vienna Dict., f. 70v.). [As a synonym of *ah uaytan*, it apparently means a wizard of the werewolf type (San Francisco Dict., Maya-Span.)].

Ez: something (or someone) enchanted or bewitched. *Ez en tumen Juan*, Juan has bewitched me.

Ezyah: enchant, bewitch.

Kaxcuntah: to bind (or exorcise) with certain spells.

Naual: a dance of men and women, "which is not very decent" (*Landa's "Relación,"* 128).

Naual: to stagger, as from weakness or intoxication.

Pul abich ḵiḵ: a spell that is cast to cause blood in the urine.

Pul abich puu[h]: to cast a spell causing pus in the urine, and such a spell.

Pul chacuil: a sort of evil eye, by which fevers are cast on children.

Pul chub chii: to bewitch infants so that they can not suckle.

Pul hau yoḵol ti: to bewitch, causing leprosy (*hau*).

Pul ḵiḵ ta: to bewitch, causing bloody stools.

Pul noḵ ti yit uinic: to bewitch, casting worms from the rectum on the floor. (Vienna Dict., f. 121r.). [This could also mean "casting worms into the rectum of a man."]

Pul xan kik: to bewitch women, causing hemorrhage, *lluvia*, also such a spell. [*Xan-kik* is defined as bloody flux.]

Pul xe-kik: to bewitch, causing blood-vomit.

Pul yaah: to bewitch generally, cast spells, to poison by spells, and a spell of that sort.

Tak yah: to bewitch bringing on some illness. [Today it would apparently refer to a contagious disease.]

Uaay: a familiar spirit, which the necromancers, wizards, or enchanters have. It is some animal, into which they change in a fantastic manner, through a pact which they make with the devil; and any harm that comes to such an animal comes also to the wizard whose familiar it is.

Uaayben, or *uaayben uinic*: wizard (*brujo*), who takes the form of some animal (Vienna Dict., f. 30*v*.).

Uaayinah: to become a wizard or take the fantastic form of another.

Uaaytan: wizard (*brujo*).

Uay-xibalba: wizard or magician, who speaks with the devil (*demonio*).

APPENDIX C
A Modern Witch Story

[Related by Arsenio Ceme of Izamal. Text supervised by
Victoriano Dzib of Pisté. Translation by Sr. Ramón Arzápolo
Marín, who has also corrected the notation of this modern text.]

IN THE TOWN OF ACANCEH there was a woman, whose name was
Petrona Ucán, and she had three daughters. The mother was a very
competent witch, so even to her three daughters she taught what she
knew. There was a boy named Victoriano Santos. Then he started
visiting one of these girls; and then he made love to [this] Francisca
Kumul; and a child was born of this girl. When this boy saw that a
child was born to this Francisca, he left her, so he did not marry
this Francisca.

Well, the mother of this Francisca knew well how to bewitch.
Little by little he began to feel sick. [It was] just his belly that was
enlarging.

Since the father of this Victoriano was living, then a *yerbatero* was
called, whose residence was at Cansahcab. This *yerbatero's* name was
Crescensio Escamilla. In order to see what illness this boy had, it was
recognized by this Escamilla, [who stated] the illness that this boy
had. So it was ascertained by this Escamilla what illness this Victoriano
had. "He is bewitched."

So, when he heard this, the father of this boy informed the
Presidente Municipal of Acanceh. Then these women were sum-
moned by the authorities before the *yerbatero*, and they were told that
they had bewitched this boy. Then they said, [together with] Francisca's mother, that they had not done it. But Mr. Escamilla made the

authorities realize that it was really a disease caused by witchcraft that the boy had.

This Mr. Escamilla gave some medicine for the boy to drink. It was twelve o'clock at night when he voided two snakes. One was a rattlesnake; the other was a boa.

Then the *Presidente* seized the mother of this Francisca, and she was forced to tell how they did the evil to that boy. But first she was frightened because of a pretense that she would be hanged. Then she said how she truly did it. Then she said she grieved over the deceit by the boy. We have to investigate. Then the mother of that girl said she had given that boy just a light punishment.

Then she was told by the *Presidente* that she had to pay for the work done by Mr. Escamilla. By the time she paid for the treatment given to that boy, they were told that the day they did it again, they would be killed.

Maya text

Tu cahi Acanceh yan[hi] huntul x-ch'up Petrona Ucán u kaba yetel oxtul 'u x-ch'upul paalal Le ma'ma ti'lo hach ma'loob pulyah pues tac le oxtul 'u paalaloob tu camzah ti' le baax yohlo' Yanhi huntul xibpaal Victoriano Santos 'u kaba ca hopp 'u bin 'u ximbaltic huntul ti' le x-ch'upalo' ca yanhi 'u yacuntic Francisca Kumul ca yanhi huntul champaal le x-ch'upal Cu yilic le xibpaal dzoc 'u yantal 'u champaal le Francisca ca tu ppatah ma dzoc 'u bele yetel le Francisca

Pues 'u ma'ma le Francisca yohel ma'loob pulyah Hunhumppi'tile ca hoppol 'u kohaantal chen 'u nak cu bin 'u nohochtal

Co'mo cuxaan 'u tata le Victoriano ca bini' than huntul yerbatero cahnal Caansahcab 'U kaba le yerbatero Crescencio Escamilla yohlal 'u yilic baax kohaani' yan ti' le paalo' Ca tun kaholtab tumen le Escamilla baax kohaanil yan ti le Victoriano Pulbi yah yan ti'

Cu yubic tun 'u tata le xibpaalo' ca tu dzah yohelte 'u Presidente Municipal Acanceh Ca thanoob tumen le autoridado' tu tan le yerbatero ca 'alab ti'obe leti'o pulyahmi le xibpaalo' ca tu yalahoob le

'u ma'ma le Francisca ma' leti'o tu betoobi' Pero yum Escamilla tu
betah 'u yilic autoridade de que hah pulbi yah yan ti' le xibpalo'

Le yum Escamilla tu dzah humppel dzac 'u yuk le xibpalo Las
doce ti' akabe' ca tu manzah ca'tul can huntul tzabcan, huntul ochcan

Pues le Presidente tu machah u ma'ma la Francisca ca betab 'u
cantic bix tu betiloob le lo'b ti' le xibpalo' Pero tanil dzab zahcil ti'
tumen tuz u hi'ch'il u cal Ca tun tu yalah bix 'u hahil tu betil ca tu
yalahe' tu ya oltah uchic u tu'zul tumen le xibpaal ma' dzoc u bel yetel
le x-ch'upalo' Yan ch'a 'u than yetelo' Ca tu yalah u ma'ma le
x-ch'upalo chen tu chan castiga[r]ta le xibpalo'

Catun 'alab ti' tumen le Presidente leti' cun bo'tic le meyah tu
betah le yum Escamilla Le cu dzocol u bo'tic le dzac betab ti' le
xibpalo' ca 'alab tiobe' le kin cu ca zut 'u betoobe' cu cimzalob.

[*Note*: Both Arsenio Ceme and Victoriano Dzib told me that the
former neither spoke nor understood Spanish; but as he was a former
resident of Izamal, it would seem probable that he understood a
little. Thus it is interesting to find repeated use of the words *autoridado, c'omo, ma'ma, Presidente, pues*, and *yerbatero*. *Tata* ("father")
does not appear in the early colonial Maya dictionaries, nor can I find
it in Beltrán's vocabularies. I first find it used about the year 1769, but
not again until 1811 (Roys, *The Titles of Ebtun*, 290, 336). Molina's
Mexican dictionary, first published in 1571, gives it as a child's way of
saying *tayta* or *tatli* ("father").]

CORRELATION
OF MANUSCRIPT PAGES
as Numbered in
the Gates Reproduction

MS pp.

1-12   The usual hand of this MS, hereinafter called Bacabs hand.
       Pp. 1-3 have been neither transcribed nor translated.

[13]   Blank page.

14-15 Bacabs hand.

[16]   Blank page.

17-19 Bacabs hand.

20-21 Intrusive incantation, different hand; see Appendix A.

22-61 Bacabs hand.

62-63 Intrusive incantation, same hand as pp. 20-21; see Appendix A.

64-69 Bacabs hand.

70   Medical prescription, different hand; omitted here.

71   Blank page.

72-88 Bacabs hand.

197-98 Bacabs hand.

189-96 Bacabs hand.

199-214 Bacabs hand.

[The remainder of the MS. has been neither transcribed nor translated. I do not feel competent to comment on the handwriting.]

215-26 Apparently ordinary medical prescriptions.

227   Probably a medical prescription.

228   Blank page.

229-30 Medical prescriptions.

231   Probably part of an incantation.

232 Blank page.
233 Probably part of an incantation.
234 Blank page.
235 Probably part of an incantation.
236 Plant lore.
237 Plant lore?

Verso of pp. 236–237 is a printed Indulgence dated 1779.

REFERENCES

Andrews, E. Wyllis
1937 "Notes on Snakes from the Yucatán Peninsula," Field Museum of Natural History *Zoological Series*, Vol. XX, No. 25, pp. 255–359. Chicago.

Barrera Vásquez, Alfredo
1943 "Horóscopos mayas ó el pronóstico de los 20 signos del tzolkin según los libros de Chilam Balam, de Kaua y de Mani," *Registro de Cultura Yucateca*, Vol. I, No. 6, pp. 4–33. Mexico.
1957 See Calkiní, Códice de
——, and S. Rendón
1949 *El Libro de los Libros de Chilam Balam*. Mexico.

Beltrán de Santa Rosa, M. P.
1859 *Arte de el idioma maya reducido a sucintas reglas y semi-lexicón yucateco*. Mérida. (1st ed., Mexico, 1746.)

Berendt, C. H.
Nombres proprios en lengua Maya. Manuscript. Berendt Collection, No. 48, University Museum, Philadelphia.

Calkini, Crónica de
[Chronicle and geographical description of the province of Ah Canul in Maya.] Manuscript. Photostat by W. E. Gates.

Calkiní, Códice de
1957 Proemio y versión del Profr. Alfredo Barrera-Vásquez. *Biblioteca Campechana* 4. Campeche.

Codex Dresden
1892 *Die Maya-Handschrift der Königlichen Bibliothek zu Dresden* . . . . Dresden. (Originally published in 1880, Leipzig).

Codex Madrid (Troano Section)
1869–70 *Manuscrit Troano. Etudes sur le système graphique et la*

langue des Mayas. By C. E. Brasseur de Bourbourg. 2 vols. Paris.

Codex Paris

1933 *The Codex Pérez* . . . . Reproduced by T. A. Willard. Glendale. (Not to be confused with Codex Pérez, a nineteenth-century copy of a series of colonial Maya manuscripts.)

Codex Pérez

c. 1837 Manuscript owned in Mérida. Photograph made for the Carnegie Institution of Washington.

Gann, T. W. F.

1918 "The Maya Indians of Southern Yucatán and Northern British Honduras," *B.A.E. Bulletin 64.* Washington, D.C.

Gates, W.

1910 "Commentary upon the Maya-Tzental Pérez Codex with a concluding note upon the linguistic problem of the Maya glyphs," *Papers* of the Peabody Museum, Harvard University, Vol. VI, No. 1. Cambridge, Mass.

Gaumer, George F.

1917 *Monografía de los mamíferos de Yucatán.* Mexico.

Guiteras Holmes, C.

1961 "La magia en la crisis del embarazo y parto en los actuales grupos mayances de Chiapas," *Estudios de cultura Maya,* I, 159–66. Universidad Nacional Autónoma de México, Facultad de Filosofía y Letras: Seminario de Cultura Mayo. Mexico.

Judio, Libro del

Manuscript in Maya language. Peabody Museum, Harvard University, Cambridge, Mass.

Kaua, Book of Chilam Balam of

Manuscript, photographic reproduction by Gates, Peabody Museum, Harvard University, Cambridge, Mass.

Landa, D. de

1941 *Landa's "Relacion de las cosas de Yucatán."* Translated and edited by A. M. Tozzer. *Papers* of the Peabody Museum, Harvard University, XVIII. Cambridge, Mass.

Lizana, Bernardo de

1893 *Historia de Yucatán. Devocionario de Ntra. Sra. de Izamal y
       conquista espiritual en 1663.* Museo Nacional de México,
       Mexico. (1st ed., Valladolid, 1633.)

Lundell, C. L.

1937 *The Vegetation of Petén.* Carnegie Institution of Washington
       Publication 478. Washington, D. C.

Maler, Teobert

1908 "Explorations of the Upper Usumacintla and Adjacent
       Region . . . ," *Memoirs* of the Peabody Museum, Harvard
       University, Vol. IV, No. 1, pp. 1–49. Cambridge, Mass.

Means, P. A.

1917 "History of the Spanish Conquest of Yucatán and of the
       Itzas," *Papers* of the Peabody Museum, Harvard University,
       Vol. VII. Cambridge, Mass.

Millspaugh, C. F.

1895–98 *Contributions 1–3* to the *Flora of Yucatán.* Field Museum of
         Natural History *Publications 4, 15,* and *25. Botanical Series,*
         Vol. I, pp. 1–56, i–vii, 281–339, 345–410. Chicago.

Molina, Alonso de

1880 *Vocabulario de la lengua Mexicana.* Leipzig.

Morley, Sylvanus G.

1946 *The Ancient Maya.* Stanford University, Calif.

Motul Dictionary

1929 *Diccionario de Motul,* Maya-español, atribuido a Fray An-
       tonio de Ciudad Real, y *Arte de lengua maya,* por Fray Juan
       Coronel. Edited by J. Martínez Hernández Mérida.

Pacheco Cruz, S.

1939 *Léxico de la fauna yucateca.* Mérida.

1958 *Diccionario de la fauna yucateca.* Mérida.

Pérez Dictionary

1866–67 *Diccionario de la lengua Maya.* Compiled by J. Pío Pórez;
         completed by C. H. Berendt. Mérida.

Pío Pérez, Juan

1898 *Coordinación alfabética de las voces del idioma Maya que se hallan en el arte y obra del Padre Fr. Beltrán de Santa Rosa.* Mérida.

Ray, V. F.

1963 *Primitive Pragmatists: The Modoc Indians of Northern California.* Seattle.

Redfield, Robert

1941 *The Folk Culture of Yucatán.* Chicago.

——, and Margaret Park Redfield

1940 "Disease and Its Treatment in Dzitas, Yucatán," Carnegie Institution of Washington *Publication 523, Contributions to American Anthropology and History,* Vol. VI, No. 32, pp. 49–82.

——, and Alfonso Villa R.

1934 *Chan Kom, a Maya Village.* Carnegie Institution of Washington *Publication 448.* Washington, D. C.

Rejón García, M.

1905 *Supersticiones y leyendas Mayas.* Mérida.

Relaciones de Yucatán

1898–1900 In *Colección de documentos inéditos relativos al descubrimiento, conquista y organización de las antiguas posesiones españolas de ultramar.* 2nd ser., Vols. XI, XIII. Madrid.

Roys, Ralph L.

1931 *The Ethno-Botany of the Maya. Middle American Research Series, Publication No. 2.* New Orleans.

1933 *The Book of Chilam Balam of Chumayel.* Carnegie Institution of Washington *Publication 438.* (Trans. and ed. by R. L. Roys). Washington, D. C.

1939 *The Titles of Ebtun.* Carnegie Institution of Washington *Publication 505.* Washington, D. C.

1940 "Personal Names of the Maya of Yucatán," Carnegie Institution of Washington *Publication 523, Contributions to American Anthropology and History,* Vol. VI, No. 31, pp. 31–48. Washington, D. C.

1943 *The Indian Background of Colonial Yucatán.* Carnegie Institution of Washington *Publication 549.* Washington, D. C.

1944 "The Vienna Dictionary," Carnegie Institution of Washington Division of Historical Research, *Notes on Middle American Archaeology and Ethnology*, No. 41. Cambridge, Mass.

1949 "The Prophecies for the Maya Tuns or Years in the Books of Chilam Balam of Tizimin and Mani," Carnegie Institution of Washington *Publication 585*, Contribution 51. Washington, D. C.

1954 "The Maya Katun Prophecies of the Books of Chilam Balam," Series I, Carnegie Institution of Washington *Publication 606*, Contribution 57. Washington, D. C.

1957 *The Political Geography of the Yucatán Maya*. Carnegie Institution of Washington *Publication 613*. Washington, D. C.

———, France V. Scholes, and Eleanor B. Adams

1940 "Report and Census of the Indians of Cozumel, 1570," Carnegie Institution of Washington *Publication 523*, *Contributions to American Anthropology and History*, Vol. VI, No. 30, pp. 1–30. Washington, D. C.

Sahagún, Fr. Bernardino de

1938 *Historia general de las cosas de Nueva España*. Ed. by Pedro Robredo. 5 vols. Mexico.

Sánchez de Aguilar, P.

1937 *Informe contra idolorum cultores del obispado de Yucatán* .... Mérida. (Originally published in 1639, Madrid.)

San Francisco Dictionary

1870 Diccionario Maya-Español del Convento de San Francisco en Mérida. Copiado por C. Hermann Berendt, M.D. Manuscript, Mérida. Photographic copy by the University of Pennsylvania Library, Philadelphia.

1870 Diccionario Español-Maya del Convento de San Francisco en Mérida. Berendt copy; photographic copy by the University of Pennsylvania Library, Philadelphia.

Scholes, France V., and Ralph L. Roys

1948 *The Maya Chontal Indians of Acalan-Tixchel: A Contribution to the History and Ethnography of the Yucatán Penin-*

sula. Carnegie Institution of Washington *Publication 560.* Washington, D. C.

Seler, E.

1902–23 *Gesammelte Abhandlungen zur amerikanischen Sprach- und Alterthumskunde.* 5 vols. Berlin.

Solis Alcala, E.

1949 *Códice Pérez.* Traducción libre del Maya al Castellano. Mérida. Standley, P. C.

1930 *Flora of Yucatán.* Field Museum of Natural History *Publication 279, Botanical Series,* Vol. III, No. 3. Chicago.

Thompson, J. E. S.

1930 "Ethnology of the Mayas of Southern and Central British Honduras," Field Museum of Natural History *Anthropological Series,* Vol. XVII, No. 2. Chicago.

1934 "Sky Bearers, Colors and Directions in Maya and Mexican Religion," Carnegie Institution of Washington *Publication 436, Contributions to American Archaeology,* Vol. II, No. 10, 209–42. Washington, D. C.

1937 *Mexico Before Cortez.* 2d ed. New York and London.

1939 "The Moon Goddess in Central America with Notes on Related Deities," Carnegie Institution of Washington *Publication 509,* Contribution 29. Washington, D. C.

1950 *Maya Hieroglyphic Writing: An Introduction.* Carnegie Institution of Washington *Publication 589.* Washington, D. C. 2d ed., Norman, 1960.

1954 *The Rise and Fall of Maya Civilization.* Norman.

1958 "Symbols, Glyphs, and Divinatory Almanacs for Diseases in the Maya Dresden and Madrid Codices," *American Antiquity,* Vol. XXIII, pp. 297–308. Salt Lake City.

1961 "A Blood-drawing Ceremony Painted on a Maya Vase," *Estudios de cultura Maya,* Vol. I, pp. 13–20. Universidad Nacional Autónoma de México. Facultad de Filosofía y Letras: Seminario de Cultura Maya. Mexico.

1962 *A Catalog of Maya Hieroglyphs.* Norman.

1963 "Merchant Gods of Middle America," *Homenaje al Ing. Roberto Weitlander*, II. Mexico.

Tizimin, Book of Chilam Balam of
Manuscript original in Mexico City. Reproductions by Gates in the Peabody Museum, Harvard University, Cambridge, Mass., and Edward E. Ayer Collection, Newberry Library, Chicago.

Tozzer, A. M.
1907 *A Comparative Study of the Mayas and the Lacandones.* New York.

1921 *A Maya Grammar with Bibliography and Appraisement of the Works Noted, Papers* of the Peabody Museum, Harvard University, Vol. IX. Cambridge, Mass.

1941 *Landa's "Relación de las Cosas de Yucatán."* A translation; edited, with notes. See Landa.

———, and G. Allen
1910 "Animal Figures in the Maya Codices," *Papers* of the Peabody Museum, Harvard University, Vol. IV, No. 3. Cambridge, Mass.

Vienna Dictionary
c. 1625 *Bocabulario de Mayathan por su abeceario* (Spanish-Maya). Manuscript in Nationalbibliothek, Vienna.

Villa Rojas, A.
1945 *The Maya of East Central Quintana Roo.* Carnegie Institution of Washington *Publication* 559. Washington, D. C.

Villagutierre y Soto-Mayor, Juan de
1701 *Historia de la conquista de la provincia del Itza.* Madrid. Reprinted 1933, *Biblioteca Goathemala*, IX, Sociedad de Geografía y Historia de Guatemala. Guatemala.

Xiu Family Tree
Manuscript in Peabody Museum, Harvard University, Cambridge, Mass. See Sylvanus G. Morley, *The Ancient Maya*, pl. 22.

Yerbas y Hechicerías del Yucatán
  Manuscript in Library of Middle American Research Institute, Tulane University, New Orleans.
Zimmerman, G.
  1956 *Die Hieroglyphen der Maya Handschriften.* Universität Hamburg. Abhandlungen aus dem Gebiet der Auslandskunde. Vol. LXVII—Heihe B (Völkerkunde, Kulturgeschichte, und Sprachen Band 34). Hamburg.

INDEX

P AGE NUMBERS in the following index refer to the pages in this book. Maya names for plants, fauna, deities, and ritualistic items are indexed by manuscript page numbers in three glossaries (Plant Names, pages 114–28; Fauna Names, pages 129–42; Proper Names, 143–61). Entries without page numbers below refer to these glossaries. Known English and Latin names for fauna and flora, as well as some less important Maya names in these categories, are included in this index with cross-references to the glossaries. In the case of a few items (i.e., birth, creation, cursing) it is not always clear whether they refer to diseases or to deities associated with diseases; such items are indexed only under diseases.

Maguey: 12, 59
Maize: *see* Uaxac-yol-kauil (person)
Man, stone: xvi, 16, 22, 23, 26, 28, 34, 35, 41, 46, 48, 66; green, xvi, 31, 32, 33, 43, 44; white, 24; black, 50
Man, wooden: xvi, 16, 22, 23, 26, 28, 34, 35, 41, 46, 48, 50, 51, 52, 66; green, xvi, 31, 32, 33, 43, 44, 150ff.; red, 24
Mat: 162
Medical problems: *see* disease
Melochia pyramidata: *see* chichibe
Moon: red-ringed, 10; face of, 31, 32, 33, 34; *see also* Ix U-sihnal (person)
Moth, clothes: *see cuyil*
Mut (bird of tydings): xii, 7, 8, 9, 10, 34, 36, 41, 45, 47, 60, 70

Nabal-bacte worm: 55
Nagualism: 7, 166–67
Needle: 22, 26, 43, 53, 54, 55, 163; *see also* Ix Hun-pundzub-kik (person)
Nettle: 33 & n.; *see also ppoppox, sac-la*
Night: snake of, 49; *see also* diseases (creation and birth)
Nopalea cochenillifera: *see pakam*
Notoptera Gaumeri: *see puc-ak*
Numbers, ritualistic: three, 163; four, 8, 12, 14, 15, 16, 17, 18, 22, 23, 27–28, 33, 35, 38, 40, 42, 44, 48, 49, 51, 53, 54, 57, 59, 61, 67, 163; five, 6, 8, 9, 39; six, 36; seven, 9, 66, 163 (*see also uuc-*); nine, 32 (*see also bolon-*); ten, 32; twelve, 163; thirteen, 11, 16, 18, 22, 24, 25, 32, 39, 48, 50, 51, 52,

54, 60, 64–65, 70 (*see also oxlahun-*); fourteen, 54, 163
Nymphaea ampla: *see nab*

Oriole: *see kubul*
Ox-chochola: 163
Ah oxou: 70

Paklah-sus: 52
Palum-cit: 37
Papaya: 13
Phragmites communis: *see halal*
Piscidia communis: *see habin, toncuy*
Pithecolobium sp.: *see ton -cuy*
Pleiades (Tzab): 7, 25; *see also* Ix Hun-tip-tzab, Ix Ko-ti-tzab, Ix Pic-tzab, Ix Ti-ho-tzab
Plumeria: hummingbird, 11; erotic charm, 167–68; *see also* diseases (seizures), Ix-Canlahun-nicte, *nicte, nicte-max, sabac-nicte, sacnicte*, Ix Tan-yobal-nicte, Ix Uucyobal-nicte
Ix Pokol-pic: 42
Ppocinbe (ant?): 36
Ix Ppohal-mum: 53
Prayers, absence of: xxv
Puhi rush: 39
Pule bird: 10
Puma: 26
Puns: xvii, xix, 10n., 14n., 24, 27n., 30, 30n., 41 43, 44n., 53, 55, 59, 60, 64, 65, 70n.
Punab tree: 10
Putrefaction, place of: 45

Quetzal: *see kuk, yaxum*
Quicksand: 15, 21

Rain: storm, 31; *see also* Ix Chaclahyeeb, Chac-Pauahtun-Chac, *water*

Ritual of the Bacabs has been set on the Linotype in eleven-point Granjon, a book face worthy of rank with the time-honored Caslons. The book has been printed on paper bearing the watermark of the University of Oklahoma Press and designed for an effective life of at least three hundred years.

UNIVERSITY OF OKLAHOMA PRESS
Norman